# Traveler's Rest and the Tugaloo Crossroads

Robert Eldridge Bouwman

UNG
UNIVERSITY *of*
NORTH GEORGIA™
UNIVERSITY PRESS
Dahlonega, GA

Published by:
University of North Georgia Press
Dahlonega, Georgia

Printing Support by:
Booklogix Publishing Services, Inc.
Alpharetta, Georgia

Cover Photo: Front view of Traveler's Rest circa 1953
Cover design by Jon Mehlferber, April Loebick, and Corey Parson.

ISBN: 978-1-940771-14-4

Printed in the United States of America, 2015
For more information, please visit: http://ung.edu/university-press
Or e-mail: ungpress@ung.edu

# Table of Contents

# Preface to New Edition

Traveler's Rest and the Tugaloo Crossroads was first published by the State of Georgia in 1980, by the Historic Preservation Section of the Department of Natural Resources. As acknowledged in the first edition, this book was made possible by many "interested individuals." The same is true of this new edition, published by the University of North Georgia Press.

When Traveler's Rest was researched and written in the late 1970s, the historic site had two full-employees and was open six days a week. Today, Traveler's Rest is open for part of the day only on three Saturdays per month. The tour-guide is paid by the Friends of Traveler's Rest, a group of private individuals dedicated to the sites preservation, and maintenance for the site comes from private donations with occasional contributions from the State of Georgia, providing for Traveler's Rest to be open once a month. School groups can visit the site by making arrangements with the Friends of Traveler's Rest. There is an annual gathering called Pioneer Day and a Christmas program, mostly attended by interested people from Toccoa and nearby.

Funding from the state has been reduced by means of gradual cutbacks. Traveler's Rest was nominated as a "place in peril", and when selected, received a much-needed new roof in 2012. Today, Traveler's Rest is neglected by the State of Georgia and most of the state's citizens.

How has this happened? The state's neglect must be understood as the result of public disinterest. Yet Traveler's Rest remains a fascinating place where people can take a look into Georgia's past, catching glimpses of interesting characters and the way they lived. Traveler's Rest is a treasure that is still appreciated by visitors and those who love it. I am grateful to those people, past and present, who serve Georgia by maintaining this treasure. I am grateful to Dr. Jack Wynn for the idea of re-issuing Traveler's Rest and the Tugaloo Crossroads, and to the University of North Georgia Press for taking up the project.

# Acknowledgments

This book was made possible by the assistance of numerous interested individuals, and acknowledging all of them would be impossible. The Traveler's Rest files were painstakingly collected over several years by employees of the old Georgia Historical Commission, as well as researchers for the Historic Preservation Section. Their work has been much appreciated.

In finding materials on Traveler's Rest and the history of the Jarrett family, I was greatly aided by Henry B. and Elizabeth Hayes, Mabel Ramsey, and Rose Jarrett Taylor, all of the Toccoa vicinity.

My genealogical research was facilitated by Mrs. R. E. O'Donnell of Fort Worth, Texas, and Mrs. E. L. Stephenson of Covington, Georgia.

Thomas J. Lumsden, M.D., of Clarkesville, Georgia, generously contributed the results of his research on the Unicoi Turnpike. Many of the maps in this book were discovered with the assistance of Pat Bryant, Marion Hemperley, and Janice Blake of the Georgia Surveyor General Department. The maps were ably prepared by Mel Wolfe, Leonard Chester, and Stephanie Low of the Site Planning Section of the Department of Natural Resources. The modern photographs of Traveler's Rest were taken by David J. Kaminsky in 1977.

Frances Wilbanks, curator of Traveler's Rest, was an unending source of aid, information and inspiration.

Patricia Eldridge Bouwman was indispensable as ever, especially in preparation of the manuscript.

# Location of the Site

On Georgia Highway 123, amid the foothills of the Blue Ridge Mountains, stands Traveler's Rest Historic Site. Six miles southwest is the town of Toccoa, and nearby is Lake Hartwell—which was created by the damming of the Tugaloo River.

Traveler's Rest is located in a portion of Stephens County which was originally Franklin County. A treaty of May 31, 1783, between the Cherokees and the State of Georgia resulted in the Cherokees ceding these lands along the Tugaloo to the state. Franklin County was then created on February 24, 1784. In 1818, Habersham County was formed when the state took the northern portion of Franklin County and combined it with lands recently ceded by the Cherokees. From this time until 1906, Traveler's Rest was located in the southeastern portion of Habersham County.

In 1874, the nearby town of Toccoa was incorporated, and area residents clamored for the new town to replace Clarkesville as county seat. Their efforts failed in this, but legislation was enacted to create a new county of which Toccoa would be the seat. On August 18, 1905, Stephens County was created from portions of Habersham and Franklin counties, Traveler's Rest being included in the new county.

# Preface

Traveler's Rest is one of many historic properties in the state for which the Georgia Department of Natural Resources has responsibility. It is the ultimate goal of the Department to provide historical documentation, in published form, on each of the sites. This documentation is required to authenticate the site, provide information supporting the development of the site, and prepare the groundwork for the interpretive program to center on Traveler's Rest.

The Georgia Historical Commission, with the assistance of the Toccoa Chamber of Commerce and the Jarrett Manor Foundation, purchased Traveler's Rest and 2.995 acres from Mary Jarrett White on July 25, 1955. On July 28, 1971, the State of Georgia bought an additional .329 acre from Clyde McClure and George Ramsey, Jr. Traveler's Rest is located six miles east of Toccoa, in Stephens County, on Riverdale Road near Lake Hartwell, approximately one half mile west of U.S. 123. In 1964, Traveler's Rest was recognized as a National Historic Landmark by the National Park Service.

The house stands within two miles of the site of Old Tugaloo Town, an important Cherokee village. It is situated on a crossroads at the southern end of the Great Wagon Road, down which a wave of European-American migration poured to fill the land east of the Appalachians in the mid-eighteenth century. The first known white settler on the site of Traveler's Rest was frontiersman Jesse Walton in 1784. He was followed by others including Joseph Martin and James R. Wyly, prior to occupation of home and land by Devereaux Jarrett in the 1830s. The history of Traveler's Rest is then intertwined with the history of the Jarrett family until the State's purchase in 1955.

It is a history encompassing the Cherokees, migration, frontier war, and gold rush; it includes the development of Traveler's Rest as stagecoach inn/tavern into its long years as a plantation center; through Civil War and Reconstruction, the gradual decline of land and family is taken to the present century, where Traveler's Rest becomes the physical embodiment of history transfigured into legend.

The architectural development of Traveler's Rest mirrors the people and the years through which the site matured. In its evolution are clues of an early cabin (ca. 1784), replaced by a simple frame house (ca. 1815), and enlarged to its present size sometime in the late 1830s.

The history of Traveler's Rest is the history of a people and a heritage, reflected in the structure that developed with the years.

# Introduction

Traveler's Rest and the Tugaloo Crossroads is a history based on intensive historical, archaeological, and architectural research. It has not been possible to coordinate all of the studies closely with the development of the site. Some restoration of the site had taken place prior to the beginning of archaeological investigation, and virtually all restoration had been completed when architectural analysis was undertaken. Nevertheless, these studies have assisted in the final stages of restoration and have given us a clearer picture from which to view the events and individuals who comprise the history of Traveler's Rest. With this broader perspective, the site can be appropriately interpreted for the public.

The history begins with the Cherokees who were drawn to the lands along the Tugaloo at the foothills of the Blue Ridge prior to the sixteenth century. Although they apparently were not in conflict with Spanish conquistador Hernando de Soto in 1540, the Cherokees seldom enjoyed peace. From the beginning, the cluster of villages which included Old Estatoe and Tugaloo Town [see Maps 1-4] were caught up in a long struggle—first with other tribes, and then with the Europeans. The Europeans' arrival triggered a revolution in Cherokee life, and it generated the competition and crisis that was played out at Tugaloo Town, until 1715 the Cherokee capital in this area. During the Revolutionary War, Georgia wrested the Tugaloo Crossroads from the Cherokees, and it was opened to white settlement by 1784. The land at the ford was surveyed in 1785 and granted to Major Jesse Walton.

Both the ford and the creek emptying into the Tugaloo nearby were named after Walton. Born in the backcountry of Colonial Virginia, Walton had been a hunter, trader, settler, and Indian fighter on the frontier, as had many of his neighbors. Following the Revolution, these backwoodsmen brought their families to the lands along the Tugaloo. Among Walton's neighbors were long-time Cherokee trader Bryant Ward and General Joseph Martin, one of the foremost heroes of the Revolutionary War.

In the summer of 1789, Jesse Walton was ambushed and killed by Creek Indians. The Walton's Ford tract then passed to Jesse's heirs. For about twenty years, his four sons, two daughters, and their families lingered at the Tugaloo, after which they were drawn west by the lure of new lands. In 1813, Walton's heirs relinquished a small house and the land at the ford to a Joseph Martin, husband of Walton's daughter Mary. It may have been Martin who replaced the cabin at Walton's Ford with the first section of the house which now stands at Traveler's Rest. Martin sold the house and land to James R. Wyly in 1818.

A militia officer, road builder, entrepreneur, and public servant, Wyly appears to have been the first to have operated an inn at Walton's Ford. Wyly held title to Traveler's Rest for about twenty years, but by 1833 (at the latest), he had sold this to a man named Devereaux Jarrett and moved to Clarkesville.

Jarrett, who had lived in this area for most of his life, enlarged the house into a comfortable inn, named it Traveler's Rest, and probably left it much as it is today. A man of whom far too little is known, Devereaux Jarrett died in 1852, leaving more than 10,000 acres and numerous slaves to be divided among his four children. They lived prosperously in plantations along the Tugaloo, with Charles Kennedy Jarrett, the youngest son, maintaining the inn at Traveler's Rest. C. K. Jarrett married Elizabeth Lucas of Athens, Georgia, but soon the Civil War came, putting an end to slavery and to the Jarretts' accustomed manner of living.

The postbellum years brought an era of economic woe to the South, and the Jarretts' once-considerable estate dwindled steadily. It is from this period that the bulk of the surviving personal documents come, providing the most detailed material about the lives of the people at Traveler's Rest.

At the turn of the century, only Sally Grace and Mary Elizabeth were surviving of C. K. Jarrett's children. During the first half of the twentieth century, Traveler's Rest—then known as Jarrett Manor—was a faded remnant of Devereaux Jarrett's plantation-inn. Eventually, Mary Elizabeth Jarrett White became the sole occupant of the old inn, which was rotting away around her. To her, Traveler's Rest was the "old home place," and in reminiscences, newspaper articles, and in conversation with friends, she kept the memories alive.

Her dedication in preserving the home and its history was rewarded in 1955, when the Georgia Historical Commission acquired Traveler's Rest and began restoring it. This picturesque old home in the foothills of the Blue Ridge has a history well worth retelling. And Traveler's Rest and the Tugaloo Crossroads has grown from the efforts of a number of people over several years to recall this history.

# ARCHAEOLOGY AND ARCHITECTURE AT TRAVELER'S REST

The history of an individual or a society cannot be comprehensively interpreted using verbal documentation alone, and the history of Traveler's Rest is not limited to the written record. In the summer of 1968, archaeologist Dr. William M. Kelso conducted excavations of Traveler's Rest for the Georgia Historical Commission. Architectural historian Paul Buchanan conducted an architectural analysis of Traveler's Rest in the fall of 1977. The complete text of both these reports appears in the Appendices, but an overview of their findings is presented here to set the scene for the historical narrative.

The building known as Traveler's Rest was building two primary stages, hereafter referred to as Period I and Period II. Period I dates at ca. 1815 and concerns the south end of the structure. Archaeology suggest that there was a structure on the site before 1815, and architect Buchanan gives the construction date as 1815, plus or minus five years, but suggest 1815 as the most likely date. It was probably built, therefore, by Joseph Martin, who owned the land on which it is situated until 1818. However, since the land changed hands during the possible range of years which the reports have assigned to the construction, it is difficult to be conclusive. Historical data does favor Martin as the builder, since he sold the land for $100 per acre, a high price for land—unless there were substantial improvements.

Traveler's Rest, as it appeared circa 1815 or Period I (1815-1835), was approximately half its present size. It was a two-story, frame building, eighteen feet and two inches by fifty feet and ten and one-half inches. On the west or front façade was a one-story, shed porch with six posts connected by a balustrade, except in the center, where steps led to the front doors. On the east or rear façade was a similar shed, but only the center portion was open. There were shed rooms on either end of this east façade.

The exterior was weatherboarded, and there were end chimneys with stone foundations and brick stacks. The foundation of the building was stone, and the structure had a gable roof.

The first floor contained two rooms of equal size with a door between them. The rooms matched, each having two windows and a center door on the west, a fireplace with flanking windows on the exterior ends, and two doors on the east, one leading to a shed room and one to the east porch. The south room, known as the "hall," had a quarter-turn stair leading to the second floor from the northwest corner of the room. The north room was the "parlor."

The second floor had three rooms and a stair passage. The space above the "hall" of the first floor was partitioned to give two small bedrooms and the stair passage. The space above the north room or parlor of the first floor was of equal size with the parlor. The second-floor rooms on the south had no fireplaces, but were heated with wood stoves. The north bedroom had a fireplace.

There were probably a number of outbuildings during the period, but none have survived. Neither the archaeological nor architectural reports were able to address that topic for this early period. No doubt, however, there were at least privies, a detached kitchen, slave quarters, and probably a smokehouse, and a well or spring house.

Soon after Traveler's Rest was purchased by Devereaux Jarrett in 1833, the main building underwent major alterations and additions, almost doubling its size. Period II of the construction history was between1835 and 1840. When the building was enlarged, it was over ninety feet long. The front shed porch was extended the new length of the building, and a second entrance was added to the old porch area.

The old south rooms of the first floor yielded space for a new central hall and stair and a stair passage for a new stair leading only from the second floor to the west porch. The fireplaces in these rooms were given new Greek Revival mantels.

The only change on the second floor of the old house was an east west partition in the large north room. This created one unheated room.

Like the older portion, the new addition had four rooms downstairs, two of which were rear shed rooms. The north main room was the dining room. A stair led from the south main room to the second floor. Below the dining room was a large, cellar kitchen to replace an earlier, detached kitchen. Upstairs, the new portion included a large, north bed chamber, stair passage, a small chamber and a north-south hall connecting the new section to the old second-floor section. Architect Buchanan believes that the north addition was built primarily as family quarters, with the old south end reserved for tavern use.

A cursory glance at the building gives the impression that it was built as a single unit. The north addition matches the south end superficially with regard to architecture. A thorough analysis of this building, based on architectural design, building materials, moulding profiles, brick bond, structural techniques and archaeology, belies the overall impression, revealing the major changes noted above, as well as more subtle ones which are noted in the full reports.

The archaeological excavation yielded data on two outbuildings. Fifty feet to the northwest of the main house, the stone foundations of the smokehouse were uncovered. It measured eighteen feet, six inches square. The artifacts recovered place its earliest occupation date at circa 1830. It was probably built, therefore, by Jarrett. Historical research turned up a circa 1890 photograph of the building, which shows a hewn-log building with an overhanging porch roof, said to be the smokehouse.

Still in existence, though greatly restored, is the outbuilding traditionally known as the "loomhouse." The architect's report states that it was built after 1850, while the archaeologist believes that it was there in the 1820s and was used as a dairy. The building has two levels, the lower being brick and the upper, frame. It seems plausible that either there was another building on the same site in the 1820s, or that some portion of the present structure dates to the 1820s. However, the building as it exists today is post-1850. Other outbuildings known to have existed during Jarrett years were a store, barns, stables, smithy, mills, slave dwellings and bridges.

Architect Paul Buchanan refers to the building as a "combined residence-tavern" and states that the amount of space allocated to the family fluctuated, depending on the "numbers and type of the traveling public who had to be accommodated." Of the significance of the building architecturally, he notes that it is a "good remaining example of early-nineteenth-century pioneer vernacular architecture of the Georgia Piedmont and its growth up to the 1860s." He states that the native materials used, as well as the building style and techniques, were especially suitable for an area that had little skilled labor and that lacked available materials for purchase, while accommodating the climate as well.

Traveler's Rest is open to the public as a house museum and contains period furniture, much of it from the Jarrett family, and artifacts found on the site.

The historical, architectural and archaeological research on which this report is based will ensure an accurate interpretation of the site in the future. To visit Traveler's Rest today is to step back in time to the days of stagecoach, roadside tavern and pioneer living. Traveler's Rest is a fine structure exemplifying our nineteenth-century heritage.

# Chapter 1

## Cherokee Villages

People have been living in the vicinity of Traveler's Rest for scores of generations, thousands of years. When the Cherokees settled at the mouth of Toccoa Creek at about 1300 A.D. (at the earliest), they built their lodges around a mound beneath which lay evidence of lengthy Indian occupation. Perhaps driven south by the Iroquois and Delaware tribes, the Cherokees took over the Southern Appalachians (see Map 1), pushing the Creeks southward and the Shawnees northwest. A few generations of adaptation passed, and by the time European explorers visited them, the Cherokees had largely forgotten their own usurpation, regarding their territory as an ancient homeland, occupied by them throughout history. So the Cherokees explained: "Time out of mind, these lands have been the hunting grounds of the Cherokee."[1]

Little is known of the Cherokees' predecessors in the Tugaloo region; however, archaeologists at the site of Tugaloo Town on Toccoa Creek have designated several distinct periods of occupation. There, the pre-Cherokees lived in Stone Age simplicity, casting aside over the years the bones, broken tools, and pottery which are our only record of them. At least eight layers of occupation were unearthed at the Tugaloo mound. These excavations undertaken in 1957 revealed that as population ebbed and flowed, people were again and again attracted to the area.[2] The mysterious message left on the "Indian Rock" or petrograph [petroglyph] at Traveler's Rest is a lasting testimony to the continuing efficacy of the Tugaloo Crossroads.

Much more is known of the Cherokees, the "mountaineers" of the South. Related to the Iroquois group of tribes, the Cherokees proudly called themselves the *Ani-Yunwuja*, the "Real People."[3] The name "Cherokee" is apparently of foreign origin.[4] The word could mean "Ancient Tobacco People," "Children of the Sun," or "Brave Men."[5] A relatively large tribe, the Cherokees were certainly not the Lost Tribes of Israel, as some early traders and settlers wished to believe.[6] Members of the tribe built their principal

The Cherokee Country in the Southern Appalachians, 18th Century. *Site of Traveler's Rest.

**Map 1:** The Cherokee Country in the Southern Appalachians, 18<sup>th</sup> Century

towns on the headwaters of the Savannah, Hiwassee, and Tuckasegee rivers, and all along the Little Tennessee, as well. There, they strove to adjust themselves to the southern mountain climate, while surrounded on all sides by hostile rivals.[7]

By the late seventeenth century, when they were contacted by European explorers, the Cherokees had become a tribe of great power and influence. They controlled 40,000 square miles of territory in what is now southwest Virginia, the western Carolinas, eastern Tennessee, and the northern areas of Georgia and Alabama. Indian expert James Adair estimated them to number between 16,000 and 17,000, with 6,000 warriors, inhabiting sixty-four towns in 1735. With their huge territory and relatively large population, the Cherokees were strategically situated to hold the balance of power in southeastern North America. Whether they favored the English settlements to the east, or the Spanish and French along the Gulf of Mexico and up the Mississippi to a point north of the Ohio River, would prove to be a vital factor in determining the course of history. This potential was offset, however, by the loose nature of Cherokee organization, which frequently kept the tribe from wielding a more powerful influence.[8]

On the Tugaloo River, several generations of Cherokees followed the tribal patterns by living in a cluster of small villages along the streams which fed the river. Tugaloo Town (Tugaloo meaning "rough or muddy waters") was at the mouth of Toccoa Creek, about a mile up the river from the eventual site of Traveler's Rest. Nearby were Old Estatoe, six miles up the river; Noyowee, across from Estatoe; Tetohe, up Toccoa Creek; Chagee, down the river and in South Carolina; and Tussee, to the south. Old Estatoe was the "mother village" of the cluster, and also the largest, having a population of about 600. In all, the Lower Towns included about eleven villages, with a population of roughly 2,000.[9] All the towns in the Tugaloo cluster were bound together by footpaths—a northeastward trail led to the important Cherokee town of Keowee, and a northwestward trail ran through Chota and climbed the mountains to the important Middle Towns of the Cherokees (see Map 2).[10]

When Colonel George Chicken visited the Cherokees as the special emissary of South Carolina in 1725, he described Old Estatoe as:

> ...a large Town and very well fortified [*sic*] all round with Punchins and also ditched on the outside of sd [said] Punchins (wch [which] Ditch) is Stuck full of light wood Spikes so that if the Enemy should ever happen to fall therein, they must without doubt receive a great deal of damage by those Spikes.[11]

Chicken labeled "Tugelo Town" the "most Antient [*sic*] town in these parts." Apparently Tugaloo was dominant, for there the Cherokees held their most important councils with the settlers, and Chicken singled out the "Warriour of Tugelo" for special presents. No estimates of the size of the town have been found; since it was smaller than Estatoe, its population could have ranged anywhere from 100 to 400.[12]

At Tugaloo, the Cherokees spoke their "eastern" dialect, being characterized by its rolling R's. They lived as most Eastern "Woodland" Indians lived by farming, hunting, and trading. Tribal structure was dominated by seven clans, to which the individual clan members were intensely loyal. Each village was largely autonomous, ruled by a daily council in which both men and women participated.[13]

Indeed, Cherokee women were extremely powerful in the tribal councils. As James Adair reported, "They have been a considerable time under petticoat government." The head of the women's council was the "Beloved Woman" of the tribe, "whose voice was considered that of the Great Spirit speaking through her." The influence of the Cherokee women was to prove of tremendous importance later to European traders and settlers.[14]

At Tugaloo Town and elsewhere, the Cherokee houses were oblong. To build them, the Cherokees would set up a row of posts, fill in between these with wicker-work, and cover the result with a "plaster of mud and grass." After putting on a bark roof, they would then whitewash the lodge inside and out. Furnished with fur couches, stools, and house keeping implements, these lodges were often found unbearably stuffy by European visitors, but not nearly so "close" as the small, air-tight "hot-houses" the American Indians inhabited in the winter.[15]

The life of these Cherokees occupying the area near the future site of Traveler's Rest was a true test of their ability to survive. It is conjectured that a typical Indian woman spent her day gathering fruit and nuts; tending crops of maize, potatoes, and squash; and performing household tasks such as preparing food, tanning hides, weaving, and making pottery. Men at home made tools and weapons and assisted with crops, but much time was spent away from the village in hunting or raiding the tribe's many enemies.[16]

In addition to all these tasks, however, the Cherokees managed to make time for religion and entertainment. Men and women observed a calendar of religious ceremonies, by which they commemorated the seasons and the tribe's relationship to nature. Before contact with European culture had completely revolutionized tribal patterns, a "priestly cult" of both men and women dominated Cherokee leadership. This "cult" was especially powerful in the Tugaloo Town cluster, though its power waned with the changes of the eighteenth century.[17]

The Cherokees also took their games seriously. They joined most eastern tribes in a thorough addiction to *chungke*, a game played by throwing poles at a rolling, discus-shaped stone. A player took great pride in his

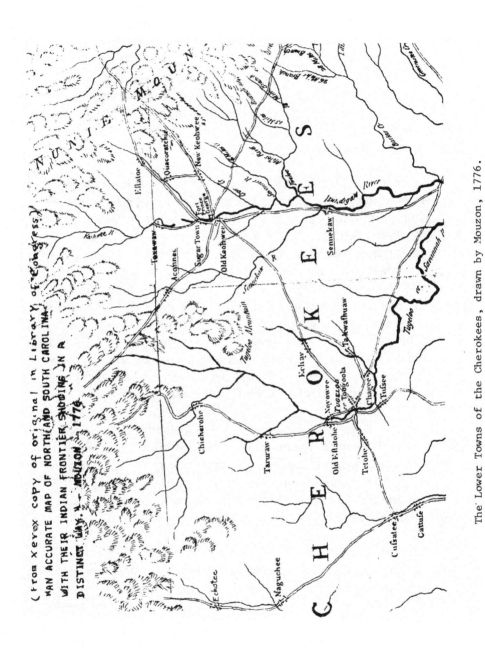

**Map 2:** The Lower Towns of the Cherokees, drawn by Mouzon, 1776

*chungke* stone, shaped and ornamented "with prodigious labor." Every village had a *chungke* yard, and the men loved the game so much that clearing a field for this purpose was supposedly their first activity when founding a new village. *Chungke*, as well as all other games, was accompanied by vigorous gambling.[18]

According to Brown's *Old Frontiers*, the "whole population" participated in "ballplay." Playing on a level field, the American Indians enjoyed a brutal sort of lacrosse, endeavoring to maneuver the ball through the opponent's goal. Sometimes one village's team would play another's in a match: sometimes the entire community would join in. On such occasions,

> In the desperate struggles for the ball, with hundreds running together and actually leaping over each others heads, darting between their adversaries' legs, tripping and throwing, every voice raised to the highest key in excited shrill yelps, there are rapid feats in succession that astonish and amuse one far beyond the conception of one who has not had the singular good luck to witness them. The spectator loses his strength, and everything else but his senses, when the confused mass of ball sticks, shins, and bloody noses is carried off to different parts of the ground for a quarter of an hour at a time without any of the mass being able to see the ball, which they are often thus scuffling for when it has been thrown off and played over another part of the grounds. And so on until the successful party arrives at one hundred, which is the limit of the game.[19]

Both the villages of Tugaloo and Old Estatoe had ball teams whose players traveled to games even in war time. The seriousness with which the Cherokees took this "sport" even extended to the testing of the capacities of their conjurors by demanding winning magic.[20]

To Europeans, the Cherokee men presented an intimidating, "savage" visage. Of the braves, one visitor, Henry Timberlake, wrote in 1762:

> The Cherokees are of a middle stature, of an olive colour, tho' generally painted, and their skins stained with gun-powder, pricked into it in very pretty figures. The hair of their heads is shaved, tho' many of the old people have it plucked out by the roots, except a patch on the hinder part of the head, about twice the bigness of a crown-piece, which is ornamented with beads, feathers, wampum, stained deers hair, and such like baubles. The ears are split and stretched to an enormous size, putting the person who undergoes the operation to considerable pain, being unable to lie on either side for near forty days. To remedy this, they generally slit but one side at a time; so

soon as the patient can bear it, they are wound round with wire to expand them, and are adorned with silver pendants and rings, which they likewise wear at the nose.[21]

On the appearance of the women of the tribe, explorer-naturalist William Bartram observed in 1776:

> The dress of the females is somewhat different from that of the men; their flap or petticoat, is made after a different manner, is larger and longer, reaching almost to the leg, and is put on differently; they have no shirt or shift but a little short waistcoat, usually made of callico [sic], printed linen, or fine cloth decorated with lace, beads etc. They never wear boots or stockings, but their buskins [short leather boots] reach to the middle of the leg. They never cut their hair, but plait it in wreathes, which is turned up, and fastened on the crown, with a silver broach, forming a wreathed top-knot.[22]

Such were the American Indians that the European explorers and settlers found living in the area near what would later become Traveler's Rest, convinced that, "We are the first people that ever lived on this land; it is ours."[23] But the Cherokees possessed a drastically different concept of land-ownership from that of the settlers. As the American Indians saw it, the Creator had provided land, along with air, water, and sunlight. Tribes claimed jurisdiction over the hunting grounds in the vicinity of their villages, but they had considerable trouble understanding and accepting the concepts of sovereignty and individual ownership of property. They were perplexed and infuriated by the settlers' practices of parceling, transforming, exploiting, and often squandering the land. As the tide of white settlement expanded with apparently irreversible, insatiable voracity, the Cherokees joined other American Indians in a desperate, violent, hopeless resistance. The American frontier was the scene of one of history's vast dramas. The Tugaloo Crossroads was a focal point in that drama.[24]

The Cherokees loved their Tugaloo lands with good cause, for there they prospered in spite of the fact that they were never to know peace in those lands. From the time they arrived in the Alleghenies and the Tugaloo area, the Cherokees struggled to adjust to rapidly developing events and situations which continued to have a shattering impact on their culture.[25]

Actually, the Cherokees never had a chance to find their place among the southeastern tribes. No sooner had they arrived in the mountains, expelling rivals from the territory and making enemies of the surrounding Shawnee, Iroquois, Creek, Yamassee, and other tribes, than they found themselves at a tremendous disadvantage in accessibility to the revolutionary weapons and tools of the Europeans. With all their enemies becoming comparatively well supplied with the fruits of a devastating technology, the Cherokees, by the late 1600s, were desperate to redress the balance of equipment. For the next few generations, Cherokee life was dominated by the adjustment to the presence of the whites and their goods.[26]

For Cherokee men, hunting and warfare mushroomed in importance. The braves had to hunt as never before to obtain the skins needed to trade for guns, ammunition, knives, hoes, cooking utensils, ornaments, and other trade goods. Meanwhile, old tribal antagonisms became exacerbated with the European powers' imperial struggle over the resources and territory of the southeast. The pressure to hunt was complicated by the unrelenting necessities of attack and defense. The story of the Tugaloo Crossroads continued as it became the early frontier. Conflict and turmoil took place among the Cherokees as they reacted to the shock of the Europeans' arrival.[27]

The story of the Tugaloo Crossroads continued as it became involved in the frontier conflict and turmoil taking place among the Cherokees as they reacted to the shock of the European's arrival in the southeast.

## NOTES

[1] Quotation from John P. Brown, *Old Frontiers: The Story of the Cherokee Indians* (Kingsport, Tenn.: Southern Publishers, Inc., 1938), p. 15. On the origins of the Cherokees, see also James Mooney, *Myths of the Cherokee* (New York: Johnson Reprint Corp., 1970), p. 15; William S. Willis, *Colonial Conflict and the Cherokee Indians, 1710-1760* (Ann Arbor, Mich.: University Microfilms, 1955), pp. 1-12; and Grace Steel Woodward, *The Cherokees,* (Norman, Okla.: University of Oklahoma Press, 1963), p. 99; J.R. Caldwell, "Appraisal of the Archeological Resources of Hartwell Reservoir," National Park Service, 1953.

[2] *Anderson [S.C.] Independent*, February 17, 1957, p. 15.

[3] Brown, *Old Frontiers*, p. 14.

[4] Mooney, *Myths of the Cherokee*, p. 15.

[5] Woodward, *The Cherokees*, p. 21.

[6] Mooney, *Myths of the Cherokee*, p. 21.

[7] Ibid., p. 14.

[8] Ibid., p. 34; and Willis, *Colonial Conflict*, pp. 1-3.

[9] Kathryn Curtis Trogden, *The History of Stephens County, Georgia* (Toccoa, Ga.: Toccoa Woman's Club, Inc., 1973), pp. 2, 3. Mouzon's map, (Map 2) is "An accurate map of North and South Carolina with their Indian frontier showing in a distinct way" (1776); original in possession of the Library of Congress, Washington, D.C. Brown's map appeared in his book, *Old Frontiers*. Also, for a complete listing of the three general divisions of Cherokee towns [Lower, Middle and Upper] and their locations, see John R. Swanton, *The Indian Tribes of North America* (Washington, D.C.: Smithsonian Institution Press, 1968), pp. 216-18.

[10] Verner W. Crane, *The Southern Frontier, 1670-1732* (Ann Arbor, Mich.: University of Michigan Press, 1929; reprinted 1956), p. 130.

[11] Newton D. Mereness, *Travels in the American Colonies* (New York: MacMillan Co., 1916), p. 150.

[12] Mereness, *Travels in the American Colonies*, pp. 137, 145.

[13] Brown, *Old Frontiers*, pp. 15-25; Woodward, *The Cherokees*, pp. 11-21; and Mooney, *Myths of the Cherokee*, pp. 14-16.

[14] Brown, *Old Frontiers*, p. 18.

[15] Ibid., p. 20.

[16] Willis, *Colonial Conflict*, p. 104.

[17] Ibid., p. 257; and Woodward, *The Cherokees*, p. 49.

[18] Brown, *Old Frontiers*, pp. 21, 22.

[19] Ibid., p. 21. Brown's reference is George Catlin, a contemporary who was a trader with the American Indians. A more recently published source is Charles Hudson (see footnote below), who maintains that only the men participated in the ball games, p. 411. See George Chicken's "Journal of the March," *Yearbook of the. City of Charleston*, 1894, pp. 315-354.

[20] Charles Hudson, *The Southeastern Indians* (Knoxville, Tenn.: University of Tennessee Press, 1976), p. 411.

[21] Henry Timberlake, *Memoirs* (London, 1765; reprinted by S.C. Williams, Watauga Press, 1927), p. 49.

[22] Woodward, *The Cherokees*, p. 37.

[23] Ibid., p. 99.

[24] On land-ownership, see Dale Van Every, *Ark of Empire* (New York: Mentor Books, 1963), pp. 56-58.

[25] Willis, *Colonial Conflict*, pp. 21, 78, 104.

[26] Ibid., entire work.

[27] Ibid., pp. 73, 78, 90.

# Chapter 2

## Tugaloo and the Cherokee Frontier

The Cherokees first encountered Europeans when the expedition of Spaniard Hernando de Soto visited them in 1540. Strange as they must have appeared, however, with their guns, armor, silk clothes, bloodhounds, horses, and crosses, the Spaniards' arrival could not have adequately forewarned the American Indians of the total revolution which would soon come about in their way of life.

The Spanish expedition, consisting of 500 to 700 Europeans and several hundred Indian slaves, passed to the east of Tugaloo Town, where the Cherokees may not have yet settled. The Spanish saw their first "Chalaque" towns on the Keowee River, where the "naked and lean" American Indians nonetheless gave the Spanish several hundred wild turkeys and some deer. Later, at Nacoochee (northwest of present-day Clarkesville), the Cherokees provided the Conquistadors with 300 dogs to eat. The Spanish passed through this territory without leaving their customary legacy of raping, burning, looting, and enslaving, and perhaps due to this lack of lasting trauma, the Cherokees retained little memory of de Soto or the visit of Juan Pardo in 1566-1567.[1]

Indirectly, the wandering "conquistadors" and the longer-lasting missions that the Spanish established along the South Atlantic and Gulf of Mexico coasts had a considerable impact on Cherokee culture. From the Europeans, the Cherokees eventually acquired horses; Samuel C. Williams maintains this occurred about 1700 through trade with the Chickasaws, who had obtained horses somewhat earlier. As generations passed, the American Indians apparently bred them in considerable numbers. According to Logan's *History of Upper South Carolina*: "On the luxuriant cane pastures of the Tugaloo and Keowee Rivers...the Cherokee kept immense droves of horses that roamed as wild and free as the deer of the same region." Early Franklin County deeds indirectly support this claim, for they occasionally mention "old fields" near the sites of the former Tugaloo towns.[2]

For over a century, the Cherokees continued their adjustment to the Southern Appalachians and the Tugaloo region, and they experienced little direct contact with the Europeans. Major changes, however, were signaled around 1673, when the first contact between the Cherokees and the white traders was recorded. In 1674, an adventurous South Carolinian, Dr. Henry Woodward, passed through the towns at the headwaters of the Savannah, quite possibly the first white man to pass by the future location of Traveler's Rest.[3]

In spite of a few such tenuous contacts, the Cherokees remained remote from the English until after 1700. Extensive involvement between Cherokees and Europeans did not come until the colonists' economic and territorial rivalry had spread to include the land of the Cherokees. From the vantage point of the English colonists, the Cherokees were an unknown "quantity" before 1700.[4]

When 150 settlers disembarked on the Southern frontier in 1670, founding the South Carolina colony, they were immediately caught up in all-out imperial rivalry. "Wee [sic] are here settled in the very chaps of the Spaniards," they reported. The Spanish had an old base at St. Augustine and outposts well up the South Atlantic coast, which they considered to be theirs.[5] (See Map 3.)

The English, Spanish, and French quickly involved the American Indians in their struggle for empire. As Vernor Crane maintains in *The Southern Frontier*, "In the interior of North America rivalry centered in competition for the Indian trade and Indian alliances." Among the South Carolinians awoke a "dawning consciousness" of the "ultimate stake" in this contest—"the dominion of the continent." Such a prize produced a bitter and lengthy struggle, much of which took place in the neighborhood of Tugaloo Town. The conflict did not diminish for over a century and a half, after the land had passed into the hands of American settlers and the Eastern Cherokees were all but destroyed. But in 1700, the fate of this struggle was uncertain.[6]

In the late seventeenth century, the South Carolina colony was controlled by the same group of Englishmen who ran Hudson's Bay Company. Members of this group were well aware of the value of a fur trade with the American Indians, so by 1700, South Carolina was the vanguard of British imperial expansion. Enterprising traders of the colony had already penetrated beyond the Mississippi River, "the spread of English influence [being]...accomplished...by obscure and often nameless explorers and traders."[7] South Carolina held a key position just south of the Alleghenies, with access to the tribes of the Southeast denied to the northern English colonies. The English were almost always able to out-trade the Spanish and the French, and this ability was the "fundamental reason for the success...of the English in the tortuous politics of the wilderness..."[8]

Sometime before 1696, Jean Couture, a French *coureur de bois* of great experience, deserted the French in order to pursue the more lucrative

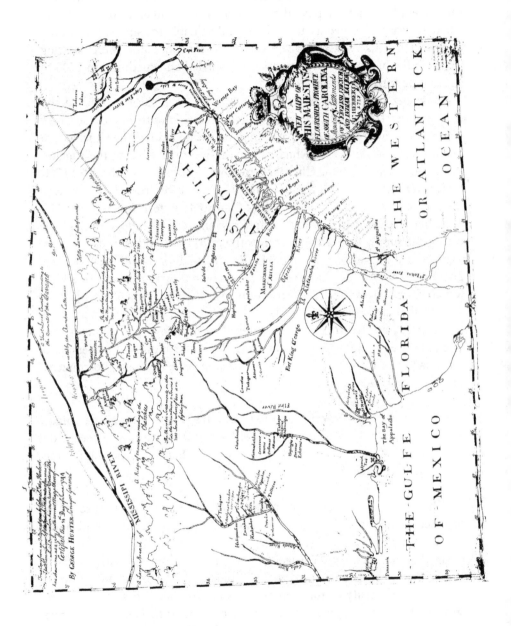

**Map 3:** South Carolina and the Southeastern Frontier, ca. 1775.
*Site of Traveler's Rest

possibilities of trading with the American Indians for the English. Couture passed through the Cherokee territory from the northwest, descended the ancient Unicoi Trail, passed by Tugaloo Town, and arrived in Carolina, where he was welcomed as an explorer and valuable Indian expert. Associated with various Western trade promoters—some of whom were "seeking riches in the bed of the Savannah River"—he led an expedition in 1700 to open trade with the Cherokees.[9]

A trader setting out from Charles Town in the early 1700s had the choice of two trails: the main path, which led overland from Ochese Creek to the Coosa and Talapoosa rivers, then on to the land of the Chickasaws; and the less-traveled route, which ran up the Savannah River to the Tugaloo towns, and then on up the Cherokee trail to the mountains. Soon after 1700, traders regularly followed a path up the Tugaloo to get from the Cherokees the deer skins that furnished the bulk of the Southeastern Indian trade. "Infinite herds" of deer were killed, their skins tanned and shipped to England before the supply and trade fell off in the mid-eighteenth century. Goods were carried in and out of the mountains in small pack trains of well-laden horses. Sometimes, Cherokee burdeners would carry thirty skins all the way to Charles Town for "two yards of blue duffields [a type of cloth]."[10]

On the navigable rivers, such as the Savannah, small craft were used to facilitate transportation. It was stated that "a periago paddled by seven or eight slaves could load 500-700 skins." Years later, however, traders used much larger boats. In 1748, the *South Carolina Gazette* advertised concerning one such boat:

> Stolen, or gone adrift, from Mr. Elliott's wharf, last Tuesday night, an Indian-trading Boat, 42 Feet long and upwards of 7 feet wide, with a Cabin in her Stern, and Staples in her Side, and a king bolt in her Head.[11]

These long, narrow boats, by necessity, displaced only three or four feet of water, as the rapids just above the site of Augusta were a major obstacle to river transportation. Nonetheless, such trading boats were quite likely navigating the waters of the Tugaloo to Tugaloo Town in the early 1700s.[12]

As the Carolinians expanded their trade and settlement, they also increased the intensity of the imperial rivalry. The Spanish and French responded to Carolina's growing Indian trade by founding Pensacola in 1698, Biloxi in 1699, and Mobile soon afterwards. The French expansion especially aroused in the English a fear of the "menace of French encirclement," and the French avidly courted the American Indians, including the Cherokees.[13]

All of the tribes had been provided with ample reasons for hating the Charles Townians by this time. A great many of the Cherokees owed the traders for goods received in advance, and it had also become obvious that the English settlements were spreading rapidly, eliminating coastal tribes. Furthermore, the growing English slave trade in American Indians was terrifyingly ruthless. Matters were also aggravated by the fact that most traders were "not (generally) Men of the best Morals," frequently exploiting the American Indians' fatal susceptibility to "fire-water" to perpetrate unfair exchanges. The situation was so bad that it was said,

> There are a number of Idle Desolate People White men who under the notion of Traders live a Debauched and wicked Life and have nothing to do, and for want of Subsistence become a burthen [sic] to the Cherakee [sic] Indians.[14]

These factors combined to provoke the Yamasee War of 1715, when all the Southern tribes, with the exception of the Chickasaw, conspired to destroy the Charles Town settlers because of their hatred for the traders. In a surprise attack, the Cherokees wiped out the English traders among them, except for one who escaped to Charles Town with a dire warning. The 17,000 Cherokees then prepared to add their numbers to the other Indian hordes arrayed against the 5,000 Carolinians. The French gloated, as the very survival of the Southern English colonies seemed to be in doubt, but the English rallied to defeat the Yamasee, the Apalachee, and some of the Northern tribes as well, causing the Cherokees to waver in their hostility. Also, at this point, the Cherokees must have considered the consequences of their actions where trading was concerned, for in spite of numerous honeyed promises, few goods had found their way to the mountains from the French.[15]

At this critical juncture, late in 1715, Colonel Maurice Moore led 300 men to Tugaloo Town to persuade the Cherokees to renew their friendship with the English. The small colonial army marched up the Tugaloo to the village at the mouth of Toccoa Creek, shadowed by Indian scouts for the last several days. Captain George Chicken, already something of a hero, kept a vivid journal of the march. Upon arriving in the Cherokee country, Chicken reported:

> Thorsday ye 29 - This day we drewe up ower men and marched to tugaloe where ye Indens meat us with the Eigalles Talles [feather and dresses] and made their semimoneys [ceremonies] then come sem ould [sic] men with black drinke to give us when they retorned back they tould us to march into ye Town they made [a] lane of there men to ye Round Howes where ye Congyer ["Charity Hayge" of Tugaloo, archi magnus of the Lower Towns and firm friend of the English, who greatly esteemed him] satt in State to Receive us after we toucke him

by ye hand We stept back then he came and strode before us with his hands oupen to Receive ye 2 white flages with he did then gave them to one of his men to seat one of ye Tope of ye Round Howes [*sic*]

On December 30ᵗʰ, the Colonials met with the Conjuror and began "ye discours." The leader of Tugaloo Town told the soldiers that "he and ye English was all one that he nore none of his men should ever fitte ageanst us aney more...[*sic*]." The Cherokees did not want to fight the Yamasees either, "as for ye Crickes [Creeks] they hade promised to com down when we came up...[*sic*]" to negotiate. The Conjuror told the English that he did not wish to fight the Catawbas and Yamasees, but that he had no objections to taking on the Yuchis and Apalachees. He continued, saying that the Creeks had promised to negotiate with them, and they were expected soon.

Staying at the Lower Towns, the English observed two parties among the Cherokees; the Conjuror of Tugaloo, who led a peace faction comprised mostly of leaders of the Lower Towns, closer to the English; and the Cherokees of the mountains, who were inclined not to turn against the other tribes, but rather to continue the war against the English. For the time being, however, the Cherokees promoted negotiations with the oncoming Creeks, and the English agreed to wait, their force scattered among the Lower Towns to make provisions more accessible.

The Cherokees' involvement in these crucial negotiations, however, did not abate their love for the ballgame. On January 7, the team from Tugaloo Town traveled twenty-five miles to Tohowee, on the Salwege River, for "a greatt ballplay." Four days later, "ther was a greett ballplay att Esttohee (Old Estates) agenst ye peaple of Tugaloe [*sic*]."[16]

In three weeks, a large war party of Creeks secretly arrived (on January 27), consisting of perhaps 200 to 500 warriors. The English at Tugaloo saw only a dozen Creek chieftains, who went into the "Round Howes." Suddenly, there came a war-whoop and outcries, as the Creek emissaries were "put to the knife" by the Cherokees. Later, the English found out about the Creek war party and its proposal to massacre the scattered Carolina army and then to fall upon the frontier settlements. The Carolinians greatly appreciated the closeness of the call, for the Creeks had almost convinced the Cherokees to agree to their plan when, "as Providence order'd it, they chang'd their minds and fell upon the Creeks and Yamusees [*sic*] who were in their towns and kill'd every man of them." The remainder of the Creek war party was then driven off.[17]

This "massacre" at Tugaloo Town had far-reaching consequences. Disaster for the Southern English colonies was thus narrowly averted, and the foundation was laid for a trading alliance between Charles Town and the Cherokees, which waxed and waned for the next 50 years. The Yamasee War opened the eyes of many English colonials to the overall importance of the imperial struggle, and, finally, the Creeks were motivated to remove from northwestern Georgia and retire closer to the French at Mobile. For the next few generations, the Creeks would seek to wield the balance of power in the southeast, and they still sought this as late as the 1780s, when a Creek raiding party ambushed and wounded Jesse Walton on his Tugaloo land.[18]

In 1717, a trading factory was established near Tugaloo Town close to the site where Devereaux Jarrett's bridge would one day cross into South Carolina, and the Tugaloo Crossroads increased in importance as trade between the English and the Cherokees developed. During the eighteenth century, Charles Town traders reached the Cherokees by water routes or "well-beaten roads." The Indian trading paths "really began," Vernor Crane observes in *The Southern Frontier*, "at the fall-line of the rivers," and Fort Congaree, built in 1718 and situated "at the head of the Santee Swamp," was a major stopping-place on the trails to the Catawbas and the Cherokees. From Congaree, traders could reach Tugaloo and the Lower Towns. According to Crane, from Congaree,

> [The] path followed the southern margin of the Congaree watershed, through Saluda Old Town and Ninety-Six, so-called because ninety-six miles from Keowee, and then crossed over to the headwaters of the Savannah River. From Dividing Paths near Apple Tree Creek one path ran westward to the heart of the Lower Towns on the Tugaloo River, the other to Keowee. At Tugaloo…the English maintained one of their principal factories…Westward from Tugaloo, at the head of the Chattahoochee, fifteen to thirty miles distant, were the frontier towns towards the Creeks: Soquee or Sukeki, Naguchee, and Echota. From Echota a difficult mountain path led by way of Unacoi [sic] Gap over the lofty Blue Ridge, then through the Valley Towns to the Head of the Hiwasee, a branch to the Tennessee, and ultimately across the high Unakas by the Northwest Passage of the traders to the Overhill Cherokee.

Rather than turn southward through the Lower Towns, however, most traders went to the mountain Cherokees by way of Keowee and Rabun Gap. From Charles Town, the nearest Cherokee village was 300 miles; the farthest, 500.[19] (See Map 4.)

As the trade developed, more and more traders used the Savannah River route to the Cherokees. Vernor Crane describes this path as follows:

> Long before the founding of Georgia, the Carolina traders followed a path to the Cherokee from Old Fort, opposite Savannah Town, along

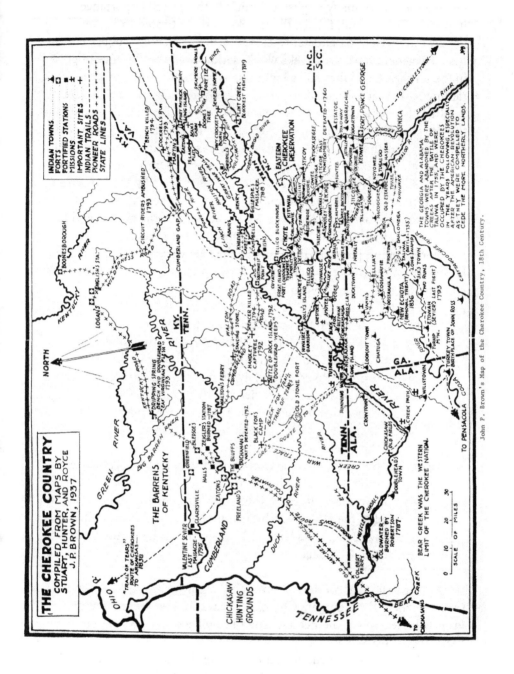

**Map 4:** The Cherokee Country

the right bank of the Savannah River. Later, this became the main highway between Georgia and the mountain towns. But the usual Carolina route from Savannah Town ran northeast of the river. Both trails entered the Cherokee country at Tugaloo, where also ended the Indian path, sometimes used by traders, from Coweta Town on the Chattahoochee.[20]

The Yamasee War established an alliance between the South Carolinians and Cherokees that never satisfied the American Indians. Indeed, for the Cherokees, the eighteenth century was a troubled, even disastrous, time. The warriors could never seem to get enough guns and ammunition from Carolina to put them on a secure basis with other tribes, and they constantly sought a more abundant source of trade. The headmen sent numerous emissaries to the Virginians, Pennsylvanians, and the French, seeking trade. While almost constant warfare made armament a necessity, it also distracted braves from the deer-hunting they must do to gain purchase power for guns and other trade goods. Add to these problems the unsavory character of traders, their eagerness to develop the rum trade, the ravages of plague, and the steady growth of settlement, and it becomes easy to understand why this century was one of continuing crisis for the Cherokees at Tugaloo and elsewhere.

By the middle of the eighteenth century, the wise among the Cherokees were aware of the degree to which the tribe had become dependent on manufactured goods. Skiagunota, an old at chief of the Lower Towns, expressed this realization:

> My people…cannot live independent of the English…The clothes we wear we cannot make ourselves. They are made for us. We use their ammunition with which to kill deer. We cannot make our guns. Every necessity of life we must have from the white people.[21]

At the Tugaloo villages, the quality of life suffered. Decades of fighting, hunting, and living near the white men and their trade had revolutionized Cherokee lifestyle. But the benefits of metal goods, clothing, and decorations were more than offset by the evils of disease, war, indebtedness, and drunkenness. Farming suffered from the distractions of disease and war. The religion and power of the "priestly cult" declined, while the position of women became increasingly one of alienation. Meanwhile, village rivalry for tribal leadership—mostly among the Chota, Keowee, and Tellicoe—rent the Cherokees. Only the bounty of the land saved the American Indians from poverty.[22]

The war with the Creeks was a constant problem for the exposed towns on the Tugaloo. Raiding parties could strike at any time, and it seemed to the Cherokees that the English were favoring their enemies. The Charles

Townians set the Creeks' prices for trade goods at a lower rate, and when the Conjuror of Tugaloo, a proven friend of the English, was murdered by Creeks just outside Charles Town in the early 1720s, the Cherokees suspected English connivance.[23] In 1724, they looked the other way when a party of Creeks under "Gogel Eyes" looted the station at Tugaloo, wounding trader John Sharp and making off with slaves and goods. It was reported that the Cherokees felt that Sharp had been living up to his name.[24]

In 1725, Colonel George Chicken set out from Charles Town on a mission to patch up the relationship between the English and Cherokees. He visited a score of towns, explaining the Carolinians' position, pressing gifts on the headmen, including the "Warrior of Tugelo," one of the "Most Noted Men in the Nation." In mid-September, Chicken climaxed his mission at Tugaloo Town, where "At the said Town they fired a Volly [sic] at my Entrance of their Council House and Ussed [sic] their Ceremony before me...." Chicken informed the American Indians that the English had demanded satisfaction of the Creeks for their raid on Sharp's trading post, and the Creeks had already returned the slaves.[25]

In October of that year, an event occurred which indicates something of what life must have been like for the Cherokees in the towns on the Tugaloo during those years. In the "dead of night," four Creeks stealthily approached Old Estatoe, the best fortified town in the area, fired against the village and fled into the night with the Cherokees in hot, but futile pursuit. Finally, in 1755, the Cherokees alleviated some of the tension of such surprise attacks by defeating the Creeks in a battle at Taliwa, just southwest of present-day Dahlonega.[26]

Far worse than war, however, was the devastation wrought by smallpox, especially an epidemic which swept the whole Cherokee Nation in 1738-39. In two years, the tribe's population was reduced by half. Although the American Indians were particularly susceptible to this white man's disease, possessing little immunity against it, they worsened its impact by treating the accompanying fever in a traditional manner: taking steamy sweat-baths, followed by plunges into disastrously cold water.

At first, according to *Old Frontiers*, the tribal "magi and religious physicians" attributed the plague to "aldulterous [sic] intercourses" of the young people, who had been accused of having "violated" marriage customs "in every thicket." As they had supposedly earned their illness through exposure to "night dews," the shamans prescribed staying outside all night, splashing on cold water, and singing "Yo Yo etc. with a doleful tone." These remedies, of course, did not cure the smallpox. Thus,

> When they found their theological regimen had not the desired effect, but that the infection gained upon them, they held a second

consultation, and deemed it the best method to sweat their patients, and plunge them into the river,—which was accordingly done. Their rivers being very cold in summer, by reason of the numberless springs, which pour from the hills and mountains—and the pores of their bodies being open to receive the cold, it rushing in through the whole frame, they immediately expired: upon which, all the magi prophetic tribe broke their old consecrated physic-pots, and threw away all the other pretended holy things they had for physical use, imagining they had lost their divine power by being polluted; and shared the common fate of their country. A great many killed themselves; for being naturally proud, they are always peeping into their looking glasses, and are never genteelly drest [dressed], according to their mode, without carrying one hung over their shoulders: by which means, seeing themselves disfigured, without hope of regaining their former beauty, some shot themselves, others cut their throats, some stabbed themselves with knives, and others with sharp-pointed canes; many threw themselves with sullen madness into the fire, and were slowly expired, as if they had been utterly divested of the native power of feeling pain.[27]

The French seized this opportunity to spread rumors that the English were purposefully circulating the disease in order to exterminate the Cherokees and claim their lands. The American Indians were inclined to believe them.[28]

The prevalence of warfare and the decline of religion and farming all tended to undermine the Cherokee women's general position in the tribe. Nonetheless, many English traders found it expedient and desirable to marry high-placed women of the various villages. Although the Cherokee women were often attracted to the wealthy traders, they were also inclined to marry them in order to regain lost status, and the English married into the Cherokee tribe to an unparalleled extent on the North American frontier. Hundreds of mixed marriages took place over the years, but mixed-bloods did not exercise any considerable leadership in the tribe before the 1760s. However, as hostility developed between the Cherokees on the one hand and the traders and settlers on the other, intermarriage was to achieve great historical significance, for many women were forced to choose between white husbands and tribal loyalties. During the course of the Revolution, some—led by Nancy Ward—came to favor reconciliation with the American rebels over continued hostility and bloodshed in service to the English Crown.[29]

The founding of Georgia did not relieve the Cherokees from the pressures of war, trade, and change, although the Georgia colonists did attempt to compete with South Carolina for Indian trade after 1735. They soon built

Fort Augusta, in 1739, and were well-located to offer the Cherokees better prices than the Carolinians could. However, this competition gave the American Indians only short-term relief, for apparently the colonists found it more profitable to compete in rum-trading than in useful goods, and colony prohibitions against the liquor trade were never enforceable.[30]

By 1751, settlers were nearing the Tugaloo area, and their steady advance gradually brought about a change in the tribe's thinking. Historians such as Woodward and Willis discern by the 1760s a trend in the Cherokee tribe to put less effort into warring against other tribes, as well as less disunity and competition among the Cherokee towns. From the time of the French and Indian Wars (1754-1761) and the Cherokees' disastrous war against the English colonies (1760-1761), the tribe was increasingly preoccupied with defending its lands from the encroaching white settlers.[31]

The French and English struggle to control North America erupted into armed clashes in the mid-1750s. The Cherokees had accumulated plentiful grievances against the English and made the fateful choice during this time of siding with the French. As the Cherokees and colonists traded bloody blows, the Lower Towns led in anti-English sentiment. Tugaloo Town had harbored a grudge after 1751, when Carolina thieves stole over 300 deerskins from Tugaloo hunters. The Tugaloos suspected Justice James Francis of Ninety-Six of protecting the culprits, and young Cherokee warriors retaliated by mingling with Seneca war parties on the Georgia frontier. War came to the Tugaloo towns in June of 1760, when Colonel John Montgomery led a surprise night-time attack on Keowee and Estatoe, routing the American Indians and burning the towns. Just a year later, the whole Tugaloo cluster was laid waste by Colonel James Grant and 2,000 men. The English came as before in "Green Corn Month"—June—and gave the Lower Towns a ransacking from which they never recovered. Grant's daily journal captured the tenor of the campaign:

> We halted (at Etchoe). Corn about the town was destroyed. Parties were sent out to burn the scattered houses, pull up beans, peas, and corn, and to demolish everything eatable in the country. Our Indian scouts, with one of our parties, destroyed Neowee and Kanuga. A scout of our Indians killed a Cherokee and wounded another at Ayore. A miserable old squaw from Tasso was brought in and put to death in the Indian camp by one of the Catawbas.[32]

Grant's army carried the attack into the Middle Towns and then abandoned the campaign in July, out of provisions. Fifteen towns and 1,500 acres of crops had been razed, and 5,000 Cherokees fled into the mountains, only to face starvation. The Lower Towns' "immense" herds of horses soon starved also, with some perhaps being eaten by the hungry American Indians. While some historians say the Lower Towns were never rebuilt, Brown, in *Old Frontiers*, maintains that some of the towns at the Tugaloo cluster were restored after the colonists reoccupied Fort Prince George in the early 1760s. It is reasonably certain, however, that Tugaloo Town never recovered from Grant's onslaught in 1761. At the onset of the Revolution in 1776, Colonel Samuel Jack and 200 Georgians completed the destruction of the towns at the headwaters of the Tugaloo. Colonel Jack was accompanied by Lieutenant Leonard Marbury, who later took out grants to land near Tugaloo Town and Old Estatoe. Tugaloo Town was ransacked again in August by Andrew Williamson and several hundred soldiers from South Carolina (see Map 5). After that, the lands on the river must have been relatively empty until the acreage was plotted out to settlers a decade later.[33]

## NOTES

[1] Willis, *Colonial Conflict*, p. 11. Willis says that the Cherokees did not settle on the Tugaloo until after 1600. Also, Woodward, *The Cherokees*, pp. 22, 23.

[2] Samuel C. Williams, ed., *Adair's History of the American Indians* (New York: Promontory Press, 1930), pp. 242, 340. John H. Logan, *A History of the Upper Country of South Carolina* (Charleston, S.C.: S.G. Courtenay Co., 1859), Vol. 1, pp. 158-59.

[3] Crane, *The Southern Frontier*, pp. 15, 16.

[4] Ibid., pp. 16-21. Also, Willis, *Colonial Conflict*, p. 16.

[5] Crane, *The Southern Frontier*, p. 3.

[6] On the story of this struggle, read Willis, *Colonial Conflict*; Crane, *The Southern Frontier*, p. v.; and David Ti. Cock ran, *The Cherokee Frontier, Conflict and Survival, 1740-1762* (Norman, Okla.: University of Oklahoma Press, 1962).

[7] Crane, *The Southern Frontier*, p. 22.

[8] Ibid., p. 23.

[9] Ibid., pp. 30, 42, 43.

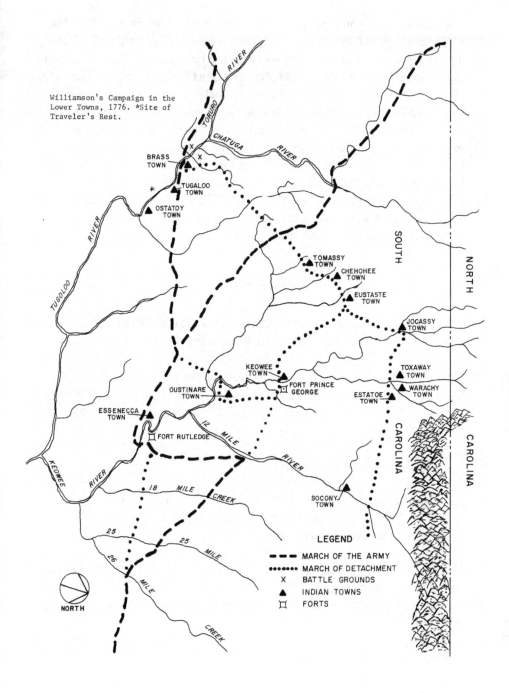

**Map 5:** Williamson's Campaign in the Lower Towns, 1776

[10] Ibid., pp. 109-12, 126, 128.

[11] Ibid., p. 128. See also, A.R. Kelly and Clemens de Baillou, "Excavation of the Presumptive Site of Estatoe," *Southern Indian Studies*, Vol. 12, October 1960, pp. 3-31.

[12] Crane, *The Southern Frontier*, p. 128.

[13] Ibid., pp. 48, 61, 62. Also, E. Merton Coulter, *Georgia: A Short History* (Chapel Hill, N.C.: University of North Carolina Press, 1942), p. 11.

[14] Willis, *Colonial Conflict*, pp. 61, 62, 68.

[15] On the Yamasee War, see Crane, *The Southern Frontier*, pp. 175-85.

[16] Trogden, *The History of Stephens County*, p. 5, 28

[17] Willis, *Colonial Conflict*, pp. 41-43; and Crane, *The Southern Frontier*, pp. 150-52.

[18] On the results of the Yamasee War referred to here and on Page 20, see Willis, *Colonial Conflict*, pp. 43-47; Crane, *The Southern Frontier*, pp. 182-85.

[19] Crane, *The Southern Frontier*, pp. 129, 130; Willis, *Colonial Conflict*, pp. 41-43.

[20] Crane, *The Southern Frontier*, pp. 132, 133.

[21] Corkran, *The Cherokee Frontier*, p. 14. Also, Willis, Colonial Conflict, p. 9.

[22] Willis, *Colonial Conflict*, pp. 4, 125.

[23] Ibid. p. 50.

[24] Crane, *The Southern Frontier*, p. 266.

[25] Mereness, *Travels in the American Colonies*, p. 145.

[26] Ibid., pp. 160, 161; and Brown, Old *Frontiers*, p. 26.

[27] James Adair, *History of the American Indians* (New York: Promontory Press, 1930), pp. 244, 245.

[28] Brown, *Old Frontiers*, pp. 51, 52.

[29] Willis, *Colonial Conflict*, p. 125; and Woodward, *The Cherokees*, p. 86.

[30] Willis, *Colonial Conflict*, pp. 60, 61.

[31] Ibid., 4; and Woodward, The Cherokees, pp. 86, 87.

[32] Brown, *Old Frontiers*, pp. 90-96, 110; and Woodward, *The Cherokees*, pp. 75, 77, 78.

[33] Brown, *Old Frontiers*, p. 154. Also, Corkran, *The Cherokee Frontier*, p. 247. Corkran indicates that Old Estatoe may have been defunct by the time of Grant's mission. He also reports that the treaty forced on the Cherokees at the end of the French and Indian Wars included a cession of hunting lands within 40 miles of the Tugaloo towns, p.262. Samuel Jack's expedition of Georgians did not finish off the Cherokee Lower Towns for good. Ben Hawkins visited the Nacoochee town of Little Chote as late as 1796; "Nacoochee Valley: Early Crossroads," an unpublished paper by Dr. Thomas L. Lumsden, Clarkesville, Georgia. On Williamson, see Colonial Records of North Carolina, Vol. X, p. 746; on Marbury, see Charles C. Jones, The *History of Georgia*, Vol. V (Boston: Houghton, Mifflin and Company, 1883), pp. 245-47. On the horses, see Logan, *History of Upper South Carolina*, p. 159.

# Chapter 3

## Jesse Walton: Frontiersman and Settler

The Tugaloo River and its surrounding areas were pioneered by white settlers at the climax of a wave of settlement which began in Pennsylvania, rolled through Virginia and North Carolina, down the eastern slopes of the Blue Ridge, and into northern Georgia by the mid-1780s. Most of the first grantees to acquire land in what would become Franklin County, Georgia, were from North Carolina and Virginia. Obese and somewhat rapacious, Colonel Ben Cleveland took out a grant to the site of Old Tugaloo Town in 1785 while another veteran frontiersman, Major Jesse Walton, obtained a survey to land spanning the river at a ford slightly downstream. The ford became known as Walton's Ford, and the good-sized creek, which entered the river nearby, became Walton's Creek. Traveler's Rest would one day stand at the southern border of Walton's 400-acre grant.[1] (See Map 6.)

Jesse Walton led a life of remarkable adventure and accomplishment on the Southeastern frontier. The location and year of his birth are not precisely known, but it probably took place in Goochland County, Virginia. When his father, William, died in 1746, Jesse was mentioned in his will as the youngest son, and since the next older, William, was born in 1736, Jesse's birth must have occurred around 1740. This makes him a contemporary of his frontier compatriots—Joseph Martin, John Sevier, and the Cleveland brothers, Ben, John, and Larkin.[2]

The major route of the great mid-eighteenth century migration down the eastern slopes of the Appalachian Mountains was known as the "Great Philadelphia Wagon Road," which skirted the mountains from Pennsylvania to Georgia, following "an ancient warrior's path" of the Iroquois. Settlers—a great flood of English, Scotch-Irish, German, and, later, their African slaves—began to utilize this route along the frontier of every colony south of Pennsylvania in 1744. After 1760, this migration reached dramatic proportions. As Carl Bridenbaugh observed in *Myths and Realities, Societies of the Colonial South*,

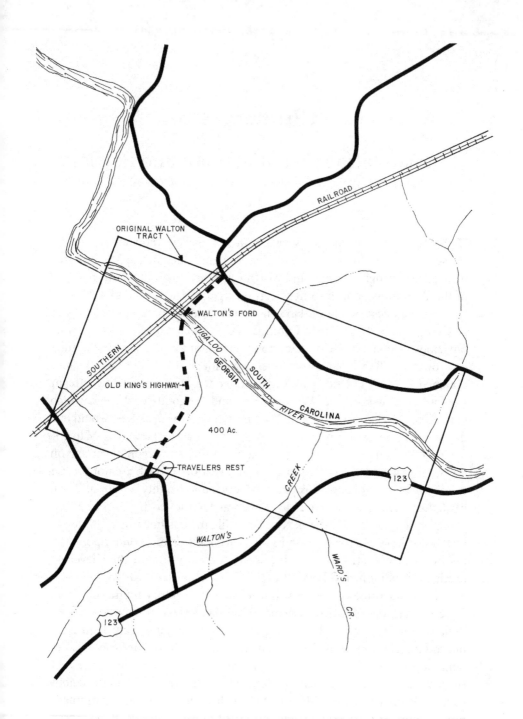

**Map 6:** Walton Grant on the Tugaloo River, 1785

In the last sixteen years of the colonial era, southbound traffic along the Great Philadelphia Wagon Road was numbered in tens of thousands; it was the most heavily traveled road in all America and must have had more vehicles jolting along its rough and tortuous way than all the other main roads put together.[3]

In the mid-1760s, this land-hungry tide of people swept up three young men in Virginia—Ben Cleveland, Jesse Walton, and Joseph Martin—and eventually carried them to the Tugaloo River. Like twigs in a stream, Walton and Cleveland lodged for a time in western North Carolina. In those years, the wagon road was hardly more than a trail in that state, yet, by 1765, most of the road had been cleared for horsedrawn vehicles; its maintenance was supposedly overseen by countyappointed commissioners, while local farmers earned "off-season" income by filling holes, endeavoring to defeat the mud with gravel. From the Yadkin River, the main portion of the wagon road ran on to Augusta, and later, a lesser branch found its way to western South Carolina and crossed the Tugaloo into northeastern Georgia—to the famous crossroads known as "The Dividings," at the site of Clayton in Rabun County, the ancient Indian crossroads near Apple Tree Creek. According to Joan A. Sears:

> Settlers coming into Georgia could come along the trail [the Great Wagon Road] to "the Dividings," turn south, and continue along a major Indian trail called the Unicoi…This route, which later became the first vehicular way in northeast Georgia, began at the Tugaloo River.[4]

By the time Jesse Walton began to impinge on historical records, he was a restless settler in western North Carolina married to Mary Walker. Around 1770, however, he and his neighbor in Surry County, Ben Cleveland, set out—along with William Hightower, Jesse Bond, and Edward Rice—to sample the hunting grounds of fabled "Kaintuck." Late that summer, they traveled over 300 miles into the wilderness, stopping on the Kentucky River. They had a fine time pursuing game, but in October, when they prepared to depart

> …with the profits of their hunt…pelfry and fur-skins, they was discovered by sum Cherokee Indians who at first manifested friendship but err long they all was made prisoners and all their property and fire arms taken from them—their hats and shoes; and an old shot gun was given in return.

According to one account, the Cherokee leader told the hunters that all the game on Indian land belonged to the American Indians, pointed east, and said, "That is your way home, walk." The hungry hunters had time to contemplate these words as they trod the 300 barefoot miles back to North Carolina. Finally, they slaughtered a faithful friend, Walton's dog. "They killed Toler," it was said, "and found him very fat, for a dog..."[5]

Ben Cleveland, however, was not one to let his property go quite so easily, and he resolved to return to the Cherokee country "in opposition to wishes of his friends, to whose remonstrances he replied 'that they (the American Indians) had robbed him of all he had, that he would as soon die as to be left in so destitute a condition.'"

A few months later, Ben

> ...got sum of his confidential friends and after making the necessary arrangements visited the Town where the Indians resided that had plundered him and his party. The head man after being sattisfyed [sic] made ample sattisfaction [sic] for their losses.

Historians agree that upon Cleveland's return, "he saw the lands on the Tugulo [sic] River, now Pendleton District, So. Carolina but as the Revolution was came [sic] on, he never had it in his power to Explore the country untill [sic] it was over."[6] The record does not say what Cherokee towns they had visited, to be returning by way of the Tugaloo, and this memoir of Devereaux Jarrett's neighbor, Ben Cleveland, Jr., fails to mention whether or not Walton accompanied the "rescue mission."

When the colonies opted for independence, Jesse Walton was an experienced militia officer in Surry County, North Carolina. According to the Draper Manuscripts, Walton's company of minutemen was the first to be raised in that county.[7] In August of 1775, Walton and Ben Cleveland were on the Surry Committee of Safety, which took a stand against taxation without representation, resolving:

> ...that those who now would subject all America or this Province to Dependency on the Parliament of Great Britain are guilty of a very Dangerous Innovation injurious to the Crown and inconsistent with the Liberty of American subjects; and that by the Law of Nature and the British Constitution no man can be Legally Taxed, or have his property taken from him without his consent, given by himself or his Representatives.[8]

Soon, Walton and Cleveland were appointed to confiscate Tory ammunition, and in September of 1775, Walton became a member of the Special Committee of "secrecy and intelligence." During that winter, he fulfilled the position in investigating the loyalty of the Moravians at Wachovia, North

Carolina, who were subsequently cleared of charges of aiding the British. The Moravians, however, apparently took a dim view of Walton and his company, for when under investigation by the "Committee of Safety," they wrote that one day, "Capt. Walton and his company drew up before the tavern; some of the men spoke joyfully of the booty they were going to get." At this time, the Moravians reported that Walton had tested their loyalty through their willingness to accept the Patriots' tender: "Capt. Walton and his Lieutenant, Benjamin Cleveland...went into the store and workshops and took what they wanted, charging it to public account." In February of 1776, the Moravian *Records* again briefly mentioned Walton's company, also in an unfavorable light. The community at Bethabara (near Wachovia) "had been frightened by men wearing buck-tails in the hat, presumably...from [Walton's] Company, which has been roughly treating people on the Atkin."[9]

Also in February, agent Walton was active in leading the militia in the capture of two of the area's foremost Tories, who were charged with conspiring to help the British. Before long, Walton's company was on the march, along with General Griffith Rutherford, to confront 3,500 Loyalists at Cross Creek. Before the Surry County men could arrive to gather any laurels, the Patriots had won the Battle of Moore's Creek, and Walton's men were allotted the unsatisfying task of guarding prisoners. The watchful Moravian wrote:

> March 13. Capt. Walton and his company spent the night in the tavern [at Salem] on their return from Cross Creek, which caused a great deal of disturbance there, though it was fairly quiet in the town.[10]

Early in the Revolution, the traders' custom of marrying into the Cherokee tribe became a prime factor in the course of the war on the frontier. Nancy Ward, a "Ghighau" or "Beloved Woman" of the Cherokees since she fought in her husband's place at the Battle of Taliwa in 1755, took an active role in promoting peace between the Cherokees and the settlers. Respected by both peoples as "queenly and commanding," Nancy married Bryant Ward, a trader, around 1760. When she could not keep the Cherokees off the warpath through persuasion, she warned the whites of impending attack in July of 1776. One of those who felt that the two peoples should learn to live together, the "Ghighau" acted to save lives on both sides.[11]

By May of 1776, Jesse Walton held the rank of major. That summer, the Cherokees of the Middle Towns in North Carolina were perpetrating bloody raids on the frontier settlements, just as Nancy Ward had warned. Rutherford's brigade was ordered after the "hostiles," and Walton was dispatched with a force of 300 under Lieut. Col. Joseph Williams to protect the settlers on the waters of the Holston, Watauga, and Nolachucky Rivers. They were to join Colonel William Christian at the Long Island of the Holston (Joseph Martin's Station) and combine for an attack on the Overhills. The Cherokees were forced to sue for peace, and were granted it on the condition of their meeting at Long Island to cede a portion of much-coveted land to Virginia and North Carolina.[12]

Some of the Surry County troops remained in the western country to build and garrison a fort, and under Jesse Walton's command, Fort Williams was placed on the Nolachucky River near Jacob Brown's settlement. Walton must have been quite attracted to the region for, in spite of the dangers, he bought a plantation in the neighborhood in 1777. Nearby, Ben Cleveland was commanding a garrison at John Carter's Fort on the Watauga, and the two North Carolina outposts cooperated with Joseph Martin's Station in an endeavor to protect the frontier settlements.[13]

That summer, all the soldiers attended the treaty conference at the Long Island of the Holston. Fort Williams was taken over by Colonel John Sevier and western troops, and when Sevier moved to a plantation near Walton's, he and Jesse are presumed to have developed an "abiding friendship."[14] Soon Walton exercised political leadership in becoming a justice of the Court of Pleas for Washington County in February of 1778. Before taking a seat on the bench, however, he apparently returned to Surry County to gather his possessions and move his family. In May of that year, Walton and Sevier were commissioned to oversee confiscated Tory property. (Years later, Draper's sources claim Cleveland had grown wealthy through his leading role in confiscating Tory property; however, the present author has not seen any speculation along these lines regarding Walton, and it is not definitively known how Walton acquired his wealth.)[15]

In the fall of 1778, Walton was instrumental in the founding of what would one day be Tennessee's first town, Jonesborough. He had been appointed in November to "lay off the place for erecting the courthouse, prison, and stocks." He aimed to make an impact in North Carolina politics, for he chose to name the town after one of the state's leading Patriots, Declaration of Independence-signer Willie Jones. Walton was chosen to serve as Washington County's representative in the state legislature, and, in Halifax in 1779, he introduced a bill officially establishing Jonesborough. He was appointed,

> ...to lay out and direct the building of said town...and to make or cause to be made a fair plan of said town and number the lots, and take subscriptions for said lots, which shall be done by ballot in a fair and open manner...Every grantee of any lot shall within three years build on said lot one brick, stone, or framed house, twenty feet long and sixteen feet wide...with a brick or stone chimney.

Walton acquired nine of these lots in 1781, although he could have hardly planned to put a house on each. However, these lots made him Jonesborough's most substantial property owner. His old Kentucky hunting friend, Jesse Bond, apparently a tag-along, bought two lots.[16] Walton was the "leading spirit" in the town and the most active town commissioner; his duties included executing deeds, keeping accounts, and sitting on the county court—all this when he was not away serving in the North Carolina Legislature or in combat. Unfortunately, Walton's lot speculation was undermined by Jonesborough's slow growth in the beginning.[17]

Washington County records also show that Jesse Walton often sat with the court at Jonesborough. Beset by the dangerous difficulties of the Revolution, intermittent Indian wars, and a semi-barbarous populace, this court was determined to establish law and order on the frontier through stern justice. Horse thieves were punished by being pilloried for one hour, having both ears cut off, receiving thirty-nine lashes each, and having H and T branded on their cheeks.[18]

Apparently, citizens of the Watauga region were not all Whigs, for the court minutes show frequent efforts to deal with the Tory problem, several individuals being tried for high treason. In the summer of 1779, Walton and Jesse Bond appeared as witnesses accusing Benjamen Holley of that very crime. Holley must have fled, however, for the records contain no mention of his trial, but it is reported that his property was confiscated. Another somewhat mysterious case was that of James Gibson, who was called before the justices in February of 1781 while Jesse Walton sat on the bench. Gibson seems to have publicly expressed an unacceptable opinion of the court, for the records only state:

> James Gibson being brought before the court for throw-out Speeches against the Court, to wit, saying that the Court was perjured and would not do Justice, and other Glaring Insults—the Court on Considering the matter are of opinion: That the said James Gibson is Guilty of a flagrant breach of Peace and for the Same and the Glareing [sic] and dareing [sic] insults offered to the Court do order that the said James Gibson be fined the sum of fifteen thousand pounds and that he be kept in custody till the same be paid.[19]

The outcome of this case is not given, nor do the records reveal any details of the trial and Gibson's potent accusations.

Meanwhile, the Revolutionary War continued. Fearing and hating the encroaching settlers, many Cherokees were eager to lay waste to the frontier. In 1779, Joseph Martin, Virginia's Cherokee agent, wrote to Governor Patrick Henry that the Chickamauga branch of the tribe was planning to ravage the western settlements. Henry proposed a joint attack on the American Indians from North Carolina and Virginia, and Colonel Charles Robertson was chosen to lead the Watauga forces while Walton would be commissary. He refused the post but did agree to be contractor for the army and was given £5,000 to provide supplies. Samuel C. Williams, historian of Tennessee, reported that Walton went along on the ensuing campaign, which moved down the Watauga from Big Mouth Creek, where the Americans "wholesomely chastized [*sic*]" the Chickamaugas.[20]

Walton rounded out his Revolutionary career by serving as one of three auditors who settled claims by citizens against the state for property impressed during the war, participating in the Battle of King's Mountain, and joining another campaign against the Cherokees. History books yield no special mention of Walton's part in the heroics at King's Mountain.[21] On September 26, 1780, several hundred "overmountain men," including Jesse Walton, gathered at Sycamore Shoals on the Watauga and resolved to march southeast and confront a Tory army led by a redoubtable British Regular Colonel Patrick Ferguson that controlled the Carolina "Upcountry." On the same day, Colonel Elijah Clarke led 400 refugees from Dennis Mill, Georgia, heading for the Watauga settlement—the nearest area then under the control of the American rebels. The Patriot cause had suffered calamities in Georgia, and in mid-September, Clarke led a small force in an attack on Augusta. Its repulse brought about the arduous march which the Whig refugees then faced. Eating little besides nuts and berries gathered on the way, Clarke's people made an eleven-day journey, harassed by the specter of defeat and hostile American Indians. The illiterate Clarke bitterly dictated a report:

> Colonel Cruger, from Ninety-Six, with a body of Tories and Indians, followed us into the upper settlements of Georgia and, finding us out of reach, fell on the sick and wounded together with old men, women and children of the families of those that adhered to or retreated with us. Lads were obliged to dance naked between two large fires until they were scorched to death; men stripped, dismembered and scalped, and afterwards hung up; It is too painful for me to dwell on this subject.[22]

At the Watauga, the refugees were sheltered with the Seviers, Waltons, and other families in the area. Meanwhile, the frontiersmen rode and marched down the mountains by another route, encountered Ferguson's Tories, and bloodily defeated them at the Battle of King's Mountain on October 7.[23]

The Georgia refugees arrived at the Watauga settlement where events proceeded rapidly. Clarke joined the fighting in South Carolina, was wounded, and came back to winter at the Watauga. Soon after returning from King's Mountain, John Sevier led an expedition, which included Clarke and Walton, against the threatening Chickamauga Cherokees. The backwoodsmen burned several towns, sparing only Nancy Ward's Echota; their most decisive victory occurred at Boyd's Creek. There, on December 16, 1780, a small army of frontiersmen marching south of the French Broad River discovered a Cherokee ambush and turned the tables on the American Indians. Walton capably commanded the right wing of the frontiersmen "briskly wheeling" his men in a pincers maneuver designed to trap the Cherokees. The left wing failed its part in the task, but nonetheless, a decisive victory was achieved.[24]

At Echota, Nancy Ward sent the hungry troops some cattle, a few of which Clarke immediately ordered slaughtered. This action greatly piqued the recently-arrived Joseph Martin who was apparently already chagrined over Sevier's invasion of the Cherokee country without waiting for him. Martin reclaimed the gift of the cattle from his mother-in-law, an act which enraged Clarke. When Clarke came up,

> ...hot words were exchanged until Martin drew his sword. Clark, with a stroke like lightning, thrust aside the sword, jumped him with his fists, and a lively fight ensued. Both were large men and of impulsive temperments, Colonel Sevier had difficulty separating them and adjusting their differences.[25]

Back at Watauga, the restive Clarke decided late in the winter of 1781 to return to the field in Carolina and Georgia; Jesse Walton and 130 Wataugans went along to help the Georgians "in struggles which were growing bitter instead of ameliorating."[26] After a few battles, Walton must have led the Watauga men back to Tennessee. There can be little doubt that his association with Clarke was a factor in his moving to Georgia about four years later.[27]

In spite of his great successes in Tennessee, however, Walton was apparently dissatisfied in Washington County, and in 1783, he visited Georgia "with a view toward removal." Like his comrades-in-arms, he was always on the lookout for more and better land.

> It was taken for granted on the frontier that any man worth his salt would reach for as much land as he could possibly hope to get. The acquisition of land was one means by which any man might aspire to wealth, and it was an American principle as well established then as it has remained since that material advancement should constitute any man's major purpose in life.[28]

No doubt Walton's decision to move to the Tugaloo River was influenced by the issuance of bounty grants in Franklin County by Georgia. It happened that General Elijah Clarke was again visiting Sevier on the Watauga in 1783, and historian Samuel C. Williams hypothesized that Clarke may have lured Walton southward.[29] Certainly Walton would have been influenced by the plans of his old comrades—the Clevelands, Jesse Bond, and Edward Rice—to settle on the Tugaloo. Whenever possible, frontier people preferred to migrate in groups of several families, and, thusly, Elijah Clarke had come to Georgia in 1773. The advantages of ready familiarity with neighbors were numerous in those years of mutual dependency. Several of Jesse Walton's Watauga neighbors appear in both the Washington County, Tennessee, and the Franklin County, Georgia, records among them being Jesse Bond and Edward Rice; William Gray and James Wyly also lived near Walton in Tennessee before moving to the Tugaloo. It is not known whether these families moved together, but they well may have.[30]

Other Revolutionary War veterans Walton probably knew also settled there, for the attractive lands were easily available to veterans.[31] The list of Walton's neighbors who were veterans included Leonard Marbury, Elijah Isaacs, William Clark, James Blair, James "Horse Shoe" Robinson, and John Stonecypher. Samuel C. Williams stresses the presence of George Walton, one of Georgia's signers of the Declaration of Independence, and his family near Franklin County as an explanation for Jesse Walton's move, but since Jesse settled near the Clevelands, it seems that this friendship was the stronger lure. The relationship of the two Walton families was not as close as Williams thought it to be.[32]

In 1785, Jesse Walton began to take out grants on the Tugaloo River. Of his several tracts, only one, 287.5 acres on Walton's Creek, was close to the Walton's Ford tract and in the vicinity of the future site of Traveler's Rest. Sometime soon after deciding to settle on the Tugaloo, he faced the unenviable task of moving his family and belongings down from Washington County, a journey which was surely accomplished by 1786. Walton had to organize the transportation of his large family, slaves, and possessions along Indian trails from the Nolachuchy to the Tugaloo. The removal was accomplished without wagons—perhaps along the route which Clarke had followed when fleeing Augusta in 1780.

From the inventory of Walton's estate, it is possible to hypothesize the difficult journey of the family. An unknown number of people and animals made up the Walton caravan. There was likely more than one family making the journey, but in any case, well-armed men and boys led the way down forest paths. Some may have been mounted on a few of Jesse Walton's eight or so horses; however, most of the horses were utilized to transport the household furniture, kitchen utensils, tools, and other belongings. The pack horses, women, and slaves followed the party's vanguard, and behind these were driven the few score of cattle and hogs, and a handful of sheep. The livestock set the pace for such caravans—a slow one—and were herded by slaves and boys. Behind these, no doubt, followed an alert rear-guard, for the mid-1780s were years of intermittent warfare, and the Waltons were traveling through hostile Indian country. Such caravans were loosely organized, with dogs and children ranging up and down the column. At best, the Waltons could make only a few miles a day. As one astute observer on the Great Wagon Road noted, "It's a great life for dogs and men, but it's hell on women and steers."[33]

A surprising number of the King's Mountain veterans came to settle on the Tugaloo. In addition to Jesse Walton, Ben Cleveland, James Wyly, William Gray, and James Blair, there was James "Horse Shoe" Robinson, who lived to see his Revolutionary adventures fictionalized in a popular romantic novel by John Pendleton Kennedy.[34]

Walton left no record of his reasons for leaving Tennessee. Perhaps the availability of Tugaloo lands, favorably remembered from his pre-Revolutionary War visit, coupled with the other reasons mentioned previously, is sufficient explanation. Nonetheless, other factors may have inclined Walton toward Georgia.

Possibly he was influenced by factors which undoubtedly persuaded his acquaintance Joseph Martin to follow him a few years later. Walton may have been repulsed by the Tennessee attitude toward the American Indians, summed up in John Sevier's condemnation of American Indian children as "Nits that make lice."[35] Continued war between the Cherokees and the settlers, many of whom stubbornly violated the Treaty of Long Island, seemed certain. The year after the Revolution ended, frontiersmen reported at least 200 killed, and this danger may have influenced Walton to move to the apparently more secure—and empty—Tugaloo lands. Some of his new neighbors, especially Bryant Ward, Joseph Martin, and William Wofford, had close ties with the Cherokees.

Living on the North Carolina frontier west of the Blue Ridge in the early 1780s, Walton must surely have felt the insecurity evinced by his neighbors, Sevier and Martin. The United States government had proven unable to protect the frontier people, and the American Indians constituted a grave threat. Even George Washington believed the western territory would be difficult to hold,[36] and Martin and Sevier secretly courted Spain for southwestern land grants. This uncomfortable situation must have influenced Walton's decision. Then came the move to create the state of Franklin in 1784. Walton, who had invested considerable effort in North Carolina politics developing eastern connections, may have opposed the Franklin movement, and as a local leader, he was conspicuously absent from the first

Franklin Convention in August of 1784. His sale of Jonesborough property was the first recorded under the Franklin government.[37]

Economics may have also been a factor; before Walton sold his land in Franklin, the Spanish declared the Mississippi River closed to American traffic, and even at that early date, the westerners were well aware that this tightened an economic noose around their necks. All these elements made life west of the Blue Ridge appear rather insecure, and when the empty lands of the Tugaloo became available, Jesse Walton decided that they were worth the difficult move.[38]

Doubtless Walton felt that he could breathe more easily when he witnessed the negotiations and signed the Treaty of Hopewell in the summer of 1785. In this treaty, the Cherokees ceded the land of their former Lower Towns on the Tugaloo, along with the lands at the Tugaloo Crossroads, soon to become Walton's Ford.[39] Any feelings of security enjoyed by the Waltons, however, were short-lived, for in 1786, the Creeks began raiding the Georgia frontier.[40]

By the 1780s, the Creeks were being heavily pressured in their lands in the old Southwest. They wanted, above all, to maintain a supply of trade goods and hold onto their lands, and both of these goals led them to accept the ready friendship of Spain. Alexander McGillivray, the mixed-blooded and well-educated leader of the tribe, began a skillful game of diplomacy and warfare to gain the Creeks' end. Assured of Spanish supplies, he collected;

> a Sufficient Number of Warriors &…set [them] out without loss of time & to traverse all that part of the Country in dispute & whenever they found any American settlers to drive them off…Parties of Warriors Set out in every direction to wherever the Americans were Settled, & where they were forming new establishments.

McGillivray sought to curtail settlement without provoking a retaliatory invasion on the part of the Americans, and for the rest of his life, succeeded in this aim of perpetuating tension and danger to settlers on the Tugaloo.[41]

The Tugaloo settlers responded to these Creek attacks with alacrity. When the American Indians struck and stole Jesse Walton's horses in March of 1786, Joseph Martin happened to be at the river. Not knowing "what Savages" were attacking, the next "morning Col. Martin with a party of men pursued on tract overtook them on the Fryday [sic] evening following, at a Village lately erected on Hightower River occupied by the Creek Indians." The borderers' report to the governor continued:

> There [at the Hightower] found in possession of the said Creek Indians the above mentioned horses, brought away two the Property of

Major Jesse Walton, the other three being the Property of the Cherokee Indians Col. Martin thought best not to concern with them. Those Depredations has obliged us to act on the Defensive which we hope will meet your Honors approbation.

(To wit)

That Col. Martin take command of Twenty men and go to said village and Request to be at peace with said Indians and to know their reasons for such conduct, this is a Step we have taken for our own Safety being drove to it by dire necessity....

*Benj. Cleveland*       *Jno. Barton*

*Tho. Payne*       *Lewis Shelton*

*John Gorham*       *Moses Guest*

*Larkin Cleveland*       *Sheriff*

*Jesse Walton*[42]

Despite this peace overture, however, the "hit-and-run" warfare continued to beset the Tugaloo people. By May, Ben Cleveland, Jesse Walton, and John Cleveland reported to Governor Telfair:

Our people is [*sic*] Much Alarmed at the late hostilities Acted by the Creek Indians on the Ocone [*sic*] and Expect Every Moment When it Will be our unhappy fate and should it be the Case the Consequence Will Certainly be Desperate Our Settlement at this time is Verry [*sic*] Weak not consisting of more than 45 men in the upper company which have the Greater part of the frontier to face and them are so Incumbered [*sic*] with their families So that they cannot do Duty and expect to get weaker Every day Some moving and others talking of Moving that we are Doubtful we Shall be able to Stand through Weakness and Scarcity of Provisions. We therefore humbly beg you'l [*sic*] send us a Relief of men and Provisions to support themselves. We are Verry [*sic*] Scarce and hardly can make out to Support our family.[43]

The settlers sent a wagon down to Augusta for arms and ammunition, but although Telfair had promised prompt action, no powder and ball were available. The governor then told the settlers to obtain aid from Elijah Clarke should an emergency arise. The immediate crisis passed; nonetheless, the Tugaloo was the scene of sporadic violence for years to come. In July of 1788, William Walker Walton, Jesse's oldest son, was wounded. Others were killed.[44]

Walton did not let the uncertainties of life on the Tugaloo deter his political career, however. When the first Franklin County Superior Court convened under George Walton at Warren Philpot's house, Jesse Walton was there to serve along with Ben and Larkin Cleveland. He was elected to Georgia's Executive Council in 1786 and 1787; he served in the General Assembly in 1789, and he appeared, at early middle-age, to be on the verge of consummating his promising career.[45] Meanwhile, Walton contributed to the early settlement of Franklin County, building a gristmill and helping with construction and improvement of roads, probably supervising the laying of the road from Walton's Ford to the Indian trading path that ran along the south side of the river.[46]

The Waltons and their neighbors still lived with danger on the Tugaloo. Every spring and summer in the late 1780s, Creeks raided the frontier, "to carry off stock and work animals, to burn the housing and fences…and to massacre some of the inhabitants."[47] In 1787, Joseph Martin observed, concerning the continuing outbreaks of Indian raiding:

> Could a diagram be drawn, accurately designating every spot signaled by an Indian massacree [sic], surprise, or depredation, or courageous attack, defense, pursuit, or victory by the whites, or station or fort or battlefield, or personal encounter, the whole of that section of country would be studded over with delineations of such incidents. Every spring, every ford, every path, every farm, every trail, every house, nearly, in its first settlement, was once the scene of danger, exposure, attack, exploit, achievement, death.[48]

In those years, the settlers attempted to live and work in groups. The militia policed the forests, and although their scouting was mostly uneventful, it was occasionally interrupted by violent skirmishes.[49] According to Brice Martin, son of Joseph and sometime inhabitant of the Tugaloo, Jesse Walton resettled on one of his Tugaloo grants.

Martin wrote:

> Some years after the Indian troubles commenced he [Walton] removed his family 15 or 16 miles from his settlement [perhaps across the river to Ben Cleveland's], but every Season he brought up his force and tended his plantation on the Tougalo [sic].[50]

In 1788, Walton may have participated in an ambush of a raiding party of Creeks. The story has it that a party of Cherokees warned Cleveland and his son John that the Creeks were approaching, and a party of settlers then surprised and drove off the marauders. Cleveland, by all accounts an easy target, was severely wounded and had to be cared for by the Cherokees.[51]

In "Green Corn Month," June of 1789, Jesse Walton was "at his plantation tending to his crop," when he and Sheriff Moses Guest were surprised by some Creeks. Both were wounded, but "as they were on horseback, were able to get away." Walton was taken to Ben Cleveland's, where he "suffered intensely" for three weeks before he died. From Cleveland's house, Joseph Martin wrote to Patrick Henry in July of that year:

> I attended the intended treaty with the Cherokee [on the] 25th. last month at French Broad River, where the Commissioners waited 12 days over the time appointed for holding the treaty without hearing a word from the Indians. They then decampt [sic] and went on to meet the Creeks...About the time the Indians were expected, they made a surprise attack on this quarter, killed and wounded several, among which was Major Walton, who is now at my elbow, who I expect to expire in a few minutes from this time.[52]

So Jesse Walton paid the price of frontier living. In later years, a vivid but fanciful legend of his family's death at the hands of the American Indians developed. The origin of this legend is obscure, but it seems quite likely that much of the story derived from the fun-loving imagination of Mary Jarrett White, Traveler's Rest's last private owner. According to the myth, vengeful Cherokees, eager to redress the balance with Indian-fighter Walton, laid siege to an already-completed Traveler's Rest, trapping Jesse's family within the house. For several days the heroic Waltons held out, shooting at the savages from the "loopholes" still present in the attic. Finally, the American Indians burst in and slaughtered all the Waltons save one lad who hid in a secret hiding place over the porch. Other versions provide other details, few of which are in accord with the known facts. Eventually, grave sites were found to go along with the story that Walton's family was massacred, and some hinted that the dark stains on the upstairs hallway floor were surely some unfortunate Walton's blood.[53]

Although the actual details of Jesse Walton's death are scarce, they clearly refute almost every account of the massacre legend. First of all, it is certain that Jesse did not build any portion of the house which now stands at Walton's Ford. Second, it is known that he was ambushed by Creeks, not Cherokees. Furthermore, a glance out of the supposed "loopholes" in the attic reveals their complete inadequacy for defense purposes. A crushing blow to the massacre legend, however, can easily be found in the early Franklin County records, including Jesse's will, for the entire Walton family appears in the these records years after the mythological massacre. In spite of such conclusive evidence, material from the stains on the upstairs floor was sent to the Georgia Institute of Technology in Atlanta, where laboratory tests revealed that the dark spots were a type of paint thinner.[54] Although historical legends die hard, there is no longer any basis for belief in the traditional story of the Walton massacre. The known facts provide sufficient inspiration for those who love exciting history.

Walton was a victim of McGillivray's and the Creeks' efforts to halt the spread of settlements. He lived and died in the vanguard of the frontier and is remembered as "a man with a large family, extensive property, and of unbounded hospitality."[55]

Before dying, Walton found strength to dictate his will:

In the name of God Amen,

I Jesse Walton of the state of Georgia, Franklin County, being in a low state, altho [*sic*] in perfect mind and memory, being disirous [*sic*] of settling all my affairs in this life, do constitute this my last will and testament replacing all others &, first I request that I be decently buried, and all my just debts paid, the remaining part of my estate to be disposed of in the following manner

(Item) I give and bequeth to my loving wife Mary all my household furniture the balance of my estate I request to be equally divided between my wife and my children, as soon as my son George arrives to the age of twenty one years. It is to be rembered [*sic*] that I did some time past give my son Walker Walton two negrees (towit) [*sic*] Smart and Kyne, together with some land, all which is to be considered in part of his dividend of my estate. I do also request that my loving wife Mary and my friend Larkin Cleveland, be Executor of this my last will and testament, revoking all others, I acknowledge this to be my last will and testament, in witness whereof I have hereunto set my hand and seal this thirteenth day of June Annodom [*sic*]. one thousand seven hundred and eighty nine

*Jesse Walton*
[seal]

Witness
*Abner Franklin*
*Jesse Bond*

Recorded this 10th day of August 1790 in my office
*Nathaniel Payne R.P.*[56]

The inventory of Jesse Walton's estate reveals that most of his property was in land, farming equipment, livestock, and slaves. In addition to twenty-two slaves, Walton owned:

| | |
|---|---:|
| Horses | 8 |
| Ploughs | 4 |
| Hoes | 10 |
| Axes | 3 |
| Crosscut Saw | 1 |
| Cattle | 30 |
| Hogs | 40 |
| Sheep | 5 |
| And household furniture | |

There is no mention in the inventory of houses or a gristmill, however.[57]

## NOTES

[1] Robert W. Ramsey, *Carolina Cradle, Settlement on the Northwest Carolina Frontier, 1747-1762* (Chapel Hill, N.C.: University of North Carolina Press, 1964); George Gilmer, *Sketches of Some of the First Settlers of Upper Georgia, of the Cherokees and the Author* (New York: D. Appleton & Co., 1855); *Index to Headrights and Bounty Grants of Georgia 1756-1909* (Vidalia, Ga.: Genealogical Society, 1970). See Jesse Walton and Ben Cleveland.

[2] Samuel C. Williams, "The Founder of Tennessee's First Town: Major Jesse Walton," *East Tennessee Historical Society Publications*, No. 2, 1930, pp. 70-80.

[3] Carl Bridenbaugh, *Myths and Realities, Societies of the Colonial South* (New York: Atheneum, 1968), p. 130.

[4] Joan A. Sears, "Town Planning in White and Habersham Counties, Georgia," *Georgia Historical Quarterly*, No. 54, 1970, pp. 20-40; Parke Rouse, Jr., *The Great Wagon Road, From Philadelphia to the South* (New York: McGraw-Hill Book Co.), pp. ix, 70, 93, 94.

[5] Lyman C. Draper Manuscripts, King's Mountain Papers, 5DD104, 5DD13-3; the Draper Manuscripts are now in the possession of the State Historical Society of Wisconsin, Madison, Wisconsin. The Cherokees' bitterness at the hunters' presence is understandable. The tribe's declining livelihood was dependent upon a diminishing supply of deer; white hunters such as

Walton and Cleveland were in effect stealing the Cherokees' main source of "income." The Draper Manuscripts, painstakingly collected over forty years of the ninteenth century, are especially valuable to this historian of the frontier in the Revolutionary and post-Revolutionary South. They include some interesting documents concerning the Tugaloo frontier.

[6] Ibid., 5DD13-3.

[7] Ibid., 3DD311-20. Upon returning from Kentucky to North Carolina, Walton and Cleveland must have been robbed by Cherokees from the Lower Towns. Only thus can Cleveland's coincidental visit to the Tugaloo be accounted for.

[8] Williams, "Jesse Walton," p. 70.

[9] Adelaide L. Fries, ed., *Records of the Moravians in North Carolina* (Raleigh, N.C.: State Department of Archives and History; reprinted 1968), III, pp. 127, 1,048; Williams, "Jesse Walton," pp. 70-71.

[10] Williams, "Jesse Walton," pp. 71-72.

[11] Woodward, *The Cherokees*, pp. 86, 91, 94. "Ghighau," or "Beloved Woman," was a title which enabled Nancy Ward to speak at all councils and make decisions regarding prisoners. In Ben Harris McClary, "Nancy Ward: The Last Beloved Woman of the Cherokees," *Tennessee Historical Magazine*, Vol. 21, 1962, pp. 352-64. In Cherokee, "ghighau" is spelled "Agi-ga-u-e."

[12] Williams, "Jesse Walton," p. 73.

[13] Ibid., pp. 73-75.

[14] Ibid., p. 74.

[15] Ibid., pp. 74-75; Draper Manuscripts, 5DD13.

[16] Williams, "Jesse Walton," pp. 75-76.

[17] Ibid., pp. 76-78.

[18] Everett Dick, *The Dixie Frontier* (New York: Alfred A. Knopf, 1948), p. 226.

[19] The Records of Washington County," *American Historical Magazine*, V, 1900, pp. 332-360, 372, 378.

[20] Williams, "Jesse Walton," p. 78.

[21] Draper Manuscripts, 15DD69; Williams, "Jesse Walton," p. 78.

[22] Samuel C. Williams, "Col. Elijah Clarke in the Tennessee Country," *Georgia Historical Quarterly,* Vol. 25, 1941, p. 151; Louise Frederick Hays, *Hero of Hornet's Nest: A Biography of Elijah Clark* (New York: Stratford House, Inc., 1946), pp. 105-06; Pat Alderman, *The Overmountain Men: Early Tennessee History* (Johnson City, Tenn.: Overmountain Press, 1970), p. 91.

[23] Hays, *Hero of Hornet's Nest,* p. 114, indicates the wrong dates. See also Samuel C. Williams, *Tennessee During the Revolution* (Nashville: Tennessee Historical Commission, 1944), p. 201; and Williams, "Elijah Clarke," pp. 151-55.

[24] Williams, "Jesse Walton," pp. 78-79.

[25] Hays, *Hero of Hornet's Nest,* p. 114.

[26] Williams, *Tennessee During the Revolution,* p. 201.

[27] Williams, "Jesse Walton," pp. 76-80.

[28] Ibid., p. 79; Dale Van Every, *Ark of Empire: The American Frontier: 1784-1803* (New York: Mentor Books, 1964), p. 104.

[29] Williams, "Jesse Walton," p. 80.

[30] Hays, *Hero of Hornet's Nest,* p. 9; "The Records of Washington County," pp 76, 88.

[31] In 1776 and 1777, Georgia passed laws to encourage settlement and increase military strength. The head of every family who moved to Georgia could obtain 200 acres on the frontier, plus an additional fifty acres for each family member and slave (not to exceed ten), at only two shillings per acre. The land had to he settled within six months, and 100 more acres could be obtained through the building of a gristmill. In 1780, the period for settlement was stretched to nine months, the act being carried over into peacetime in 1783, at which time a 1,000-acre maximum was imposed. Coulter, *Georgia: A Short History,* pp. 163-64, 195.

[32] Williams, "Jesse Walton," p. 80; Draper Manuscripts, 5DD104; *Index to Headrights and Bounty Grants* (see James Wyly, William Clark, James Blair, and Elijah Isaacs).

[33] Seymour Dunbar, *A History of Travel in America* (Indianapolis: Bobbs Merrill Co., 1914), I, pp. 126-28; Rouse, *The Great Wagon Road*, p. 226.

[34] John P. Kennedy, *Horse Shoe Robinson* (New York: American Book Company, 1937), Earnest E. Levy, ed., p. 533; John H. Logan, *Logan Manuscript*, Vol. II of Logan's *History of Upper South Carolina* (Atlanta: Chas. P. Byrd, State Publisher, 1910), DAR, pp. 60, 86. In *Horse Shoe Robinson*, James, for some reason, was given the first name of Galbraith. A blacksmith, Robinson had a propensity for living at "horseshoe" bends in creeks, and when Kennedy met him, the veteran lived on a bend of Changes Creek, near Ben Cleveland's former homestead, about six miles from Walton's Ford. The cabin in which Robinson lived until the early 1820s, when he moved to Alabama, still stands. In 1818, John Pendleton Kennedy was visiting the Pendleton area, and one evening he met the middle-aged Robinson and heard his tales of the battles of "yesteryear." The stories fired Kennedy's imagination sufficiently to cause him to write and publish, years later, a fanciful account of "Horse Shoe's" adventures. Those experiences did not take place on the Tugaloo, and therefore do not enter into this story; however, the reader may form an opinion of the novel's quality from the following poem by Chevy Chase which enhances its pages:

> The Battle of King's Mountain
> They closed full fast on every side,
> No slackness there was found And many a gallant gentleman Lay gasping on the ground.
>
> Oh dread! It was grief to see,
> And likewise to hear
> The cries of men lying in their gore
> And scattered here and there.

[35] Woodward, *The Cherokees*, p. 123.

[36] Van Every, *Ark of Empire*, p. 23.

[37] Ibid., p. 195; Alderman, *Overmountain* Men, p. 189.

[38] Van Every, *Ark of Empire*, pp. 16, 31.

[39] *Colonial and State Records of North Carolina* (Raleigh, N.C.), Vol. 17, p. 584.

[40] Woodward, *The Cherokees*, p. 105; *Indian Depredations Records* (Atlanta: Georgia Department of Archives and History, 1938), Vol. I, Pt. I, p. 44.

[41] Van Every, *Ark of Empire*, pp. 83-86; Brown, *Old Frontiers*, pp. 303-04.

[42] *Indian Depradations Records*, p. 436.

[43] Ibid., pp. 44b, 44c; *Creek Indian Letters* (Atlanta: Georgia Department of Archives and History, 1938), Vol. I, p. 107.

[44] *Indian Depredations Records*, pp. 44, 44b; *Creek Indian Letters*, p. 109.

[45] *State of Georgia* (Atlanta: Department of Archives and History, Stein Printing Company, 1925), *Governor's Official Register*, p. 335.

[46] Thelma Hunter's paper on Jesse Walton, Walton research files, maintains that Walton constructed a gristmill and a road. A clue concerning this road is in Wynd's *Franklin County, Georgia, Records*, p. 82, which mentions Walton's Road.

[47] Jonas Fauche, "The Frontiers of Georgia in the Late Eighteenth Century," *Georgia Historical Quarterly*, Vol. XLVII, 1963, pp. 84-85.

[48] Mooney, *Myths of the Cherokees*, p. 64.

[49] Fauche, "Frontiers of Georgia," p. 85.

[50] Draper Manuscripts, 14DD16.

[51] Fauche, "Frontiers of Georgia," p. 85.

[52] Draper Manuscripts, Tennessee Papers, 3XX308; King's Mountain Papers, 14DD16.

[53] For various renditions of the Walton massacre legend, see: "Jarrett Manor, Stained By Indian Massacre, Hallowed By Georgia's Great, Becomes Shrine;" old Georgia Historical Commission leaflet, now in files of the Historic Preservation Section. Emory Lavender, "Pioneer Inn Is Restored," *Anderson Independent*, May 19, 1969, p. 5. Shirley Roloff, "Manor Is Steeped in History," *Atlanta Times*, August 23, 1964. Susan E. Spaeth, "Jarrett Manor Has Colorful Exciting History," *The Gainesville Daily Times*, June 29, 1969. Andrew Spark, "Jarrett Manor Mirrors Georgia's Past," *Atlanta Journal and Constitution Magazine*, September 6, 1959, pp. 6-9.

[54] Traveler's Rest Papers, Historic Preservation Section.

[55] Fauche, "Frontiers of Georgia," p. 85.

[56] Fauche, "Frontiers of Georgia," p. 85.

[57] Franklin County Court of the Ordinary, *Minutes of the Court of the Ordinary, Wills, Inventories, etc., 1785-1813.*

# Chapter 4

## The Tugaloo Neighborhood: 1790-1820

Far too little is known concerning the events which took place in the vicinity of Traveler's Rest in the months and years following Jesse Walton's death. County histories tell almost nothing about the early years of settlement. It is known, however, that Joseph Martin soon did as he had predicted in his July 1789, letter to Patrick Henry and left the Tugaloo area. Returning to the Cherokee country for a tour of the principal towns, he went back to his place on the Long Island of the Holston. But Martin was a restless soul who never lingered long anywhere. He had plenty of motivation to move out of Tennessee, and before 1790, he decided to move to the Tugaloo, thus becoming a neighbor of the Clevelands, Waltons, and Wards. He attracted to the area at least two of his sons, William and Brice.[1]

A brief biography of this man, probably the most historically significant of those to be connected with the history of Traveler's Rest, reveals that Joseph Martin was one of the foremost woods-runners of the generation of Daniel Boone, the Clevelands, and Jesse Walton. Born near Charlottesville, Virginia, in 1740, he was an irrepressible adventurer even as a youth. He took advantage of his family's efforts to provide him with a good education, but preferred "a life of adventure on the western border" to that of a Virginia planter. In 1756, Joseph and Thomas Sumter ran away and joined the British colonial army at Fort Pitt, afterwards participating in the French and Indian Wars. Martin soon gained ample satisfaction for his taste for danger: alone in a cave, he subdued a desperate American Indian; he saved a "drowning companion in the swollen French Broad;" and he ventured far into Indian country, living with the American Indians there.[2]

Martin married young and to a "superior woman," Sarah Lucas, but he would not settle down.[3] He was something of a gambler and a roustabout, more of a woodsman and hunter. Accounts tell a story of Martin's early relationship, in 1767, with Ben Cleveland, in which they shared a field in Virginia. They planned to take advantage of the farmers' custom of cooperative harvesting, and invited the neighbors over for a combined working and drinking project. A morning's preparatory libation became an afternoon's carefree debauchery, and the crop was never harvested. To escape from such associations, Cleveland left the neighborhood; Joseph Martin's maturation process occurred later on the frontier.[4]

In 1769, Martin led a party of settlers to Powell's Valley, in western Virginia, where members of this group started to construct a "station." The depredations of determined American Indians, however, forced Martin to withdraw in the fall of that year, and he did not return for five years. Back in Virginia, he settled his young family in what was to be Henry County, where he made some profits from hunting and trading with the Cherokees. The family remained on this estate until he moved them to a more sumptuous place on Leatherwood Creek in 1803.[5]

Too restless to remain anywhere for long, Martin continued to be an active frontiersman, and in 1774, he led the Virginia scouts in a war on the Shawnees. The Virginians' victory in that struggle opened the way for Martin to return to Powell's Valley, and he did so with seventeen companions during mid-winter in 1774-75. Martin sagaciously built his station right on the Wilderness Road, about two miles from Cumberland Gap.[6]

This time, the station lasted for over a year, but when the outbreak of the Revolution signaled the onset of a Cherokee war, Martin again abandoned Powell's Valley in June of 1776. He had accepted the difficult task of Indian agent of Virginia, a role which brought him renown as a frontier leader. The major accomplishments of his career came in his capacity as mediator to the Cherokees, and one of Martin's historians, William Allen Pusey, wrote, "During the whole period of the Revolution, and in the uncertain times later before the establishment of Federal authority, he was the outstanding influence for peace with the Indians in this territory."[7]

Martin was put in charge of Cherokee affairs by Virginia in October of 1775, becoming well-connected with the tribe in 1777 by marrying Betsy Ward, daughter of "Beloved Woman" Nancy Ward and his later neighbor, Bryant Ward. Martin lived with Betsy Ward for most of the time he spent as Indian agent, and the marriage made it possible for him to be adopted into one of the most powerful Cherokee clans. Martin's second marriage, without dissolution of his first, apparently did not arouse much controversy with his first family. Evidently the bigamy bothered only his son William, who later wrote, "He would go home to Va., stay a while, and strange as it may seem, it never produced any discord between him and my mother." Martin quieted complainers by pointing out how the relationship to the Beloved Woman's family often saved his life.[8]

Martin collaborated with Nancy Ward, whose influence on Cherokee history was vital. They worked closely to promote peace during the Revolution, knowing from personal experience that American Indians and whites could indeed live together. One of the first Cherokees, and perhaps the first, to perceive the course by which the Cherokees might survive the era of American expansion and settlement, Nancy Ward was "purportedly the first Cherokee in the nation to own cattle." During the Revolution, she got a captive woman to teach some of her household skills to the American Indian women. William Martin wrote, "She was, I think, one of the most superior women I ever saw."[9]

Martin's influence was augmented considerably by his ability to earn and keep the Cherokees' trust in him, and his Cherokee name was purported to be "Gluglu," meaning "tall."[10] The frontier situation after 1776, however, called forth Martin's martial and diplomatic skills. The Cherokees were loyal to King George, eager to fight the encroaching settlers, and sometimes encouraged to do so by British officers and Loyalists among them.[11] In the summer of 1776, Martin joined Jesse Walton in serving in an attack on the Cherokee towns from the Long Island of the Holston. Thereafter, Martin used Long Island as his base until he moved to Tugaloo in 1789. As an Indian agent from 1777 on, Martin was remarkable. For lengthy periods during the struggle for independence, his influence was a key factor in keeping the Cherokees from attacking the American rebels.

His successful promotion of peace made it possible for the backwoodsmen to march east to the Battle of King's Mountain, the turning point of the Revolution in the South. The Cherokees did make a treaty with the British to make war on the settlers, but before they could mount a general attack, they were invaded by Sevier's expedition of frontiersmen. Joseph Martin arrived too late for this excursion late in 1780, which destroyed several towns. His fisticuffs with Elijah Clarke were apparently not conclusive (see Chapter 3).[12]

During the years 1781-83, Martin was in on almost every treaty negotiation with the Cherokees, and he also reestablished his station in Powell's Valley during this time. Ever active, he meanwhile became involved in a large Tennessee land-speculation scheme, along with William Blount and John Sevier, but their plans proved unsuccessful.[13]

In the early 1780s, when Martin's wife Sarah died, he somehow managed to crowd yet another spouse into his busy schedule, marrying Susannah Graves in 1784. They soon began what was to be his third family, Joseph, Jr., being born the following year. This family lived in Virginia.[14]

Throughout the 1780s, Martin hopped about the Southern frontier. He sought to pacify the Cherokees and get the settlers to honor the many treaties he helped negotiate, but the first task was constantly complicated by the hopelessness of the second. The State-of-Franklin controversy in the mid-1780s finally made his position in the Tennessee country unbearable, as the people of Franklin were determined to hold onto land guaranteed to the Cherokees in the most recent treaties. They hated the American Indians and anyone who supported them, and Martin's opposition to the creation of Franklin and his upholding of the American Indians' rights guaranteed that he would be unpopular among his frontier fellows. Even more so than Jesse Walton, Martin was tied to interests in eastern North Carolina, having served in the North Carolina Senate in 1787 and 1789.[15]

After 1785, Martin must have experienced a great deal of misery in his job as Cherokee agent. In 1788, his position as highest-ranking general in the territory forced him to lead a group of frontiersmen who distrusted him in an aborted expedition against the Cherokees. This, as well as other unpleasant tasks, drove him to consider a move to Spanish territory. In 1789, Martin's career as Indian agent ended, and became a private citizen again. He decided to join the Tugaloo River settlement rather than return to his young family in Virginia.[16]

Now fifty years old, Martin established himself in Georgia in his usual active way. He bought a tract of land next to Jesse Walton's Ford tract from Bryant Ward's son Samuel, and, according to his son, Joseph, Jr., he "established a fort and took an active part in suppressing Indian hostilities in that quarter." The Tugaloo neighbors lived under exposure to Creek attack:

> It was during my fathers [sic] residence in Georgia that the servant Toby and my brother Brice, who was then a boy, were guarding the Horses a short way from the fort. Two indians made an attempt to cut them off from the fort and capture them. Toby first espied the Indians and shot one dead: but quickly discovered a large party near them. He instructed his young master to reserve his fire and by that precaution, they retreated defensively, until they were relieved by men from the fort, who had rushed out from the report of Toby's gun.[17]

The maps of the 1792 and 1793 Georgia frontier show "Martin's Station" in the Middle Fork of the Broad River, about twenty miles from Walton's Ford (see Map 7). Martin apparently built a sawmill on the land purchased from Samuel Ward. The sawmill was a rarity in those days of the frontier.[18] Martin's sons stayed on the Tugaloo for the time being, but their father would not yet settle down, and in the early 1790s, he returned to his family in Virginia. A Madisonian Democrat, Martin served in the Virginia legislature throughout the 1790s, and in 1803 he retired from public service to live as a prosperous landowner. He never lost his restless ways, however, and in 1808 he made a long excursion through the Cherokee country. This journey "greatly fatigued" him, and he died in November of that year.[19]

Joseph Martin has not been given the historical attention accorded other frontier leaders of his stature; nonetheless, an ample record of his career—mostly from sketches by his sons, William, Brice, and Joseph, Jr.—has been collected in the Lyman Draper Manuscripts. These letters are sometimes lengthy documents, "written (in the case of the Martins) in excellent style. They constitute an interesting history of most of the events and leaders of the southwestern border..."[20] The Martins' and other documents in the Draper papers are valuable sources concerning the frontier era of the neighborhood of Traveler's Rest, but even so, the Martin letters offer at best only enticing—and   sometimes confusing—glimpses of expeditions and skirmishes, encounters and disputes, involving the settlers on the Tugaloo before 1800.

One of the most valuable letters is that written from William to his father in Virginia on October 27, 1793, in which he reported some of the occurrences of the recent days and notified his father of the state of the trading post:

> I have undertaken the commisaries [sic] business of six months longer, altogether myself, depending that you will let my brother Brice come & assist me, for which he shall have an equal share of the profits, which are considerable.

Contradicting William, Stephen Weeks' 1894 article on Joseph Martin maintains that Martin's trading post lost heavily, and neither source indicates where the post was located.[21]

William's letter goes on to relate continuing troubles with the American Indians: "Five horses were stole last Sunday, two from M. Shelton's plantation & three from Longnose, which is all the mischief done near here since you left here." The Tugaloo settlers responded with misdirected attacks on the Cherokees, and Martin's letter tells how Tom Kelly, who lived just above Toccoa Creek, near Elisha Isaac's, and the one-time site of Old Estatoe, led a raid on a Cherokee town:

> The Georgians have made some sham campaigns against the Cherokees...Tom Kelly being their pilates [sic] went up toward Stecoah where they found a very old harelip Indian woman and a very small boy, the old woman they killed & the boy brought in, so that was the amount of their prize...[22]

Fifty years later, Lyman Draper asked William Martin to recall what he could of another "sham campaign" staged by the settlers against the Cherokees on a town he referred to as Teuchtotee. Draper had found a 1793 Philadelphia newspaper article on the apprehension of one David McClosky, a Franklin County citizen, for leading an attack by Georgians on Teuchtotee during a time of peace. Martin could remember that he had lived on the Tugaloo at the time of McClosky's attack on "a quiet Cherokee village" located in Georgia about fifty or sixty miles from the frontier in the direction of the Creeks. Early in 1793, McClosky led a large group in pursuit of a Creek war party, but not knowing whether or not the Cherokees had any contact with the retreating raiders, McClosky's men fell on the village and killed many "because they had red skins."[23] No more details of this incident are given; however, in another letter, William Martin asserted that no attacks were made on Georgia by the Cherokees after the Revolution.[24]

As for what sort of smoking ruins the Creeks left behind them at Walton's Ford in 1789, the record is silent. Because Jesse Walton's will mentions "household furniture," it seems that the American Indians did not succeed in the total destruction of the Walton's property. Indeed, there is no way of knowing exactly where in the Tugaloo area Walton was shot, so the Creeks may not have had access to Walton's hypothetical cabin. Brice Martin's memoirs, however, do strongly imply that Walton did have a cabin at his Tugaloo "settlement."[25] Still, it does not seem likely that a veteran Indian fighter such as Walton, well aware of the dangers of the situation, would have invested much time in a house while the Creek raids continued.

It is clear, however, that some structure was built at the Walton's Ford tract before many years had passed. Walton's family, now grown up, stayed in the area, clearing and farming their land, and building small cabins or houses. Archaeological excavations at Traveler's Rest indicate that a small structure may have occupied the site before the large house was begun (probably some time between 1815 and 1820). This cabin may have been occupied by Jesse's widow, Mary. By 1798, Jesse's four sons were tax-paying landholders in Franklin County.[26]

Also by 1798, another Joseph Martin had settled in Franklin County, on the North Fork of the Broad River, but no clear connection has been established between this Joseph and the General Joseph Martin, contemporary of Jesse Walton and Ben Cleveland. Since the general's son, Joseph, Jr., was only thirteen years old in 1798, he was most likely not a Franklin County landowner. Neither is this mysterious Joseph mentioned in the memoirs of William Martin. It is not impossible that the second Joseph Martin was a "natural" son of the general, or more likely, a nephew, as the general's brother, Brice, had a son named Joseph. The likelihood of this connection is supported by this latter Joseph's marriage to Mary Walton, daughter of Jesse. This Joseph Martin is an important character in the story of Traveler's Rest. (To avoid confusion, this Joseph will be designated hereafter as the second Joseph Martin.)[27]

In the first generation of white settlement on the Tugaloo, settlers made much more rapid progress in dividing the land than in preparing it for

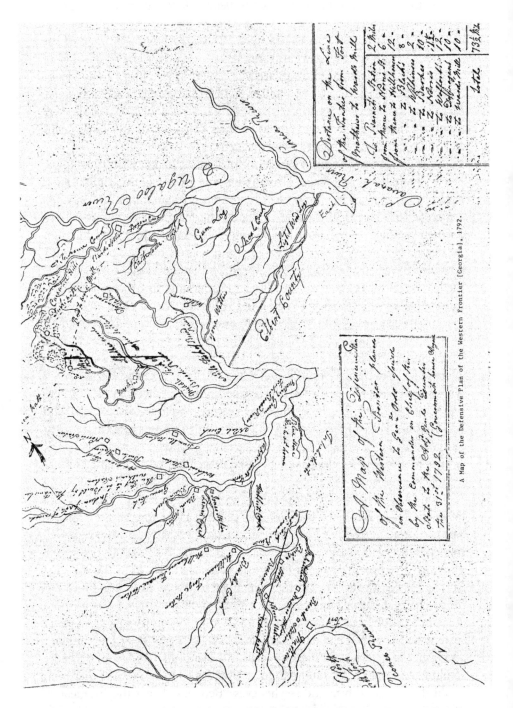

**Map 7:** A Map of the Defensive Plan of the Western Frontier, 1792

cultivation. Visitors found the area still heavily forested in the late 1830s; nonetheless, before 1800, the forest-landscape was dotted with clearings, connected by primitive paths and roads. The governor's 1792 map of the "Defensive Plan" of the Georgia frontier gives an extremely rough idea of the early Tugaloo neighborhood (see Map 7). From Franklin County deeds, it is possible to reconstruct a tentative picture of settlers' arrival and departure from the area—at least in terms of land transactions. Most of the Walton's neighbors held acreage similar to their own—small and large farms ranging from about 100 to 1,000 or so acres.[28]

Written in the mid-nineteenth century, John Login's *History of Upper South Carolina* informs readers that "[t]he cane growth of the country soon became the standard by which the early settlers estimated the value of lands. If it grew no higher than five feet, or the height of a man's head, the soil was deemed ordinary; but a growth of twenty or thirty feet indicated the highest degree of fertility." The most luxuriant cane grew on the "bottom lands" near the rivers and creeks, so the finest land at the Tugaloo Crossroads, then, was that near the river and the creek, making the Walton tracts the most valuable and, therefore, subject to the highest tax.[29]

For twenty years, the Wards were among the Walton's closest neighbors, Bryant Ward (1725-1815) being one of the first settlers near Walton's Ford. Ward had left the Cherokees at an unknown date and settled with his white family somewhere on the south fork of Walton's Creek (soon named Ward's Creek). As William Martin recalled, "When I lived in S.C. Bryant Ward, then old, sensible, & intelligent, lived my neighbor—was settled, and had a family."[30] Yet Brice Martin recalled in 1854 that he had last seen Bryant Ward in 1807, living at a farm on the Chattahoochee. On Ward's Creek, Ward had a mill, a "station," and a close partnership with his son, Samuel, until he died around 1814.[31]

Across the Tugaloo River in South Carolina, Colonel Ben Cleveland got fatter and fatter. Reported to weigh 300 pounds at the time of the Battle of King's Mountain, the five-foot-nine gentleman was thought to weigh well over 400 during his days on the Tugaloo. Born on Bull Run Creek in Virginia in 1738, Ben grew up in Orange County, six miles from the Rapidan River, where as a youth he was much inclined to eating, drinking, gambling, horse-racing, fighting, and "wild frolicking." He had a "fine and handsome appearance...one of the most martial looking men he [the narrator] ever saw; he had a walling *eye* as piercing as an Eagles [*sic*], a voice like thunder; and ever was a perfect stranger to fear." Cleveland must indeed have had a striking appearance, for one of Lyman Draper's sources claimed that "you could stand behind him and see his eyes." Ben was always the "ringleader" of a group which included his brothers—and often Jesse Walton. All his life, he liked to be surrounded by cronies.[32]

Married to Mary Graves, a woman whose father owned a considerable amount of property, Ben began to sober up. After his short-lived agricultural cooperative with Joseph Martin, he left Virginia and moved to the frontier of North Carolina, to settle on Roaring Creek at the foot of the Blue Ridge. There, he hunted, farmed, and ate. From North Carolina, he and Jesse Walton embarked on their excursion to Kentucky about 1772.[33]

During the Revolution, "Old Round-About" served his country with bravery and enthusiasm, especially when it came to hanging Tories and seizing their property. It was said of him: "It seems that Col. Cleveland was a stern military judge, as well as a patriotic partisan. If he had influence at a 'drumhead' trial, no rascally tory could escape the halter." He participated in expeditions against the American Indians, but won everlasting glory as a leader at the Battle of King's Mountain. There, he made a fiery speech, exhorting his men: "Patriots, yonder is your enemy, and the enemy of mankind. I will show you today, by my example, how to fight. I can undertake no more; you will expect nothing less." Leading the charge, Cleveland offered his mighty body as target for the enemy, who somehow still managed to hit only his horse, thereby saving it from the agonies of carrying Ben up the very steep hillside.[34]

After the war, Ben lost his North Carolina estate through a bad title and decided to move to the newly-opened lands on the Tugaloo River. It seems probable that Cleveland was a leading motivator in the migration of so many of his compatriots to the area, and the old colonel continued to be a leader in his new neighborhood. He served in the Georgia Legislature until the Beaufort Convention placed his plantation in South Carolina, and for many years he sagged the bench as a judge.[35]

In the frontier days of the Tugaloo, Ben fought the Creeks, and also led the capture of Tory river-pirate Henry Dinkins. This rogue had earned pariah status during the Revolution by his "murders and robberies"; afterwards, he hid out with the Creeks in their towns on the Chattahoochee. One night, one of Cleveland's slaves "observed" three mounted men, including two African Americans, near the plantation on the road which ran to Indian country. Alarmed by their "suspicious apperance [sic]," the slave hurried to inform those at Cleveland's house, and Ben's young "hangers-on" hurriedly formed a posse and set out in pursuit. Somewhat slower, the 400-pound judge also mounted and, "alone in the dark," began his own hunt. "Having been so much acquainted with rogues, he readily conceived the maneuver they might attempt." Ben guessed right, and he soon ambushed the outlaws on a little-used road, his "stentorian voice" and huge form frightened Dinkins and his cohorts and paralyzed them until help arrived. The posse discovered that Dinkins was accompanied by two runaway slaves, headed for the Creeks' towns when captured. Dinkins was hanged immediately.[36]

Eventually, Ben became too large to ride a horse or even wear normal clothing, "but had a kind of frock to go all over."[37] A widower, Old Ben supposedly became indulgent with his slaves, and one account reported:

> He had one old woman servant that was a great favorite and was light-fingered enough to always have a full share of the best of everything. Col. C. always kept a good supply of wine, and in order to see his servants he arranged large mirrors so he could see every movement. He would allow the servant to get her wine and then would tell her of it. Told her he had an eye in the back of the head.[38]

Another of Draper's chroniclers reported that in old age the colonel's obesity made him an object of curiosity and humor to neighbors. Once, at his place on the Tugaloo, Cleveland got involved in a strange conversation with a "half-witted, good natured beggar, Billy Vidkins," who was passing in front of the gate:

> "Hello Billy, what's the news from h_ll?"
> "Oh! nothing at all, almost, hardly," replied the easy going Vidkins, as he pushed his coon-skin cap over the left ear. "Only I heard that the devil & his wife has had a great quarrel, the other night."
> "And what were they quarrelling about?" queried the hero of King's Mountain.
> "It was about soap grease," said Billy, "but the old woman was put into a fine humor when Satan told his wife that fat old Cleveland would soon be dead, and then the fat of the lard would belong to her royal highness." It is said that Colonel Cleveland was so much pleased with Billy that he sent the little old beggar a bag of meal & a "middling" of bacon the very next day.[39]

Finally, as one admirer put it, the colonel was "smothered" by his fat, passing on in 1806 or 1807.[40]

Clevelands were numerous in the Tugaloo area. Ben's brothers, Larkin and John, were early residents of Franklin County. Larkin, a huge man like his brother and a loyal follower of Ben's, had been crippled in the Revolution. Executor of Jesse Walton's will, he lived down the Tugaloo, near the mouth of Eastanollee Creek until he moved to Tennessee, where he died in 1817.[41] The Rev. John Cleveland was a Baptist preacher, and according to the *History of the Tugaloo Baptist Association*, John founded the Tugaloo Baptist Church in 1789 with a membership of 108. Not a brawler like his brothers, John survived to a ripe old age and died in 1825.[42] In the mid- and late-nineteenth century, Tugalites Ben Cleveland, Jr., William Martin, and William Hackett remembered John Cleveland as a fiery preacher with a long white mane of hair. He baptized Martin in the Tugaloo River in July of 1791.[43]

Ben Cleveland, Sr., brought two sons to the Tugaloo region: John and Absalom, who were rather unsavory characters, both unpopular in the neighborhood. Most of Lyman Draper's sources on the Cleveland family recount a story of the teenage sons' hanging of a Tory during the Revolution in their eagerness to mimic their father. "Devil John" Cleveland grew to be a huge and intimidating bully, a "large and dreadful man." Absalom became a "lunatic."

In 1790, John bought his father's 770-acre grant at the mouth of Toccoa Creek on the Tugaloo (site of Tugaloo Town) and made it the center of a large plantation. Also known as "Drunken Jack," John was distinguished by William Martin as "one of the worst men I ever knew."[44] Some of "Devil John's" escapades are preserved in the Draper Manuscripts as stories which give an idea of the wild brutality of life on the Georgia frontier. Obviously, not all the violence which occurred at the Tugaloo was perpetrated by American Indians. William Martin's letter of October, 1793, relates two of John Cleveland's exploits:

> John Cleveland broke upon Craffords Station last Sunday [William Crawford had a mill near Tom Kelly's and Elijah Isaac's, a short distance up the river from Toccoa Creek.] and drove the whole of the people (except one woman and a few small children) and made them lie out nearly twenty-four hours, in which time Crafford went and got an officer with a party of men but he barred himself [illegible] which time they have made up. he, John moves this day with his family to Petersburger [Petersburg] in the fork, *we* hope he will never return again, since you left here, he went to David Sloands [Sloan had grants scattered all over the creeks of Franklin County]; and attempted to take of [off] that girl, Sloand interposed and John beat him largely, however, Sloand availed himself of a pan handle which stood in the corner, with which he made his way good & drove off the enemy. [The remainder of the letter goes on to say that the "old col," Ben Cleveland, had narrowly lost his election. William Martin campaigned for him, but he says he wishes he had begun his efforts earlier.][45]

In the 1840s, Martin proudly related another anecdote concerning "Devil John":

> I once took his wife from him & kept her at my house a day and night on account of his abusing her. He came after in a great rage and disgorged his fury to no purpose. After a while, moderated—

became calm, threatened to indict me and went off—Next day he returned with apparent humility—confessed his faults commended me for what I had done, and finally prevailed with his wife to return home with him.[46]

Unfortunately, however, Katherine Cleveland was not finished with husbandly maulings. William Hackett, son of Devereaux Jarrett's business partner, wrote to Lyman Draper how John's wife,

> ...became religiously inclined and proposed to join the Baptist church to which he sternly objected, and forbade her to do so; however, she joined, and when she came home, John said to Caty I suppose you have been Baptised. She said yes, "Well," said John "by G__ you shall have enough of it" he then carried her to the river a short distance and emersed [sic] her ninety-nine times more.

Eventually, Mrs. Cleveland left her husband and went to live in South Carolina with her daughters by a previous attachment.[47] John's rowdy ways caught up with him around 1803, when he was killed in a drunken brawl with a man named Bond [perhaps his father's cohort, Jesse Bond, who William Martin called "rather a worthless man"]. Hackett reported that "Devil John" perished when "he fell upon a stump and broke his back of which he died."[48]

While John Cleveland was "smart and bad,"[49] Absalom Cleveland's problem was apparently a lack of sense. William Martin recalled Absalom as slow-witted and "quite deranged." In 1786, he settled on river land granted to Ambrose Downs, between Walton's and Rocky [Thrasher's] creeks. In later years, William Hackett had vivid recollections of Absolom. He wrote:

> With Absolom I was well acquainted he was quite eccentric and cynical one of his peculiarities he drank no water for over twenty years. he died at my father's house called for water about an hour before he died and drank of it heartily.
>
> After his wife's death (about which it was said there was suspicious circumstances) he totally ignored his family—denied that they were his—refused to speak to them and to almost everybody of his acquaintance, except my Father & family, spent a good deal of his time at my Father's house always carried an old smooth barrelled [sic] gun with which he passed a good deal of his time in the woods would shoot nothing but squirrels.

Young William Hackett frequently accompanied Absolom on these "rambles" in the Tugaloo forest.[50]

In October of 1817, Absolom's sons-in-law appeared in the Franklin County Superior Court and swore, "They believe Absolom Cleveland...to be somewhat deprived of his reason and incapable of handling his own affairs." A number of neighbors, including the second Joseph Martin and Devereaux Jarrett, testified concerning Absolom's condition. He was judged to be insane, "but how or by what means he became a lunatic the jurors know not unless by the visitation of God." Cleveland was put in the care of son-in-law Thomas Harbin, who was bonded for handling Absolom's substantial property holdings. Hackett recalled that the sons-in-law soon squandered the estate. Absolom died in the early 1830s.[51]

One other Cleveland—Ben, Jr. —became a close neighbor of the second Joseph Martin, James R. Wyly, and Devereaux Jarrett. A son of "Devil John," Ben was reared by his hefty grandfather and became a person of accomplishments. A successful local politician who served along with James Blair as state senator from Habersham County, Ben, Jr., fought with distinction in the battles against the Creeks and in the War of 1812. Among the Draper Manuscripts are two letters from a cousin of Ben's, George Cleveland, a very old man who could recall but little of his youth. He did remember, however, that General Ben "took an active part in the War of 1812 & 1814—So did I: he came out a colonel, & I came out a cripple."[52]

The Wards, Clevelands, Martins, Waltons, and their other neighbors must have found life on the Tugaloo frontier much as it had been in Tennessee and North Carolina. At first, the settlers had to live with the unrelenting tension of Indian warfare, and in the first few years, they clustered around such places as Ward's Station, blockhouses indicated on the frontier map. Their initial dwellings were single-room cabins, replaced as soon as possible by double-room log houses, often incorporating a breezeway between and a loft above. While glass windows were extremely rare, wooden floors were common, and only the poorest settlers lived on clay or packed-earth floors.

As future Governor George Gilmer would one day recall, cabin raisings were the occasion of local social gatherings. The sober Moravians scolded about a typical incident, when "Wagner was very busy with his new house, and about twenty people were helping him, but things never go well at such a gathering, for more time [is] spent in drinking brandy than in working." Contrarily, the builders of the fort at Ninety-Six reported rum to be "absolutely necessary" in their work, to "encourage" them.[53]

According to Samuel C. Williams, Tennessee lacked sawmills in the "early days," and Franklin County may have, as well. *Franklin County Deeds*, however, contains a clue that indicates Joseph Martin, Sr., had a sawmill on Ward's Creek. Without a sawmill, lumber was difficult to obtain, as two men with a whipsaw could only cut rough lumber at a rate of 100 feet per day. Builders depended on wood and rocks for construction materials in the frontier days; bricks were not used at that time.[54]

The settlers cleared land by girdling trees, or cutting them down to rot or be burned. Usually a farmer would clear a few acres and use the wood for his cabin, outbuildings, and fences. According to Robert Meriweather's *The Expansion of South Carolina*, "The cleared field usually began at the edge of the narrow swamp which bordered the creek."[55]

Corn was the backcountry's primary crop, but it was not profitable unless the farmer had an opportunity to sell to incoming settlers. To plant corn or most other crops, the farmers relied heavily on their hoes, for "only the well to do had plows." A plow was not particularly useful in newly-cleared ground, which often rendered cultivation "shallow and inefficient." Largely because of the fertility of the soil, backcountry farmers grew twenty to thirty bushels of corn per acre, and between the rows of corn, they planted peas, beans, and pumpkins. Along with sweet potatoes and turnips, these augmented the farmer's diet. Orchards of peach, pear, and apple trees were rare enough in the backcountry to be "objects of extreme pride." While wheat became a popular crop, rye, barley, and oats were not prevalent.[56]

The region produced little beef or pork for export in the early years of settlement, yet a few farmers obtained enough extra stock to enhance their incomes. The scarcity of milk cows made butter a valuable commodity, but almost all owned at least one horse. Oxen were rare, while poultry was common.[57]

The earliest settlers killed off such game as buffalo, beaver, and bear, "but the deer survived in spite of the annual slaughter." Shad, perch, catfish, and trout swam the streams. Only by producing a surplus could a farmer get cash for salt, ammunition, blankets, tools, and household products such as those sold later in the few country stores (which often grew out of skin-trading and tanning operations). Early settlers had sparse furniture—a few chairs and bedsteads with straw mattresses for the poorest—while the well-off families such as the Waltons owned featherbeds, pillows, bolsters, sheets, mirrors, and dressers.[58]

Cooking was done in a pot by the open fire, and food was eaten from wooden and pewter dishes. Charles Woodmason, an Anglican minister who traveled the backcountry through much of the 1760s, commented on the poor settlers' often meager diet:

> Where I am, is neither Beef or Mutton, nor Beer, Cyder, [*sic*] or anything better than Water—These People eat twice a day…Their Bread of Indian Corn, Pork in Winter and Bacon in sumr [*sic*]. If any Beef, they jerk it and dry it in the Sun—So that you may as well eat a Deal Board.[59]

Settlers drank water, tea, and coffee. Rum, a popular drink in colonial days, was gradually replaced by whiskey and brandy.

The neighborhood streams were soon dotted with gristmills. According to one source, Jesse Walton had such a mill, yet evidence of its existence is lacking. *Deeds of Franklin County* provides clues to numerous others, such as Elijah Isaac's, which was located on a small creek up the Tugaloo River, near the site of Old Estatoe. James Blair soon had a mill on Toccoa Creek, as did Ward on Ward's Creek, and other mills were built on Rocky and Eastanollee creeks.[60]

Before 1800, most Franklin County citizens practiced handicrafts to satisfy their clothing needs, and on a day-to-day basis, the Waltons of both sexes probably wore the same sort of linsey-woolsey garments they had worn in Tennessee. Williams commented,

> Linen made from home-grown flax furnished the chain and wool supplied the filling or woof. A rough jeans was the cloth out of which the stouter garments of the men were made. Home tanning and cobbling customarily supplied the shoes or shoe-packs fashioned somewhat after the moccasins of the Indians.[61]

Throughout the frontier, health was a constant preoccupation. Common diseases were rheumatism, agues, and fevers, and smallpox was the "dreaded scourge." *Logan's History* proudly boasted, however, that in the backcountry "even the old-fashioned chill and fever were almost unknown..." The cabins were "far too recent to generate the miasm of the loathsome typhus," he said. Yet frontierspeople did occasionally suffer from plagues. Saunder's *Early Settlers of Alabama* mentions that Walton Martin, son of Mary Walton Martin and the second Joseph Martin, perished in the epidemic of 1824.[62]

Scarlet fever was also a threat to frontier settlers, and among the Jarrett papers, this medical advice on the disease provides a view of how the Jarretts handled it:

> In the mild cases of scarlet fever, little more is required than an occasional dose of salts, with mild cooling beverages, such as lemonade, or cream of tartar water sweetened—
>
> When the throat becomes infected, in addition to gentle cathartics, strong red pepper tea with salt and vinegar should be given every hour in doses of a tablespoonful to children of six or seven *years* of age; & doses proportioned to other ages—also gargles of strong red oak hark tea with alum, vinegar, myrrh, & honey should he used often: also a gargle of a strong decoction of Indigo roots.
>
> If the throat is much inflamed internally, or swelled externally, the early application of a blister to the throat is often of the utmost

consequence—At the onset if the disease appears violent, an emetic will frequently mitigate the symptoms, & render its course mild; but in any of the advanced stages must not be prescribed, but by a physician.

In those cases where the eruption is partial in its appearance, or of a pale copper hue, especially about the elbows, accompanied with cool or cold feet and hands, pale face, & symptoms of prostration apply sinaprisms & the warm bath with salt thrown into it—gently stimulate and get medical advice as soon as possible—

Salts and snake root is a good form of using salts—Feb 8th, 1836

*Haynes*

To [illegible] gills of strong red pepper tea add nearly half a pint of sharp vinegar, & two teaspoonsful of common salt[63]

No literacy figures have been found concerning early Franklin County settlers, but considering the difficulty of obtaining schooling, it is probable that illiteracy was rather high. Meriweather's study put illiteracy as low as ten to twenty percent, though certainly few of the Tugaloo neighbors were as literate as the Martins, and deeds of the period indicate that many persons signed with marks, including Bryant Ward and Mary Walton, widow of Jesse. The county histories offer no clues as to early education at the Tugaloo, and there probably was none beyond that available in the home.

When William Martin left the Tugaloo, he settled in Tennessee, near the site where the great frontier revivals originated. He recollected the advent of the early 1800s religious revival in Tennessee as "The most extraordinary in many aspects that has been witnessed in modern times…It commenced with the Presbyterians in Logan County, Kentucky, say 50 miles from here & spread to a great extent in every direction."

The revivals were circulated by means of enthusiastic camp meetings, at which Martin witnessed "exercises," including "jerks, dancing, running, jumping, wrestling, laughing, &c," and he rightly labeled the Great Revival a crucial event in frontier history.[64] Surely it found a fruitful harvest on the Tugaloo.

In 1800, the Great Revival reached Georgia in all its enthusiastic manifestations. Some feared that the evangelists were confusing the "manifestations" with religious faith, but those who objected to barking, "jerking," and dancing as Christian exercises were not heeded by most frontier people. Through the frontier, it was said that "the people fell before the word like corn before a storm of wind; and many rose from the dust with Divine glory shining in their countenances."[65]

Georgia Methodists, Baptists, and Presbyterians turned out in great numbers to be harangued by fiery Lorenzo Dow or the somewhat more decorous Francis Asbury, both of whom visited the Tugaloo area during Devereaux Jarrett's teens and may well have influenced him toward the

steadfast Methodism he later evinced. It seems likely that Jarrett heard Asbury preach when he came to Abbeville, S.C., in December of 1800. Asbury
visited the site of Petersburg, Ga., as early as 1788 and made several trips to
the Pendleton-Franklin area ca. 1800, although he had little to say about his
impressions. Staying in Pendleton in October, 1801, he wrote, "Can't record
great things upon religion in this quarter." But in November of 1807, he
reported hearing of a camp meeting in Franklin County at which 100 souls
were saved. An enthusiastic preacher, Lorenzo Dow passed through Abbeville in early 1803, but he had no comment concerning the experience.[66]

Visitors and historians do not paint an attractive picture of the average
frontier settler. Le Clere Milfort, a French adventurer who lived and fought
with the Creeks in the 1780s, occasionally visited the Tugaloo region. Milfort commented with disgusted amazement on the vicious habits of those
he labeled "Toogaloo Gaugers," ascribing the nickname to the Georgians'
practice of gouging out each others' eyes in their frequent brawls, and he
crudely joked that one-eyed men predominated on the Tugaloo.[67] Historian
Dale Van Every eloquently described the frontiersman "As a person he was
rude, uncouth, violent, greedy, cynical and brutal. He was a poor workman,
a bad farmer, and a disorderly citizen. His favorite diversions were drinking
and physical competition."[68]

In 1800, the Franklin County Grand Jury took a dim view of the county's morals, "lament[ing] the drinking, rioting, swearing, fighting and eye
gouging, the inattention of the inhabitants to divine worship…and 'even
horse swopping [*sic*] on the Sabbath Day.'" George Gilmer's assessment of
the north Georgia settlers was characterized by filial piety, yet he wrote that
"most of them would cheat for six and a quarter cents, and sue each other
for a quarter of a dollar."[69]

The settlers intimately connected with Traveler's Rest—the Waltons,
Martins, Wylys, and Jarretts—did not fit this general frontier mold, but
they do, however, appear as ambitious, grasping, and persistent individuals.
These families were part of a tide of settlement unhalted by extreme natural
and contrived obstacles for over 100 years, and the Waltons and Martins
were carried on by this tide to new lands in the West.

During the 1790s, Jesse Walton's children developed prosperous, mid-
dle-sized farms scattered on the Tugaloo. Robert Walton seems to have
lived on a Larkin Cleveland grant near the mouth of Eastanollee Creek,
while Killis, William Walker, and George Walton probably lived near Walton's Ford, where they all obtained small grants. Jesse's daughter, Mary, married the second Joseph Martin about 1803, the year in which Martin moved
from the North Fork of the Broad River. Slim evidence suggests that they
settled at the original Walton's Ford tract, for Martin lived on a Jesse Walton
grant adjacent to the plantation of "Devil John" Cleveland, and *Franklin*

*County Deeds* indicates that Killis was their closest neighbor. Rachel Walton married William Hunter [or Gunter], another local farmer. William Walker, Robert, Killis Walton, and the second Joseph Martin were all justices of the peace at one time or another.[70]

The only pre-1800 tax record for Franklin County is the *Tax Digest of 1798*, which contains a small amount of useful information on the Tugaloo people. In that year, six Waltons [the same mentioned in Jesse's will] owned thirty-two slaves and a couple of thousand acres of land. Several Waltons owned houses—William Walker owned two. All these were valued at under $100, except one of Walker's, which had three outbuildings and was valued at $150. Joseph Martin's house was worth $80, and he was listed as owning six slaves, as well. Few houses in the area were valued at higher than $100, but Larkin Cleveland's $350 dwelling was the most expensive. James Wyly, father of James R. Wyly, lived somewhere in the county in a fine $150 house.[71]

Mary Walton, Jesse's widow, lived at the Tugaloo until her death in 1800, her will being as follows:

> In the name of God Amen. I Mary Walton of the State of Georgia & the County of Franklin being sick & weak of body, but of sound mind & of perfect memory, thanks be to god for the same, & calling to mind the frailty & uncertainty of human life, have made, ordained, consti-tuted & appointed & by these prescence [sic] do make, ordain, consti-tute & appoint this to be my last will & testament, hereby revoking all other will or wills by me heretofore made, declaring this only to be my last will and testament, in manner & form following (viz)
>
> First—I give & bequeath my soul to Gog [God] my great Creator, hoping through the mediation of Jesus Christ to receive Remission of my sins, my body I leave to be decently buried at the discretion of my children, And as to what wordly [sic] things it hath pleased God to bestow on me, I give & bequeath in the following manner (viz) I give & bequeath to my Daughter Mary Carter my negro woman named Sal. I give & bequeath to my son William Walker Walton's son Jesse, a negro girl named Rhoda—I give & bequeath to my son Killis Walton all my part of this prescent [sic] crop, also my part of a legecy [sic] left to us by Henry Mullets of Virginia Dead—to pay off certain debts, and if there should be any left after the debts are discharged to be divided as other of my property, also to have a fifth part of the fol-lowing property, A negro man named Roger—a negro man named Steph. Jones—a negro boy named New Year, also a fifth part of my part of the land I now live on, also a fifth part of a mare and two colts, also a third part of all my cattle including what my son George has had, also half of my household furniture, I give and bequeath to my

son William Walker, a fifth part of the above mentioned [illegible] Lands & Houses, also I give & bequeath to my son George a fifth part of the above mentioned negroes, Lands & Houses, also a third part of all my cattle, also—I give & bequeath to my Daughter Rachel a fifth part of all my estate, also half of all my household furniture—I do hereby acknowledge this to be my last will & testament, hereby revoking and disannulling [sic] all other wills by me heretofore made, & hereby declaring this to be my last will & Testament, in witness whereof I have hereunto set my hand, & affixed my seal this eighth day of November in the year of our Lord one thousand and Eight hundred—and of the independence of the United States of America the twenty fifth—signed sealed and acknowledged in presence of us

*David* [illegible]                           her mark
*Jesse Bond*                             *Mary x Walton*
*Milbry Spark*                             (seal)

The Honorable Court of Ordinary for the County of Franklin has met according to adjournment on the 6th day of October 1801

Present                     *David Beall*
                           *Jas. H. Little*                 Esqrs
                           *Henry* [illegible]

The honorable the Court of Ordinary for the County of Franklin has adjourned until the second Wednesday of November next

                           *Jas. H. Little*
                           *David Beall*
                           *Henry* [illegible][72]


## NOTES

[1] William Allen Pusey, "General Joseph Martin, An Unsung Hero of the Virginia Revolution," *The Filson Club Historical Quarterly*, Vol. X, April, 1936, p. 58.

[2] Ibid.

[3] Judith Hill, A *History of Henry County, Virginia* (Baltimore: Regional Publishing Company, 1976 [1925]), p. 91.

[4] J.D. Bailey, *Commanders at King's Mountain* (Gaffney, S.C.: Edward H. De-camp, 1926), p. 118.

[5] Pusey, "General Joseph Martin," pp. 59-64.

[6] Ibid., pp. 65, 67, 68. Martin's Station was an essential part of the Transyl-vania Company's plans for settling Kentucky. When Daniel Boone's expe-dition went west in 1775, the people "counted on" rest and provisions at Martin's Station and got them. The station continued to be a crucial outpost on the Wilderness Road.

[7] Ibid., p. 69.

[8] Stephen B. Weeks, "General Joseph Martin and the War of the Revolution in the West," *Annual Report of the American Historical Association*, 1893, Vol. IV, p. 423; Draper Manuscripts, 3XX4.

[9] Woodward, *The Cherokees*, p. 96; Brown, *Old Frontiers*, pp. 148-49; Mooney, *Myths of the Cherokees*, p. 204; Draper Manuscripts, 3XX4; Ben Harris McClary, "Nancy Ward," pp. 352-64.

[10] Brown, *Old Frontiers*, pp. 69, 244, 245.

[11] Stanley S. Folmsbee, Robert F. Corlew, and Enoch L. Mitchell, *History of Tennessee* (New York: Lewis Historical Publishing Company, Inc., 1960), Vol. I, p. 123. Early in the Revolution, officers such as John Stuart tried to persuade the Cherokees not to attack the settlers. The militant faction led by Dragging Canoe, however, was determined to drive the settlers back from Cherokee territory; hence Cherokee raids of 1776.

[12] Pusey, "General Joseph Martin," pp. 70-74; Williams, "Elijah Clarke in the Tennessee Country," p. 155.

[13] Pusey, "General Joseph Martin," p. 76.

[14] Weeks, "General Joseph Martin," p. 477.

[15] Pusey, "General Joseph Martin." pp. 77-78; Williams, *Lost State of Frank-lin*, pp. 53, 59, 50, 190, 210, 211, 220, 245; Brown, *Old Frontiers*, pp. 197, 244, 245, 275, 278.

[16] Pusey, "General Joseph Martin," pp. 78-79; Van Every, *Ark of Empire*, p. 195.

[17] Draper Manuscripts, 3XX13.

[18] *Deeds of Franklin County, Georgia, 1784-1826*, compiled by Martha Waltus Acker (Easley, S.C.: Southern Historical Press, 1976), p. 136; Williams, *Lost State of Franklin*, pp. 248-49.

[19] Weeks, "General Joseph Martin," p. 477; Pusey, "General Joseph Martin," p. 80.

[20] Pusey, "General Joseph Martin," p. 60.

[21] Draper Manuscripts, 2XX40; Weeks, "General Joseph Martin," p. 469.

[22] Draper Manuscripts, 2XX40.

[23] Ibid., 14DD55.

[24] Ibid., 14DD113.

[25] Ibid., 14DD16.

[26] William Kelso, "Excavations at Traveler's Rest, Toccoa, Georgia, 1968" (Savannah: 1969), Georgia Historic Preservation Section files.

[27] Franklin County *Tax Digest, 1798*; John Redd, "Reminiscences of Westtern Virginia, 1770-1790," *The Virginia Magazine of History and Biography, 1899-1900*, Vol. VII, pp. 1-16.

[28] Franklin County *Tax Digest, 1798*; see Franklin County deed book: at the Georgia Department of Archives and History, Atlanta.

[29] John H. Logan, *A History of the Upper Country of South Carolina* (Charleston: S.G. Courtenay & Co., 1859), pp. 10-11; Coulter, *Old Petersburg*, p. 50.

[30] McClary's article, "Nancy Ward, the Last Beloved Woman of the Cherokees," maintains that Brian Ward left Nancy and settled in Pendleton, S.C., about 1760. This is possible, though much of this area was occupied by Cherokees up to 1776. The Tugaloo Crossroads region was not officially settled until 1784, when Brian Ward was one of the first to have land surveyed. His land and fort were on the Georgia side of the Tugaloo River. See Brian Ward in *The Deeds of Franklin County*.

[31] In 1813, Brian Ward turned his property over to Sam Ward in return for care for the rest of his life. See *Franklin County Deeds*, p. 315. A son of Brian's, John Ward, also married into the Cherokee tribe. In 1817, John Ward, "of the Cherokee Nation," and Ann Ward, gave David Humphreys power-of-attorney to try to break the will of Brian. "The legatees are not satisfied with the will and seek a more equal distribution." See *Franklin County Deeds*, pp. 362, 357.

[32] Draper Manuscripts, 5DD13 and 5DD41.

[33] Ibid., 5DD13, 5DD108.

[34] Ibid., 5DD96; Bailey, *Commanders at King's Mountain*, p. 130.

[35] Draper Manuscripts, 5DD115.

[36] Ibid., 5DD115.

[37] Ibid.

[38] Ibid., 5DD7.

[39] Ibid., 5DD96.

[40] Ibid., 5DD13; Bailey, *Commanders at King's Mountain*, pp. 114, 118, 199, 120-06, 163, 168-70.

[41] Draper Manuscripts, 5DD108, 5DD13.

[42] S.F. Goode, *History of Tugaloo Baptist Association* (Toccoa, Ga.: Toccoa Record, 1924), pp. 118, 180.

[43] Draper Manuscripts, 5DD115.

[44] Ibid.

[45] Ibid., 2XX40.

[46] Ibid., 3XX18.

[47] Ibid., 3XX18, 5DD62.

[48] Ibid., 5DD115, 5DD62.

[49] Ibid., 5DD115.

[50] Ibid., 5DD62.

[51] *Franklin County Deeds*, pp. 367-68; Draper Manuscripts, 5DD62.

[52] Draper Manuscripts, 5DD66; Trogden, *History of Stephens County*, p. 279.

[53] Robert Meriwether, *The Expansion of South Carolina* (Kingsport, Southern Publishers, 1940), pp. 65, 176.

[54] *Franklin County Deeds*, p. 336; Williams, *Lost State of Franklin* pp. 248-49.

[55] Meriwether, *Expansion of South Carolina*, pp. 165-66.

[56] Ibid., p. 167.

[57] Ibid., p. 168.

[58] Ibid., p. 169.

[59] Ibid., p. 175.

[60] *Franklin County Deeds*, p. 49; see also James Blair and Bryant Ward.

[61] Williams, *Lost State of Franklin*, pp. 248-51.

[62] Ibid., pp. 248-51; Logan, *History of Upper South Carolina*, p. 11. Yet frontierspeople did occasionally suffer from plagues. James Saunders, *Early Settlers of Alabama* (New Orleans: L. Graham & Sons, Ltd., 1899), pp. 49-50, tells that Walton Martin, son of Mary Walton Martin and the second Joseph Martin, perished "in the epidemic of 1824."

[63] Georgia Historic Preservation Section files, Jarrett Family Papers.

[64] Draper Manuscripts, 3XX18.

[65] Edmund J. Hammond, *The Methodist Episcopal Church in Georgia* (location and publisher unknown, published 1935), p. 32; Dick, *The Dixie Frontier*, p. 196.

[66] Francis Asbury, *The Journal of Rev. Francis Asbury* (New York: N. Bang and T. Mason, 1821), Vol. III, p. 236; Lorenzo Dow, *History of Cosmopolite* (Cincinnati: Anderson, Gates & Wright, 1858), pp. 159-60.

[67] Louis Le Clerc Milfort, *Memoirs, or, a Ouick Glance at My Various Travels and My Sojourn in the Creek Nation* (Savannah: Beehive Press reprint, 1969), pp. 22-24, 67-68.

[68] Van Every, *Ark of Empire*, p. 35.

[69] Ralph B. Flanders, *Plantation Slavery in Georgia* (Chapel Hill, N.C.: University of North Carolina Press, 1933), p. 129. George Gilmer, quoted in Coulter's *Old Petersburg*, p. 9.

[70] *Franklin County Deeds*, pp. 180, 279, 115, 132.

[71] Franklin County *Tax Digest*, 1798.

[72] Mary Walton's will, Franklin County *Wills, 1800*.

# Chapter 5

## The Early Days of Traveler's Rest

True to their heritage, the Walters began to vacate the Tugaloo for less expensive lands to the west soon after 1800. William Hunter (Rachel Walton's husband) sold his property in 1804, and William Walker Walton began to sell his lands in 1807. In 1810, William sold his tracts near Walton's Ford on the Tugaloo to John Hooper and moved to Giles County, Tennessee. Robert Walton deeded his lands to Kenneth Finley, James Smith, and Thomas P. Carnes and moved to Madison County, Mississippi, in 1811. On February 5, 1813, George Walton sold his small grant to Killis, his brother-in-law, and the second Joseph Martin and headed for Lincoln County, Tennessee. Several months later, in October, William Walker, Robert, George, and Killis—"legal heirs of Jesse Walton"—relinquished all their claims to the Walton estate to the second Joseph Martin.[1]

In the early 1800s, the years in which James Rutherford Wyly and Devereaux Jarrett first appeared in Franklin County records, the Tugaloo Crossroads was still a frontier outpost. The immediate danger of Indian raids was gone, but otherwise, the quality of life had not changed drastically. As saw mills began to provide lumber, it became possible for the farmers to leave behind their cabins and build more refined, frame houses. In *Old Petersburg*, E. Merton Coulter cites George Gilmer to assert that such residential moves were the occasion for "frolics" that would last "far into the night."[2]

The half-dozen slaves owned by each of the families of Jesse Walton's children were close to the average number held by slaveowners in northeastern Georgia in the frontier days. The 1790 United States Census reveals that Franklin County had comparatively few slaves, totaling 156. Jesse's twenty-two slaves had made him among the most prosperous planters in the county. In 1798, Larkin Cleveland and Thomas P. Carnes were the only slaveowners with more than twenty slaves, having twenty-seven and twenty-three, respectively. John Cleveland owned sixteen; Absolom, eighteen; Sam Ward, thirteen; James Blair, six; and James Wyly, six. Devereaux Jarrett was a relatively well-fixed slaveowner at an early age, owning seventeen chattels in 1807. It is not known how the slaves were used, but perhaps he hired them out in Franklin County in the years before he began to buy land.[3] Most of the slaves of this frontier period led lives of anonymity. Some had memorable names, such as Walton's New Year and "Devil John's" Venus, but no details of their lives have survived. An outstanding exception to this unfortunate pattern was Toby, the intrepid companion of General Joseph Martin, who saved Martin's son, Brice, from the American Indians at Tugaloo in the 1790s.[4] A young mulatto of twenty-five years, Toby was acquired by Martin in 1783 and became the Indian agent's "body and confidential servant." For years, the men were constant companions. William Martin described Toby as being of small stature, but with "great physical powers, as well as mental…few men have as fine sense." Toby was freed at Martin's death, became a Baptist preacher, and subsequently accumulated a "good estate."[5]

With or without slaves, settlers grew tobacco, corn, wheat, potatoes, and garden and orchard products, but they did not try to grow cotton to the extent that Georgians further south did. Hogs, cattle, horses, mules, and turkeys were raised. Those farmers with products to sell could take them down the "Red Hollow Road" to Augusta, from whence they were sent on by barge. According to Coulter, this was a "tobacco road…a peculiar kind of highway" constructed for rolling huge "hogsheads" of tobacco to the market at Augusta. Such roads followed the ridges to avoid "watercourses."[6] After 1805, farmers could barter goods at Devereaux Jarrett's store.

Exotic entertainment was scarce in the Tugaloo region in the early 1800s. Consequently, it seems quite likely that some members of the Walton, Martin, Wyly, and/or Jarrett families must have found time to go to the Pendleton Courthouse in South Carolina in 1810, when an elephant was displayed there for the curious. The advertisement in *Miller's Weekly Messenger* of Pendleton read:

### A LIVING ELEPHANT

To be seen at Pendleton Court House on Saturday and Monday, the 4th and 6th of August.

The elephant being not only the largest and most sagacious animal in the world, but the peculiar manner in which it takes its drink and food of every kind with its trunk, is acknowledged to be the greatest natural wonder ever offered to the public. She will draw the cork from a bottle, to the astonishment of the spectators. It will lie down and rise at command. She is nine years old, and measures upward of fifteen feet from the end of her trunk to that of her tail.—ten feet round the body, and upwards of seven feet high.

Perhaps the present generation may never have the opportunity of seeing an Elephant again, as it is the only one in the United States, and perhaps the last visit to this place.

Admittance for grown persons—Half a Dollar, children, half price.

During the remainder of the early 1800s, no spectacle to match the "sagacious" elephant was advertised in the *Messenger*. (See note 7.)

Cleveland's Ferry was the first transportation the people had for crossing the Tugaloo, it being on the road from Pendleton to Carnesville, and somewhat down the river from where Jarrett would build his bridge. One of the first wagon roads used by settlers from the north, it was probably a miserable highway, as were most Georgia roads in the early days. In frontier days, Georgia lacked a state system for building and maintaining roadways. After 1792, all male laborers were required to work on road repairs twelve days a year. Signs were to be posted at crossroads, but the roads remained "almost in a state of nature."[7]

Settlers in north Georgia and east Tennessee were well aware of the need for improved transportation between those areas. In 1796, John Sevier wrote a letter from Knoxville to the Tennessee General Assembly and urged "the making [of] a waggon [sic] road over what is commonly called the western mountains." Sevier added, "I need not point out to you Gentlemen the general utility and advantages that would be derived…in consequence of such a road." Despite Sevier's promptings and the obvious need for the road, however, the unsettled state of the Georgia-Tennessee frontier deterred action for some years.

In the early nineteenth century, the project was taken up again, this time by an enterprising group of men who formed the Unicoi Turnpike Company. The company succeeded in getting the Georgia Senate to request the federal government to allow company representatives to treat with the Cherokees for permission to open a road from the Tugaloo through the tribe's territory to the settlements in east Tennessee.[8]

The Unicoi Company soon advanced their project another step by negotiating a treaty with the Cherokees. At Hiwassee Garrison, Tennessee, on March 8, 1813, five men—Nicholas Byers, David Russell, Arthur Henly, John Lowry, and "one other person" from Georgia, Russell Goodrich (who was named later)—were commissioned to head the turnpike company. They were instructed by the treaty to:

...layout and open a road from the most suitable point on the Tennessee River; to be directed the nearest and best way to the highest point of navigation on the Tugalo [sic] River, which said road...shall continue and remain a free and public highway...for 20 years, after which to revert to the Cherokees.

The Cherokees were to be given $160 a year by the company, which was to have exclusive privileges of trading on the road for the twenty years. The treaty continued:

...And the company shall have leave, and are hereby authorized, to erect their public stands, or houses of entertainment, on said road, that is to say, one at each end...as nearly so as a good situation will permit, with leave also to cultivate one hundred acres of land at each end of the road...with a privilege of a sufficiency of timber for the use and consumption of said stands.

This treaty was apparently the genesis of Traveler's Rest, which was built near the southern end of the Unicoi Turnpike.[9]

Tennessee granted the Unicoi Company a twenty-year charter in October of 1815. The tolls were set at 12½¢ for a man on horseback, 6¼ cents for a footman, $1.00 for a wagon team, and $1.25 for a coach or carriage. Any traveler who refused to pay the toll could be fined $20.00. On the other hand, the company was required to keep the road open and repaired, or it could be fined. [10]

Georgia incorporated the Unicoi Company in December of 1816, authorizing it to open a road from the head of navigation on the Tugaloo to east Tennessee. The highway's construction lagged behind schedule, and Tennessee was forced twice to extend the time allotted for completion, the final date being November of 1818. The legislature provided that the road had to be twelve feet wide wherever digging was necessary, and twenty feet wide elsewhere.[11]

The Unicoi Company apparently contracted James R. Wyly of Tugaloo, Georgia, to supervise the construction of the highway. No direct evidence of this contract has been discovered, but an 1832 map of District 19, Cherokee County, shows the Unicoi Turnpike labeled as "Wiley's Road," traversing what is now Towns County. The road took four years to build, following the ancient Indian trail into the mountains. It seems to have begun at Mullin's Ford, the highest point of navigation on the Tugaloo (according to Sherwood's 1827 *Gazetteer of Georgia*). The road ran from "a short distance below the mouth of Toccoa Creek," passed north of the present site of Clarkesville, through the Nacoochee Valley across the Unicoi Gap and Hiwassee in Georgia, to eventually cross the Little Tennessee at Chota,[12] and end at the Merriville-Madisonville Road (see Map 8).

As the turnpike neared completion, James R. Wyly sagaciously bought Joseph Martin's farm at Walton's Ford. There can he little doubt that he was acquainted with the frontier tradition of placing inns and taverns at key fords where, during the years of maximum migration and settlement, such inns could be extremely profitable. As builder of the Unicoi road, Wyly was in a good position to determine the location of the inn which was to stand at its southern end. Inasmuch as the turnpike became a "chief route through the South for a long time," Wyly's place at Walton's Ford was certain to be lucrative.[13]

Soon after their road was completed, the men in the Unicoi Company ran an advertisement in the Knoxville *Register* of April 6, 1819, informing the public that a road was now open for safe traveling to Franklin County, Georgia, "with as much convenience as any other road through the Cherokee Country." The ad went on to say that the company had,

> ...established a number of houses for the entertainment of travellers, (which are and will be kept by white men and their families) so as not at any part of the road to have a distance of more than 20 miles without a house of accommodation of travellers.[14]

During the next few years, James R. Wyly was to emerge as a dominating force along the southern part of the turnpike. In 1821, he bought Lot 74 in the Third District of Habersham County, land acquired from the Cherokees in 1819 and divided by lottery in 1820. This lot was in the Nacoochee Valley on the upper Chattahoochee, right on the Unicoi road, and just under twenty miles from Wyly's new place at Walton's Ford (see Map 9). Within a few years, he utilized this spot with a "house of entertainment" for travelers. Next, Wyly added a holding at Hiwassee, Georgia, a few miles north of the Blue Ridge and one more day's journey up the turnpike. During the 1820s, he thus operated three inns along the Unicoi Turnpike, and he also bought a number of lots in Clarkesville, the seat of Habersham County. Wyly was thereby ideally situated to profit from the traveling propensities of his fellow Americans.[15]

Georgians traveled by foot, horse, cart, and buggy in frontier days. Stages were few, but wagoning was not. John Lambert, an Englishman, wrote this description of the wagoners and their role:

> These wagoners were familiarly called crackers (from the smacking of their whips, I suppose). They are said to be often very rude and in-

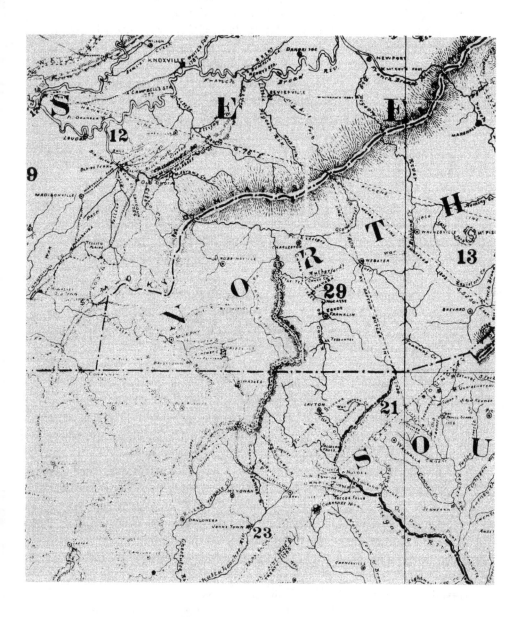

**Map 8:** The Unicoi Turnpike, showing Old Cherokee Towns and
Early Nineteenth-Century Settlements

solent to strangers, and people of the towns, whom they meet on the road, particularly if they happen to be genteel persons...In almost every part of the United States there seems to be an invincible antipathy between the towns' people and these wagoners, who take every opportunity they can to give each other a thrashing. The wagoner constantly rides on one side of the shaft horses, and with a long whip guides the leaders. Their long legs, lank figures, and meagre countenances, have sometimes a curious appearance when thus mounted; especially if a string of them happen to pass along the road.[16]

Water transportation was also a matter of extreme importance to early nineteenth-century farmers. Enthusiastic Georgians claimed that the Tugaloo River was navigable as far as Toccoa Creek, but Coulter pointed out that the river actually contained a number of difficult passages above Petersburg. *Old Petersburg* contains many details on the Georgians' efforts to improve the river. According to Coulter:

The first move Georgia made to improve the upper Savannah was in 1786, when the legislature passed a bill to promote navigation on the river from...just above Augusta to the mouth of the Tugaloo River and up that river to Tugaloo Old Town, a point near where Toccoa Creek flowed into the Tugaloo. In the introductory part of the law it was recited that "nothing contributes more to the Advantages of the Citizens, or to the opulence of the State, than making easy, and extending the Navigation of Rivers" and that as "Policy and Justice" dictated that the expense should be paid by such persons as will immediately be most advantaged thereby," a system was, therefore, being enacted to provide for the expenses...People owning land along the river were required to pay five shillings for every hundred acres of land "of the first quality" and two and a half shillings for other lands. (See note 17.)

Ben Cleveland, Sr., and Leonard Marbury were among the commissioners appointed to raise the tax.

Near Augusta, the tax was applied to all farms within five miles of the river, but upstream, the taxable distance was fifteen miles. The law was unwise and unpopular, and the revenues were not raised. A lottery was attempted to generate funds, but it too failed. Private enterprise did not get the river cleared, even with state sponsorship. For a time, citizens argued over how much to allow fishing operations to obstruct the river. The Tugaloo was "considered so precarious for navigation that the old law allowing two-thirds of the stream to be obstructed was continued."[17]

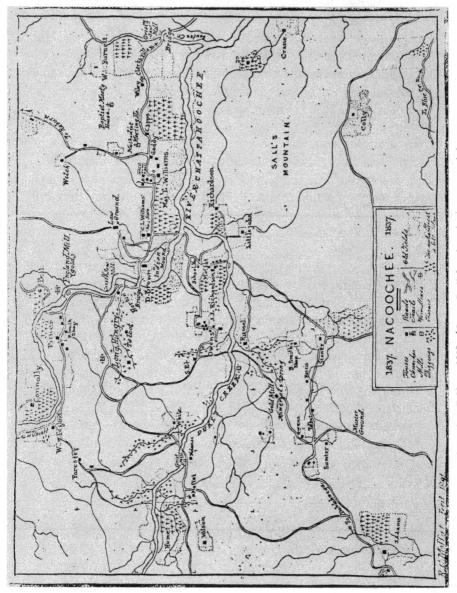

Nacoochee Valley, 1837. [James R. Wyly site shown near road in upper right. Jarrett-England sites in upper center.]

**Map 9:** Nacoochee Valley, 1837

In 1817, the Georgia Legislature appropriated $20,000 for improving the Savannah and the Tugaloo all the way up to Panther Creek, but the amount was contingent upon matching funds from South Carolina. Wyly, nearly finished with the Unicoi Turnpike, was among the river commissioners. South Carolina failed to act, so in December of 1818, Georgia repealed the matching-funds condition. The sum was then raised to $30,000, $7,000 of which was allotted for the stretch between Andersonville and Panther Creek. Wyly had once again maneuvered himself into a key position. In charge of the stretch of river between Andersonville and Panther Creek, he was in a position to greatly increase the value of his lands at Walton's Ford.[18]

By 1842, the river was cleared for navigation of boats carrying up to nine tons of cotton all the way to Andersonville, S.C. Steamboats were only an indirect help to the Tugaloo farmers, for "no steamboat could ascend the rapids at Augusta." The coming of the railroad tended to distract Georgians from river-improvement projects, and the Civil War made them out of the question.[19]

Seasonal floods, called "freshets," were a yearly trial for people on the Tugaloo and the Savannah. When spring rains joined melted snow from the mountains, North Georgia streams would swell and wash away bridges and then merge to flood the rivers. One such flood had wreaked havoc upon family Bibles and livestock when Elijah Clarke's party of settlers crossed the Tugaloo in 1773. John Lambert reported:

> Hence, when the accumulated waters of rain & snow pour down their [the rivers'] channels, the adjacent low lands and intervals are overflowed with destructive freshes or inundations. These freshes will sometimes rise to 30 or 40 feet perpendicular, above the usual level of the river. In 1701 a very destructive one occurred in part of the country; and in 1796 a very similar flood poured down the Savannah River, laying the town of Augusta upwards of two feet under water, damaging goods therein to a large amount. It tore away an extensive bridge, near 800 feet long, belonging to Mr. Wade Hampton... and carried destruction and dismay before it quit to the town of Savannah...Several bridges were carried away, and many of the Negro huts on the islands and swamp plantations near the coast, were torn up with the people in them, and carried by the torrent entirely out to sea.[20]

Perhaps transportation problems became a hit less acute for Tugaloo residents after Devereaux Jarrett opened his country "commissary." The earliest account book which has been found dates from 1805, but it refers to an even older book. The heading on the pages reads "Pendleton, S.C." The store must have been just across the river, for when it was moved in 1807, the clientele of the new store remained largely the same. Close reading of this ledger reveals that young Jarrett may have had partners or sponsors in this store, namely, his step-father Charles Kennedy and his maternal great uncle, Charles Baker. The last references in the book mention "acct. of whiskey rcd. of Charles Baker, [same] delivered Charles Baker," both dated May, 1810.[21]

The day-to-day entries for the store indicate an interesting range of products consumed by the early-nineteenth-century farmers. The ledgers provide a glimpse into the lives of those in the Tugaloo area by recording the food, kitchen items, yardgoods and so on that were sold at the store. Frequent entries for half-pints and other small quantities of brandy, rum, whiskey, and wine indicate that the store also served as a tavern. Not surprisingly, the 1805 store sold no soap, which was usually made at home, but almost amazingly, it sold no tobacco. Some of the items sold at the Pendleton store were the following:

| Tools | | Sewing and Yard Goods | |
|---|---|---|---|
| axes | 2.00 ea. | broad cloth | 2.50 yd. [at least] |
| augers | .50 | calico | .90 yd. |
| chisels | .31 | flannel | .75 yd. |
| "cotton hows" [cotton hose] | 1.75 pair | linen | .75 yd. |
| | | muslin | .62½ yd. |
| flat irons | 1.25 pair | velvet | .62½ yd. |
| hoes | 1.75 ea. | skeins silk | .12½ [⅛ yd.] |
| hatchets | .50 | skeins thread | .06¼ ea. |
| nails | .25 wt. | buttons | .75 doz. |
| penknives | .50 | | |
| scissors | .50 | | |
| "wisted hows" [worsted hose] | 1.75 pair | | |

| Food | | Kitchen | |
|---|---|---|---|
| coffee | .50 lb | creampot | .12½ ea. |
| molasses | 1.25 gal. | [coffeepots] | |
| sugar | .25 lb | knives & forks | 1.62½ set |
| salt | 1.50 bushel | pewter plates | 2.50 for 6 |
| | | mugs | .12½ ea. |
| | | pitchers | .75 |
| | | teacups & saucers | 1.00 set |

| Clothes | | Liquor | |
|---|---|---|---|
| gloves | .75 | brandy | .37½ pt. |
| handkerchiefs | .50 | rum | .37 |
| shoes | 1.00 | wine | .18¾ pt. |
| slippers | 1.50 | whisky | .12½ pt. |
| silk handker-chiefs | 1.25 | | |

Miscellaneous items also sold in the store include:

| bridles | 1.50 | combs | | "testerment" | 2.75 |
|---|---|---|---|---|---|
| copperas | .18¾ lb | | | [Bible] | |
| shot | .25 wt. | | | gimblets | .12½ |
| quire cap paper | .37½ | | | blankets | 4.00 |
| spelling book | 2.00 | | | spurs | 1.75 |

A large number of "cash lent" entries, always for small amounts, appear in conjunction with "Dev. Jarrett," demonstrating that young Jarrett was developing financial acumen. The store's customers included Ben Cleveland, Elijah Isaacs, Absolom Cleveland, George Walton, James Blair, Neely Dobson, and John Elston. They occasionally paid for goods with cash, but frequently with cotton, as well, and Jarrett also often accepted deerskins, tallow, whiskey, and, upon occasion, "bareskin" [sic], "minkskin," tobacco, sugar, beeswax, corn, hogs, wagoning, and "bawling" [sic].

The back of the ledger book contains other entries, the earliest date for these being 1807. Some pages are headed, "Franklin Ct.," the earliest with such a title appearing in 1809. The Franklin County store stocked considerably more food than the Pendleton store, and dealt less liquor. Beef, bacon, pork, corn, potatoes, and wheat appear in the Franklin entries, although

Jarrett still sold no soap and very little tobacco. Entries for this store continue until 1814, but the whole span fills far fewer pages than the 1805 entries.[22] At the Franklin County store, a few of the prices were as follows:

| | | | |
|---|---|---|---|
| beef | about .03 lb | shoes | 1.75 ea. |
| bacon | 30 wt. for 3.75 | "shewing a horse" | 1.25 |
| pork | 100 wt. for 3.25 | bridle | 1.5 |
| wheat | .75 bushel | sugar | .15 lb |
| corn | .50 bushel | coffee | .35 lb [23] |
| flour | 6.00 barrel | | |

During the years that Jarrett's store was established in Pendleton District and then moved across the river to Franklin County, the land at Walton's Ford had not yet been purchased by James R. Wyly. Wyly's first appearance in Franklin County records was not particularly distinguished. In August of 1802, 400 acres belonging to him on Lightwood Log Creek were sold at auction to William O. Whitney. This land was sold "as the result of James R. Wyly being in arrears on still taxes due to the U.S." This inauspicious introduction to one of Traveler's Rest's major protagonists, however, did not indicate a lasting trend. Regarding Wyly, the pattern is a frustrating lack of information.[24]

James Wyly, father of James R. Wyly, was a long-time landowner in Franklin County, appearing as early as 1791. A veteran of the Battle of King's Mountain, he never permanently resided in Georgia, but lived at a large farm in the (Loudon County) Tennessee country. In Franklin County, Georgia, he owned land on Eastanollee Creek and property in Carnesville, and was a tax collector for many years. James married Jemima Cleveland, daughter of Colonel Ben, and James Rutherford was born to them on June 24, 1783, in the part of North Carolina that later became Loudon County, Tennessee. *The Cleveland Genealogy* maintains that James

> grad. Greenville co. coll., Tenn.; from 1802 occupied a farm on Tenn. river, at now Landin[Loudon], Blount co. Was from 1804 during life, of the co. working out Unicory [sic] turnpike from Walton's ford, Tugalo river, to Tellico Plains, Tenn.; a State Commissioner to improve navigation of Savannah and Tugalo rivers. Served under James and Hezekiah Terrell as Sheriff of Franklin co. Tenn. for 12 years, prompt and efficient officer. Was capt. in reg. of Major Benjamen Cleveland …in Creek Indian war, under Gen. John Floyd. Fought gallantly at battles of Autossee, Ala., Nove. 29, 1813, Calibbee and Othtawalla

war, 1812. Rem. hetw. 1818 and 1820 to Habersham co., on Tugalo river, opp. Walton's ford. Planter; of good judgement; had a fine library, was well read, and accumulated a handsome property. Parents and family were Baptists.

In June of 1802, James R. Wyly married Sarah Hawkins Clark, the daughter of Elizabeth Sevier (who was the daughter of John Sevier) and William Clark [one of Jesse Walton's neighbors on the Tugaloo was a William Clark]. James and Sarah had eight sons and five daughters; according to *The Cleveland Genealogy*, the children were born in Tennessee up to 1818 and afterwards were born in Habersham County, Georgia. To this sketchy, questionable information, the Sevier Family History adds but little. It corrects Wyly's sheriffdom, however, to Franklin County, Georgia, and adds that he was colonel in the Habersham County militia.[25]

It is quite doubtful that Wyly remained in Tennessee until 1818; he apparently continued his father's practice of maintaining farms in Tennessee and Georgia. In 1806, he bought 350 acres on the north fork of the Broad River in Franklin County and paid taxes on the land for some years. In February of 1813, Wyly, along with his cousin and war buddy Ben Cleveland, grandson of old Ben, bought just over 285 acres from the John Cleveland estate, this land being near the site of Old Tugaloo Town on Toccoa Creek. Ben had sold it to son "Devil John" in 1790.

Wyly may have lived on this tract. Soon after January of 1814, he moved to a tract he bought from John's son, Fauche Cleveland. For $1,800, he received 433 acres on Toccoa Creek, "where [by August, 1815] Said Wyly now lives, adjacent Jarrat [*sic*] and land surveyed for Wyly, known as Owl Swamp." Wyly did not keep this Owl Swamp land for long, as he sold it in August of 1815 to John Elston of Pendleton, South Carolina, who had married his wife's sister.[26]

According to the genealogies, Captain James R. Wyly served "heroically" under his neighbor Ben Cleveland, Jr., in the Creek War of 1813 and 1814. Historical accounts of this Indian war are scarce, but one written by H.S. Halbert and T.H. Ball in 1895 discusses the adventures of General John Floyd's Georgia volunteers. At Autossee, in present-day Alabama, on November 29, 1813, Wyly joined 950 Georgians and 400 "friendly" Cherokees in sacking this town on the south bank of the Tallapoosa. With negligible losses themselves, the Georgians killed 400 "hostiles" and burned Autossee. The troops marched on then, Wyly with them, and destroyed Tallassee. Later, at Calabee Valley on January 27, 1814, the Georgians were part of 1,700 troops and 400 Cherokees who were ambushed seven miles from Tuskegee. It was reported that "the savages suddenly sprang from their lair in the undergrowth of the creek and made a furious assault about daylight." The volunteers countered with a charge and drove the Creeks into a swamp. None-theless, Floyd was stopped, his army "cut up," and his campaign "brought to a premature close."[27]

Meanwhile, the second Joseph Martin had accumulated a prosperous holding somewhat down the river from Wyly, at Walton's Ford (see Map 10). As a leader in the Unicoi project, Wyly must have cast admiring eyes at Martin's position on the Tugaloo Crossroads, for in 1818, Martin sold out to Wyly (1,343½ acres for $4,500) and moved to Alabama. With these lands added to his other holdings, Wyly was now a substantial farmer, as well as an enterprising road builder, river commissioner, and innkeeper.[28]

Disappointingly little is known of James R. Wyly's fellow "man-on-the-make" at the Tugaloo in those years, Devereaux Jarrett. He was born in 1785 in Georgia or South Carolina, shortly after his father Robert's death. A great many years later, Jarrett descendants would proudly recall a family tradition that George Washington had visited Devereaux's home (in Oconee or Ab-beville, S.C., or perhaps in Wilkes County, Georgia), met the youngster and pronounced him "a bright lad who would one day make his mark."[29]

Jarrett was reared and educated in Oconee County, South Carolina, where his mother, originally Dorothy Mallory, resided with her second hus-band, Charles Kennedy. Family traditions concerning Devereaux's youth do not always fit the ascertainable historical facts. For instance, one tradi-tion has it that in Franklin County Devereaux first lived in a cabin on what is now known as the Turnbull place, then moved down to Traveler's Rest about 1812, enlarging the house that Jesse Walton built. Considering the evidence in Franklin County deeds, however, this legend can hardly be true, and it becomes necessary to use all the family traditions with great care.[30]

There is good evidence that Devereaux was living on the Tugaloo by 1805, although it is not known on which side of the river. The 1805 ledgers do not carry a heading of "Jarrett's Store," but the customers are clearly Tu-galoo residents, and Devereaux Jarrett had an account book of the store. A reasonable hypothesis is that he arrived in the neighborhood by the time he was about eighteen years old, on the Pendleton side of the river. Having an inheritance of unknown size, apparently invested in about seventeen slaves, he may have owned land in South Carolina, and he almost certainly became involved in a country store in Pendleton by 1805 (probably in partnership with his great-uncle, Charles Baker, and step-father Charles Kennedy). The best evidence is his involvement in so many of the cash-loaning transac-tions in the accounts, a pattern continued in the later books that are known to be Jarrett's.[31] When the store was moved across the river in 1807, Jarrett may have crossed also, but he did not yet buy any land in Franklin County. In 1807, Jarrett made his first appearance in the Franklin County tax digest, as owner of seventeen slaves but no land. In 1808, he had only ten slaves; in

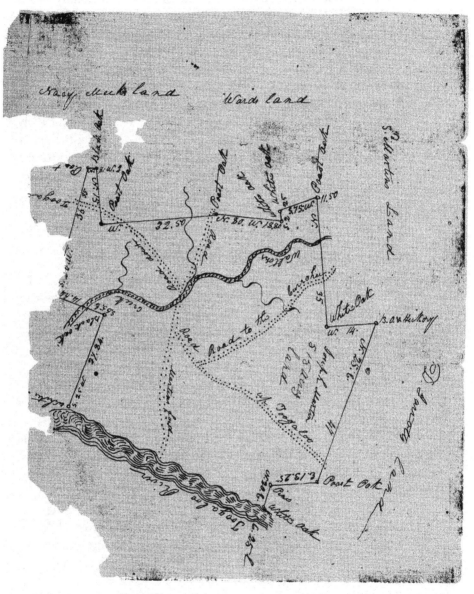

Joseph Martin Survey at Walton's Ford, 1813. *Site of Traveler's Rest.

**Map 10:** Joseph Martin's Survey of Walton Ford Tract, (c) 1815

1811, Killis Walton served as Jarrett's agent for fourteen slaves, but he still owned no land.[32]

The family tradition that Jarrett's first house in Franklin County was at the later Turnbull place is borne out by Martha Acker's *Deeds of Franklin County*. In 1814, he bought 500 acres of the John Cleveland estate from Anderson Watkins for $3,000, this land being part of Ben Cleveland's original grant on Toccoa Creek and the Tugaloo, site of the ancient and recent Indian occupation and next to Wyly's Owl Swamp. Jarrett received a grant of 300 adjacent acres the same year, and a year later, Wyly and Ben Cleveland, Jr., sold Jarrett 240 more acres on Toccoa Creek for $1,600. By the time Wyly bought Martin's plantation in 1818, Jarrett was his most substantial neighbor, owning twenty-one slaves and almost 2,000 acres, all of it along Toccoa Creek just to the northwest of Wyly's new place on Walton's and Ward's creeks. Already a farmer, juror, storeowner, petty financier, and family man, Devereaux Jarrett had not yet reached his peak of activity.[33]

Beyond his financial activities, little is known of Devereaux Jarrett, the person. His father's family had been in America since the late seventeenth Century, when Robert Jarrett I came to Virginia. Robert paid passage for seven people, and thus received 322 acres in New Kent County in 1665. His two sons, Robert Jarrett II and Devereaux Jarrett I, were born about 1698 and 1700. Robert Jarrett II became the father of Robert Jarrett III and the Reverend Devereux Jarrett II, who was born in New Kent in 1732. The Reverend Jarrett was a staunch, itinerant Anglican in Virginia and North Carolina who achieved some fame through his autobiography. He died without issue, but his brother, Robert Jarrett III, was father to Devereaux Jarrett III, Robert Jarrett IV, and Archelaus—all of whom headed for Georgia as they became adults.[34]

The three sons emigrated to Elbert and Wilkes counties in Georgia, with Devereaux III residing in Wilkes during the Revolution. At first a Loyalist, he was a Patriot by 1780. When he died in 1790, a prosperous slaveowner, his heirs received 575 acres in Franklin County. He died in Wilkes County, and his will was recorded in Elberton in 1827. Archelaus, another Revolutionary War veteran, settled in Elbert County and had numerous children. Robert IV "was a captain of horse in the Revolution either from Wilkes Co., Ga., or just across the line in South Carolina." His will (now lost) was made in Wilkes County, and "tradition has it that he died from wounds received in the Revolution." Robert IV received a Revolutionary bounty grant of 287½ acres in Washington County in 1785. His son was Devereaux Jarrett IV of Traveler's Rest.[35]

Devereaux's maternal grandparents were William Mallory and Mary Baker, who had among their children three daughters related to the story of Traveler's Rest. Ann Mallory married Colonel John Patton of Buncombe

County, North Carolina. Mary Mallory married George Blair, son of the Habersham County leader James Blair, and moved to the Tugaloo area. This couple appears in the 1807 ledger. Dorothy Mallory married (first) Robert Jarrett. Some time after his early death, she brought Devereaux Jarrett to the Tugaloo.

So Devereaux Jarrett IV spent his childhood in South Carolina and then moved to Franklin County, where he became a prosperous landowner. He married his first cousin, Sarah Patton, in Buncombe County, North Carolina, in 1807. The couple had four children—Thomas Patton, born in 1812; Robert, 1817; Charles Kennedy, 1820; and Sarah, 1824. Living after 1814 in his large cabin on Toccoa Creek, Devereaux thrived along with his neighbor, James R. Wyly, who was building what would one day be called Jarrett Manor.[36]

As prosperous, upstanding citizens, Jarrett and Wyly performed small public services for the county. By 1816, 31-year-old Devereaux Jarrett was a justice of the peace for Franklin County. In the summer of that year, he helped arbitrate a neighborhood squabble. William Edins, a substantial landowner down the Tugaloo, appeared before Jarrett and asserted that James Starrett, another farmer, "had killed & carried away 'his property.'" On reflection, Said Edins now states that he had for several days been 'addled by spiritous lickers,' and that he is sorry for what has transpired in said dispute," whereupon the proceedings were stopped.[37]

Jarrett (along with Wyly) also served on the Franklin County Grand Jury in Carnesville, a judicial body which played an interesting role in the county during those years. The grand jury reprimanded one justice of the peace for neglecting to report his accounts accurately, and the jury also sought to stir the county road commissioners into action, citing the citizens' "grievance" over "The bad & almost intire [sic] Neglected situation of our roads." Then, as now, the grand jury endeavored to serve as moral guardian for the community. Those who had taken to drunkenness, assaulting slaves, fornication, and gambling at Carnesville were condemned and rooted out. In April of 1815, the grand jury, which included Wyly, lamented the sad moral condition of Franklin County: "We view with extreme regret that so little attention is paid to those morals and principles that should be promoted in all republican governments; and presents as a grievance the frequent practice of gambling in this county..."

Those who ignored "republican" decency in one anti-social way or another could be confined, but they could also be whipped, branded, or executed, depending upon the extent of their "crimes."[38]

Architectural historians have found it far easier to determine how Traveler's Rest was built than when it was built. What sort of structures Wyly acquired on the Walton's Ford tract when he bought it from the second

Joseph Martin cannot be ascertained, but the price, $2,000 for 200 acres, suggests that a house was on the grounds. Archaeological excavations under the house have produced evidence (beneath the southern end) of an "Indian-style" cabin. There is remote chance that this cabin was built by Jesse Walton, or even earlier, but a much greater possibility is that it was put up by one of his children or by the second Joseph Martin. No one has dared any definitive speculations as to the dates of this structure, or what it looked like.[39] It is probable that this house was still standing when Wyly bought the property. If so, it appears that he soon replaced it with the south end of Traveler's Rest.

According to archaeologist William Kelso's report of 1968, the main house underwent "two major periods of construction evidenced by different materials, construction methods, and carpenter's marks." The recent study by architectural historian Paul Buchanan confirms this. Because the scaffold post-holes for the central chimney were north of the chimney, under the northern section of the house, Kelso maintained that the south end of the house must have been built first.[40] This theory is supported by the markings on the rafters of the ceiling, also. Those on the south half of the house were labeled with Roman numerals of a somewhat different style from those of the north half. Both sections of the house were fitted together on the ground, then reassembled to hold the roof.[41]

Under the extreme southern part of the house, a "back-filled root cellar" was discovered, apparently having been used in conjunction with the southern half of the house when it stood alone. Artifacts filling the root cellar show that it was closed and the southern chimney added sometime between 1816 and 1825. On this slim evidence, the experts have concluded that the two ends of the house (Periods I and II) were built about twenty years apart; the first section in around 1815-20, the second during the 1830s.[42] Evidence in the deeds does not confirm or deny this hypothesis, but it does support the hypothesis that the house was started by Wyly and enlarged by Jarrett.[43]

The house measures ninety feet by thirty-nine feet and contains in its two and one-half stories thirteen rooms and numerous fireplaces. Devereaux Jarrett arranged his house to suit the convenience of his family and his guests. Travelers could reach their rooms without going through the house, and the family quarters were provided with some privacy.[44]

Also pertaining to the structure are the rock-basement kitchen, a dug-out wine cellar, and several outbuildings. The "loomhouse," adjacent to the northern corner of the house, had multiple dirt-floor levels by the time the State acquired the site. Artifacts (a crock handle and metal lid) show that the structure was used for looming ca. 1850, and Buchanan has concluded that it was built after the rest of the house. The lower, original floor was covered with materials usually associated with a dairy.[45] (See the Appendix A for Paul Buchanan's complete report on the structural history of Traveler's Rest.)

Fifty feet northwest of the manor house, excavators uncovered the foundations of a smokehouse. It is known that Devereaux Jarrett often handled large amounts of smoked meat, so he definitely needed a place to store it. (The smokehouse may be seen in the 1890s photograph reproduced in this report.) The artifacts found in the floor excavations inclined Kelso to believe that the smokehouse was built in the early 1830s, which would correspond to the time of Jarrett's acquisition of Walton's Ford.[46] The other structures that housed Devereaux Jarrett's enterprises—the store-tavern, barns, stables, smithy, mills, slave cabins, and bridge—no longer exist.

During his first years in Franklin County, Devereaux Jarrett was also involved in a tanyard. A rough ledger survives from 1817 and 1818 and provides a hazy idea of business at the tanyard, the location of which is unknown. Jarrett had a partner in the tanyard, William Grey, a Revolutionary War veteran or the son of a veteran. Ben Cleveland, Jr., the second Joseph Martin, and James Blair brought skins to the yard, mostly deer, but some bear and mink, and they also bought leather goods there. Because this ledger refers to an "old book," it is possible to infer that Jarrett's tanyard was in business before 1817. No other tanyard ledgers survive, but the yard is mentioned in the 1830s ledgers.[47]

The kinds of artifacts found in the excavations—tableware, pipes, locks, buttons—show that the early settlers at Walton's Ford, like other American pioneers, were dependent on England for their manufactured items. The Martins, Wylys, and Jarrette were prosperous, but not to the extent that they used implements different from their neighbors. The items sold in Jarrett's store throughout its existence bear out this idea of rustic simplicity.[48]

At Walton's Ford, Wyly worked his farm, continued to father numerous children, and handled his jobs as river commissioner, militia officer, and sheriff. In addition, in 1828, he was named postmaster at Walton's Ford.[49] It seems probable that Wyly built a tavern-store near Walton's Ford, and one page of the 1831-1833 ledger, entitled "Wyly's Ferry," makes the premise appear even more likely. The items sold included alcohol in small amounts, probably consumed on the premises.

While Wyly was building Traveler's Rest, Jarrett was accumulating property. In 1819, Devereaux bought "Estatoe Old Fields" for $2,925, thereby acquiring the site of another old Cherokee town. He purchased several hundred additional acres on the Tugaloo and Toccoa Creek in the 1820s, and then he became involved in an interesting transaction in 1829 when he mortgaged "Estatoe Old Fields" to a Cherokee leader, John Martin. Martin, one-time treasurer of the Cherokee Nation, was eventually a prominent leader of the pro-removal faction in the tribe. An owner of "scores of slaves," he was a nephew of frontier General Joseph Martin.[50] By 1830, Devereaux Jarrett owned about 3,600 acres, mostly in the area somewhat to the northwest of Traveler's Rest, with a bit of acreage on Ward's Creek.[51]

Throughout the antebellum years, the Tugaloo area remained a "backwoods" region, relatively sparse in settlement, with a few tiny towns. Habersham County, thirty-one miles by twenty-three miles, was created out of Franklin County and the Cherokee cession of 1818 (see Map 11). According to Sherwood's *Gazetteer*, Clarkesville, the county seat, had thirty-three houses and stores in the mid-1820s, while Carnesville had but fourteen houses and five stores. Most of the settlers had small farms and few, if any, slaves. The lands were "adapted to wheat and corn. The climate is unsurpassed." In 1837, Clarkesville still had only 270 people and was the largest town in a county then populated by 10,671. Clarkesville was a "courthouse town," a center for transportation, commerce, schools, professions, and government.[52]

Devereaux Jarrett was a man who constantly expanded his operations. When, for some unknown reason, Wyly decided to give up his large establishment at Walton's Ford, Jarrett was wealthy enough to acquire it. A small scrap of paper from December 9, 1833, records that Jarrett agreed to pay Wyly $6,000 for his plantation at Walton's Ford. The actual deed to this exchange, drawn up in 1838, refers to 2,276½ acres "more or less…at or near Walton's Ford, being the premises whereon said Jarrett now lives…being all the lands I owned adjoining Walton's Ford…"[53] So Devereaux Jarrett moved his family and slaves down the river to the place he named Traveler's Rest, though the origin of that name has become obscure. Wyly moved to Clarkesville, but continued to hold establishments in the Nacoochee Valley and Hiwassee. He died in Clarkesville in 1855.[54]

## NOTES

[1] Martha W. Ackers, ed., *Deeds of Franklin County, Georgia 1784-1826* (Easley, S.C.: Southern Historical Press, 1976). On William Walker, see pp. 235, 288, 293; on Robert, see pp. 257, 280, 292; on George, see p. 323; on Killis, see p. 323; on the Walton heirs relinquishment to Joseph Martin, see p. 322. According to James E. Saunders, *Early Settlers of Alabama* (New Orleans: L. Graham & Son, Ltd., 1899), George Walton moved to Laurence County, Alabama, with Joseph Martin; pp. 49-50.

[2] Coulter, *Old Petersburg*, p. 26.

[3] Franklin County *Tax Digests*, 1798 and 1807; Flanders, *Plantation Slavery*, p. 52.

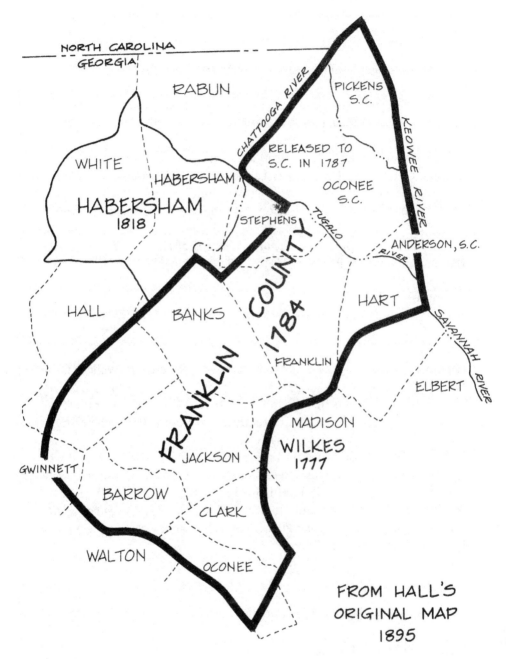

Franklin County, 1784, showing outline of subsequent counties. *Site of Traveler's Rest.

**Map 11:** Franklin County, 1784

[4] Draper Manuscripts, 3XX13.

[5] Ibid., 14DD113.

[6] Trogdon, *Stephens County History*, p. 32; Coulter, *A Short History*, p. 251.

[7] *Miller's Weekly Messenger*, July 28, 1810; Trogden, *Stephens County History*, p. 32; Coulter, *Old Petersburg*, pp. 66-67.

[8] The John Sevier letter and Georgia Senate act are from papers painstakingly collected by Dr. Thomas Lumsden of Clarkesville, Ga. Lumsden has spent years searching out materials pertaining to the Unicoi Turnpike. Most of the information available on this subject is the result of his efforts.

[9] Mrs. J.E. Hays (ed.), *Indian Treaties, Cessions of Land in Georgia, 1705-1837* (Atlanta: W.P.A. Project, 1941), p. 376c.

[10] Lumsden-Unicoi Papers.

[11] Ibid.

[12] Lumsden-Unicoi Papers; Thomas Lumsden, "Nacoochie Valley, Early Crossroads," unpublished paper. Yet on p. 105, Sherwood, in discussing Toccoa Falls, comments that the mouth of Toccoa Creek was near the head of navigation on the Tugaloo. Apparently the location of the Tugaloo's highest navigable point was not precisely known even then. See also Seymour Dunbar, *A History of Travel in America* (Indianapolis: Bobbs-Merrill Co., 1914), pp. 506-8; Cora Bales Sevier and Nancy S. Madden, *Sevier Family History* (Washington, D.C.: Kaufmann Printing Co., Inc., 1961), pp. 296-97; Edmond J. Cleveland and Horace G.Cleveland, *The Genealogy of the Cleveland and Cleaveland Families* (Hartford, Conn.: Case, Lockwood, & Brainard, 1899), pp. 2113-15.

[13] Lumsden-Unicoi Papers.

[14] Ibid.; *Knoxville Register*, April 6, 1819.

[15] Lumsden-Unicoi Papers.

[16] Coulter, *Old Petersburg*, pp. 67-69.

[17] Ibid., pp. 52-53.

[18] Lumsden-Unicoi Papers; *Laws of Georgia*.

[19] Ibid., pp. 56, 58.

[20] Hays, *Hero of Hornet's Nest*, p. 9; John Lambert, *Travels through Lower Canada and the United States* (London: T. Gillet, 1810), pp. 52-53.

[21] Jarrett ledgers, 1805-1813.

[22] Ibid.

[23] Ibid.

[24] Ackers, *Franklin County Deeds*, p. 253.

[25] *Cleveland Genealogy*, p. 2114; on William Clark, see Ackers, *Franklin County Deeds*, p 23.; *Sevier Family History*, p. 296. The *Cleveland Genealogy* apparently erred in its claims that the "Unicory" turnpike was begun in 1804, that Wyly was sheriff in Franklin County, Tennessee, and that Wyly did not move to Georgia until 1818.

[26] Ackers, *Franklin County Deeds*, pp. 323, 338, 352; *Sevier Family History*, p. 296.

[27] H.S. Halbert and T.H. Ball, *The Creek War of 1813 and 1814* (Chicago: Donohue and Henneberry, 1895), pp. 268-69, 273-74; Coulter, *A Short History*, p. 212. The author has not ascertained whether Devereaux Jarrett and Joseph Martin served with General Floyd. "Georgia's Roster of the War of 1812" shows that Jarrett was commissioned as a captain of the Franklin County Militia in 1814 (from the Jarrett family Bible).

[28] Ackers, *Franklin County Deeds*, pp. 397-98.

[29] Thomas Patton's memoir in Traveler's Rest papers in possession of Henry and Elizabeth Hayes family and the Historic Preservation Section. Thomas Patton Jarrett's memoir claims that Devereaux's mother was a Dortha Lane. Genealogical research by Mrs. R.E. O'Donnell, however, provides the information that her name was actually Dorothy Mallory. See "Research, Jarrett Family," Traveler's Rest papers.

[30] Mabel Ramsey notes; conversation with Rose Jarrett Taylor; Traveler's Rest papers.

[31] Jarrett ledgers, 1805-1813.

[32] Jarrett family papers in possession of Henry and Elizabeth Hayes. *Franklin County Tax Digests* for 1807, 1808, 1811; Jarrett ledgers, 1805-1813. It is unfortunate that Franklin County Tax Digests for the years 1812 through 1817 are lost.

[33] Franklin County records, *Superior Court Minutes, 1814-1815*; *Tax Digests*; *Franklin County Deeds*; pp. 351-52.

[34] "Jarrett-Smith Genealogy," Traveler's Rest papers, Historic Preservation Section.

[35] Ibid.; Ackers, *Franklin County Deeds*, p. 90, refers to a Robert Jarrett grant on Little Nails Creek (granted 1786), sold by Jarrett to Churnel Wallace. Page 115 refers to a 287½-acre grant to Robert Jarrett for Indian Creek.

[36] Jarrett ledgers, 1818, front page, and accounts. The 1818 ledger shows that by 1820 Devereaux was worth $20,904.50 in accounts alone.

[37] Ackers, *Franklin County Deeds*, pp. 351-52.

[38] Franklin County records, *Superior Court Minutes*, 1815.

[39] Ackers, *Franklin County Deeds*, pp. 397-98; Kelso, "Excavations," Historic Preservation Section.

[40] Kelso, "Excavations."

[41] Andrew Sparkes, "Plastic Skin Reveals Secrets of Old Inn," *Atlanta Journal-Constitution Magazine*, November 13, 1966, p. 34.

[42] Kelso, "Excavation," pp. 10, 11, 18.

[43] Ibid.; Ackers, *Franklin County Deeds*, p. 398; Sparkes, "Plastic Skin," p. 34.

[44] Sparkes, "Plastic Skin," p. 34. The students felt that the second owner, Wyly, had added the porch. They also concluded that while the first and third owners were skilled (or employed) craftsmen, the second did crude, sloppy work.

[45] Kelso, "Excavation"; Sparkes, "Plastic Skin," p. 34.

[46] Kelso, "Excavation."

[47] Tanyard ledger; 1830s ledger, p. 107.

[48] Kelso, "Excavations"; ledger, 1805-1813.

[49] Wyly ledger page in Historic Preservation Section; Wyly as postmaster, National Archives and Records Service, U.S. Post Office Records, Appointments of Postmasters, Vol. 5, p. 207.

[50] Habersham County records, Superior Court deeds; on John Martin, see Louise Hays (ed.), *Cherokee Indian Talks, Letters, Treaties, 1786-1838* (Atlanta: Georgia Department of Archives and History, 1938), p. 289. It would be interesting to find out if Jarrett used the Cherokee removal, as did so many Georgians, to avoid his debt to John Martin, but such information is not available.

[51] See Devereaux Jarrett in Franklin and Habersham county records; see Jarrett deeds in Historic Preservation Section.

[52] Adiel Sherwood, *A Gazetteer of the State of Georgia* (Athens, Ga.: University of Georgia Press, 1939), pp. 38, 44, 118; Joan A. Sears, "Town Planning in White and Habersham Counties," *Georgia Historical Quarterly,* Vol. 54 (1970), p. 26; George White, *Historical Collections of Georgia* (New York: Pudney & Russell, Publishers, 1859), p. 486.

[53] See Jarrett deeds, Historic Preservation Section.

[54] *Cleveland Genealogy,* p. 2114; Habersham County courthouse records. In September of 1836, Sarah Hawkins Clark Wyly initiated divorce proceedings against James R. Wyly. She testified that after "ten years…in much peace and harmony…And afterwards to wit in the year eighteen hundred and twelve the said James R. forgeting [sic] or disregarding his duties as a husband…commenced a course of unkind and ill treatment toward your petitioner refusing her his countenance, support and protection; reviling and abusing your petitioner [and] … had criminal intercourse with other women." The divorce was granted in 1836, with Devereaux Jarrett on the jury. See Traveler's Rest papers.

# Chapter 6

## Taverns, Travel, and Traveler's Rest

In the heyday of Devereaux Jarrett's stagecoach inn at Traveler's Rest, way-faring in America was an adventurous pastime. Not only were travelers subject to innumerable hardships and mishaps while on the move, but more often than not they also found their nights' lodgings fraught with unpleasant uncertainties. Nevertheless, travel was a popular phenomenon in the United States, even in the pre-industrial years during which Traveler's Rest thrived. Americans were a people on the move as no people had been before.

It is fortunate that many of these antebellum journeyers were literate, for an ample record now exists from their letters, journals, and memoirs of what the people, travel, and taverns in this country were like during that period. The reading world was deeply curious about the still-young United States, and many travelers (frequently Europeans) recorded their impressions with an eye to publication. Today, their observations are one of historians' main sources on the American tavern. Such travelogs are tremendously useful for the student of Traveler's Rest. From them, it is possible to reconstruct the general pattern of travel as well as taverns and to compare this pattern to conditions at Traveler's Rest. Two of these travelogs now provide the only actual views—just glimpses at that—of Traveler's Rest itself.

The only on-the-scene descriptions of Jarrett's place, in its prime, that have been discovered are those of George W. Featherstonhaugh and James Silk Buckingham—both Englishmen. Featherstonhaugh was a farmer, entrepreneur, politician, and scientist of aristocratic inclinations who had lived in the United States for thirty years before he began a series of geological-survey tours for the federal government in the mid 1830s. His book, *A Canoe Voyage Up the Minnay Sotor*, relates in vivid detail his impressions during extensive excursions through the country, including two visits to Traveler's Rest in 1836. Buckingham was a genteel Englishman who had trouble restraining his abolitionist, reformist opinions while touring the South. A "professional world traveler," he managed to produce eight books on his American adventures alone, and his *The Slave States of America* recounts an extensive journey through the South, which was supported by lectures (usually concerning his travels in the Holy Lands) in the towns he visited. Traveling with his family in 1839, Buckingham stopped at Jarrett's for a night.[1]

Europeans were apparently greatly surprised by the fact that "in America and especially in the West everybody travels." Many of these journeyers were people on the move from one home to another, but others traveled for reasons of business, opportunity, religion, or curiosity. Featherstonhaugh, who heartily disapproved of the average American, claimed, "If all the doctors, lawyers, tavern-keepers, itinerant priests, tradesmen, speculators, and bankrupts, that are roaming about this great western country, seeking whom they may devour, were to congregate in one place, it would be the most populous and extraordinary city out[side] of China."

While northern Georgia was more sparsely traveled than the "West"—meaning the northwestern and southwestern frontiers east of the Mississippi River—surely the Tugaloo Crossroads saw its share of characters.[2]

Buckingham and Featherstonhaugh were members of an exceptional group of travelers—highly cultivated people who fastidiously resented the average American's hard-drinking, tobacco-chewing and -spitting, swearing familiarity. An apparent snob, Featherstonhaugh at least was inclined to agree with Count Francisco Arese, who described the average traveler and tavern-keeper as "rude, uncivil, disagreeable, stinking: in a word, they are animals of an inferior type dressed like men."[3]

So much traveling occurred during this period that the combined American traditions of hospitality and acquisitiveness practically forced hundreds of wayside cabins and houses into the tavern business. When travelers stopped at a home by the roadside, they expected to get hospitality and to pay for it. It may be that Wyly's large house at the Tugaloo Crossroads became an inn in this manner. On the other hand, the size of Traveler's Rest and its convenient location on the highway, as well as the provisions of the Unicoi Treaty, argue for the theory that the house was actually built to be an inn.

The informality of origin of many inns led to a wide variety of accommodations, with Buckingham's and Featherstonhaugh's works providing ample testimony to the fact that weary travelers never knew what to expect at the end of a day's bouncing and jouncing on horseback or in stagecoach.[4] The average tavern was certainly not prepossessing in appearance, and unlike Traveler's Rest, the great majority of Southern inns were not picturesque and comfortable. Stopping-places were all too often like the drab and depressing one in North Carolina visited by the Buckinghams:

The bed-rooms were dark and dingy, the bedding coarse and dirty; no wash-stands, dressing-tables, mats, or carpets; broken looking-glasses, tallow candles, brass and tin candlesticks, and filthy negro servants; these were the accommodations that awaited the traveller. The dining-room was not more than eight feet high, with a whitewashed ceiling, blackened with the ascending smoke of candles; it was like a badly built soldiers' barracks; and the fare was like that of nearly all the country inns, coarse, greasy, tough, badly dressed, and cold. In short, the whole establishment was forbidding and comfortless in an unusual degree; yet here many families of opulence, and especially ladies, passed several months in the summer; were anxious to get here, and always sorry when the time came to go away.[5]

It is known that Jarrett's inn was not a fancy place, but in its rustic way, it was far more comfortable for travelers, including Buckingham, than places such as that described above.

Food, just as often as not, was untempting to the palate at most of these inns. At a decent place, one might be served a meal such as "chicken cooked with red rice and seasoned with butter and a little pepper and salt; green field peas with raw onions and green peppers, served with corn bread."[6] But Featherstonhaugh and Buckingham reported that the usual fare was inedible. Buckingham, stopping at a place in Sparta, Georgia, said,

The sight of the public table prepared for the passengers was so revolting, that, hungry as we were after our long and cold ride, early rising, and violent motion, we turned away in disgust from the table, and made our dinner in the coach on hard biscuits. There were three lines of coaches on this road, all leaving at the same hour, and arriving at the same time…The passengers from each of them took their seats at the table, and many of them appeared to dine as heartily as if they saw nothing unusual in the fare. But the dirty state of the room in which the table was laid, the filthy condition of the table-cloth, the coarse and broken plates, rusty knives and forks, and large chunks of boiled pork, and various messes of corn and rancid butter, added to the coarse and vulgar appearance and manner of most of the guests, made the whole scene the most revolting we had yet witnessed in the country.[7]

Even where the food was good, however, the traveler might find it difficult to consume. Especially on the Southern frontier, eating utensils were often primitive. In Arkansas, Featherstonhaugh found a tavern where the landlady relied on humor to overcome a limited supply of silverware. She had "no forks but them as what's on the table; thar's Stump Handle, Crooky Prongs, Horney, Big Pewter, Little Pickey and that's just what thar is, and I expec they are all thar to speak for themselves." Upon introduction, "Stump Handle" was revealed to "consist of one prong of an old fork" with one end "stuck into a stump piece of wood." "Crooky Prongs" apparently "was curled over on each side, that it might also serve as a fishhook." "Horney," fashioned from a cow horn, "was a sort of imitation of a fork," while "Big Pewter" was "the handle of a spoon with the bowl broken off." "Little Pickey" resembled "a cobbler's awl fastened in a thick piece of wood." To make matters worse, napkins were practically unknown in America before 1850.[8]

After dinner, some travelers might have chosen to sleep, but that was seldom an inconvenience to those who felt the desire to stay awake and socialize. Featherstonhaugh was continually amazed at the rudeness of these non-sleepers, and one can well imagine the discomfort of scenes in small taverns with "two-thirds of the bar-room floor...covered by the beds of weary travellers, lying closely side by side, and the remaining part occupied by people engaged in drinking and noisy conversation."[9]

Taverns often became so crowded that sleep was nearly impossible, yet even under uncramped circumstances, the would-be sleeper faced other hazards. Bedbugs and other "varmints" competed for sovereignty in almost every inn, and even those few who struggled against them could rely only on "constant cleaning with a liberal use of quicksilver as a sort of insecticide" as the most effective method. How the quicksilver worked is unknown to Paton Yoder, historian of taverns, but it must have been used as a poison. In Maryland, Featherstonhaugh awoke one morning to find "bugs running all over me and over everything else," and in Missouri, he was diverted by his roommate, who "was constantly doubling himself up on his hams, to scratch away as energetically as if he was paid for it," protesting with "deep blasphemies [which] were unequaled."[10]

In some seasons, mosquitoes were as aggravating as bedbugs, and rats and mice were also nocturnal visitors. More than one guest most have been awakened, as was the governor of Wisconsin, by a pig poking about his body. Although the Buckinghams apparently had a pleasant stay in Athens, Georgia, where the people were charming and the Planter's Hotel "peculiarly agreeable," they did encounter problems during the night:

> There was only one drawback to our comfort, which, it is true, was a large one, and that was the incessant and uninterrupted chorus kept up every night by the dogs, cows, and hogs, that seemed to divide among them the undisputed possession of the streets at night. Not less than a hundred of each of these seemed to be at large, as though they belonged to no one, each doing its best to forage for provender,

and each endeavoring to maintain the superiority of its class, in the barking, lowing, and grunting of their respective members.[11]

On another night in Athens, the Buckinghams were disturbed by a crew of slaves, well-lubricated with whiskey, who were moving a house. The worst night of all, however, must have been at the Planter's Hotel in Augusta, during which their slumbers were interrupted when the hotel burned down in a huge conflagration.[12]

Usually, lodgers were expected to share beds with strangers when necessary. Fastidious people found this sort of "gambling" with their health abominable, for it was difficult to sleep crowded together with the dirty, the intoxicated, the diseased, or the sort of person "who spent the evening telling of his eye-gouging exploits." Unscreened newcomers might arrive in a guest's bed at any hour of the night. One fellow who tried to retain a private bed by claiming to have "the itch" was rewarded with a cheerful bedmate who acknowledged the same condition.[13]

If at all possible, travelers of Featherstonhaugh's and Buckingham's ilk attempted to obtain private beds or even private rooms, and sometimes, as at Traveler's Rest, they could. In the effort, however, they exposed themselves to ridicule as snobs, and one landlady judged such privacy-seekers thusly: "Ugh! Great people truly!—a bed to themselves—the hogs!—They travel together, and they eat together—and they eat enough, too—and yet they can't sleep together."[14]

Bathroom facilities were usually primitive, and before 1850, almost all taverns provided only outside facilities. Even at that late date, only the best hotels offered washstands, basins, mirrors, pitchers, and chamberpots for the guests, and soap was an unusual luxury, as were towels. A tavern joke of the era tells of a fastidious patron cut short by the innkeeper's indignant retort, "Sir, two hundred men have wiped on that towel and you are the first to complain."[15]

Taverns could be just as useful for their neighbors as for travelers. Not only were they likely to be used as stores and post offices, but they were frequently the only useful community gathering places, and they were especially valuable as neighborhood recreational centers. The people living near a tavern-inn such as Traveler's Rest used it for promoting local politics, conversation, and conversion, as well as drinking, banqueting, and gambling.

Featherstonhaugh and Buckingham were both unfavorably impressed with American drinking habits, and another English traveler, Frederick Marryat, observed:

> There is an unceasing pouring out and amalgamation of alcohol and other compounds, from morning to late at night. To drink with

a friend when you meet him is good fellowship, to drink with a stranger is politeness and a proof of wishing to be better acquainted...Americans can fix nothing without a drink. If you meet, you drink; if you part, you drink; if you make acquaintance, you drink; if you close a bargain, you drink; they quarrel in their drink, and they make it up with a drink. They drink because it is hot; they drink because it is cold. If successful in elections, they drink and rejoice, if not, they drink and swear...[16]

The ledger books of Traveler's Rest indicate that plenty of drinking went on there intermittently, most likely in the nearby store, but perhaps in the "lobby" of the house, as well.

According to Paton Yoder, dancing was enjoyed even at the most primitive taverns, although frontier dances were not fancy affairs. Featherstonhaugh was shocked by a "ball" in Arkansas attended by a hundred men and three women, at which the men danced in full regalia, "their hats on... armed with pistols and bowie knives." As the landlord and his helpers "took pitchers of a strong whiskey-punch round the room," everyone "got amazingly drunk, but were very good natured, for there were only a few shots fired in fun."[17] At such affairs people might carouse until three o'clock in the morning or later, but it probably may be assumed that whatever dancing festivities occurred at Traveler's Rest were somewhat more genteel.

Sometimes taverns also served to help convey the "Word of the Lord." Traveler Henry Milburn told of an itinerant preacher named Peter Cartwright, who was most resourceful in finding opportunities for conversion:

There was a dance at an inn where he stopped, and no room to sit in but the ball-room. A young girl politely asked him to dance with her. He led her out on the floor, and as the fiddler was about to strike up, said to the company that it was his custom to ask God's blessings on all undertakings, and he would do this now. Instantly dropping on his knees, he pulled his partner down too, and prayed until the fiddler fled in fright and some of the dancers wept or cried for mercy; then proceeded to exhort and sing hymns, and did not cease his labors until he had organized a Methodist church of thirty-two members, and made the landlord class-leader.[18]

It is not known whether the Jarretts allowed such disruptions at their dances.

For day-to-day socializing, the tavern was extremely useful. Where else could neighbors come to talk politics, gossip, discuss weather and crops, or pair off their children? Perhaps this poem was true of the social room at Traveler's Rest:

They sat in all the different ways
That men could sit, or ever sat;
They told of all their jolly days,
And spat in all the different ways
That men could spit, or ever spat.[19]

Taverns were the scene of local celebrations and competitions, also. Target-shoots, cockfights, horse races, gander-pullings, and greasedpole contests were popular, and these may have taken place at Traveler's Rest.[20] Like modern Americans, settlers on the Southern frontier had a propensity for violent entertainment: brawling and dueling were rivaled in popularity by bear-baiting, dog- and cockfights, and gander-pulling. In Decatur, Alabama, Featherstonhaugh was invited to what he referred to sarcastically as a "polite amusement" staged at the tavern. The condescending scientist observed:

> "Gander-pulling" is a sort of tournament on horseback, and is, I believe, of European origin. A path is laid out on the exterior of a circle of about 150 feet diameter, and two saplings are sunk into ground about 12 feet apart, on each side of the path. These being connected towards the top with a slack cord, a live gander with his legs tied, and his neck and head made as slippery as possible with goose grease, is suspended by the feet to that part of the cord immediately over the path. The knights of the gander having each deposited a small sum with the manager of the game to form a sweepstakes and to defray the expenses, follow each other, mounted on horseback, at intervals round the ring, two or three times before the signal is made to pull. When that is done, the cavaliers advance, each fixing his eye steadily upon the gander's shining neck, which he must seize and drag from the body of the wretched bird before the purse is won. This is not easily done, for as the rider advances he has to pass two men, five or six yards before he reaches the potence, one of them on each side of the path, and both armed with stout whips, who flog his horse unmercifully the instant he comes up with them, to prevent any unfair delay at the cord. Many are thus unable to seize the neck at all, having enough to do to keep the saddle, and others who succeed in seizing it often find it impracticable to retain hold of such a slippery substance upon a horse at full speed. Meantime the gander is sure to get some severe "scrags," and for awhile screams most lustily, which forms a prominent part of the entertainment. The tournament is generally continued long after the poor bird's neck is broken before it is dragged from its body; but some of the young fellows have horses

well trained to the sport, and grasp the neck with such strength and adroitness, that they bear off the head, windpipe, and all, screaming convulsively after they are separated from the body. This is considered the greatest feat that can be performed at gander-pulling.

Having been over-satiated at his first gander-pulling, Featherstonhaugh had "no inclination to be present a second time," and he hastened to catch the steamer out of Decatur instead of joining the "good ol' boys" at the tavern.[21]

Featherstonhaugh could not abide American politics either, which seemed to him to be a competition of buffoons clowning for the democratic rubbish. At taverns, however, he was constantly exposed to politics, for these were always neighborhood political centers, he wrote,

> What these parsnip-looking country fellows in Georgia seem to enjoy most is political disputation in the barroom of their filthy taverns, exhibiting much bitterness against each other in supporting the respective candidates of the Union and State-rights parties which divide the State, and this without seeming to have the slightest information respecting the principles of either. Execration and vociferation, and "Well, I'm for Jackson, by _!" were the nearest approach to logic ever made in my presence.[22]

If Featherstonhaugh had happened upon a group of farmers capable of serious discussion of ideas and issues at Traveler's Rest in 1836, he surely would have heard them holding forth on religion, the Cherokee removal, the benefits of slavery, and/or nullification and states' rights.

According to Rouse's *The Great Wagon Road*, some convenient wall in any worthy establishment was utilized as a public-notice hoard. Rouse quotes a German traveler as saying:

> It is not always the custom to hang shields before taverns, but they are easily identified by the great number of miscellaneous papers and advertisements with which the walls and doors of these publick houses are plaistered [sic]; generally, the more bills are to be seen on a house, the better it will be found to be. In this way the traveller is afforded a many sided entertainment, and can inform himself as to where the taxes are heavy, where wives have run away, horses been stolen, or the new Doctor has settled...[23]

Certainly, Traveler's Rest was a stopping-place of such quality as to be graced with numerous decorative handbills. It seems probable that notices would have been concentrated in one of the public rooms—perhaps the post office—and notices probably were also posted in the nearby tavern-store.

The tavern-keepers were as unpredictable and varied as their establishments. Europeans, accustomed to obsequious innkeepers on the continent, often found their American counterparts too proud and independent a breed. Sometimes, however, they must have wished that the proprietors had more pride. In Clarkesville, Featherstonhaugh found himself embroiled in a soap-opera-like episode, when the landlord of the hotel, in over his head with debts and problems with women, sought an end to them all:

> Mr. Levy had about an hour before I reached the house attempted to liquidate all his worldly concerns by first drinking as much brandy as he could carry, and then hanging himself in a room upstairs. He was found, however, in time and cut down; and what was exceedingly odd, instead of sending for a doctor and keeping him out of sight, he was brought down-stairs and exposed drunk and half dead to the visitors and servants.[24]

Some landlords were definitely unenterprising. Yoder reports Featherstonhaugh's encounter with,

> "[a] lazy, frowzy, tobacco-chewing," innkeeper…"lantern jawed," with ill-fitting trowsers [sic] "covered with grease" and a "snuff-coloured visage" [who] had one talent…expectorating tobacco juice with a force and precision hitherto "unknown…to that branch of projectiles." While he conformed in part to the image of the landlord in that he was an active Democrat and a justice of the peace, his political methods were unorthodox, for he sometimes attempted to convince his opponents "by squirting his opinion into their eyes." He practiced his art also on the little ducklings which approached his perch on the veranda, invariably knocking them "over neck and heels"[25]

Other tavern-keepers were the centers of storms of activity. Such a man was Devereaux Jarrett. Paton Yoder, discussing the many roles of tavern-keepers, might almost be listing the enterprises of Jarrett, although the list would be incomplete even then. Yoder asserts that it was common practice for an innkeeper also to operate a store, a farm, a ferry, and a post office. Jarrett not only had all these, but he also operated mills, a bridge, a smithy, and money-lending and gold-mining activities as well.[26] Since taverns were often the centers of neighborhood political activity, the keepers were frequently local political leaders. Who would be in a better position to see everyone? Yoder comments, "Landlords became justices of the peace, county commissioners, sheriffs, judges, surveyors, United States marshal and members of state legislatures."[27] Devereaux Jarrett apparently scorned the practice of politics, however, for his only office was justice of the peace, and that came before the days of Traveler's Rest. But in his capacity as host, a proprietor was inevitably called upon to express his political opinions, as Jarrett was in his brief relationship with Featherstonhaugh, who discovered Jarrett to be an admirer of John C. Calhoun.[28]

The measure of a good landlord was his abilities as a host, with the unsatisfactory extreme perhaps personified by the suicidal landlord at Clarkesville. An able innkeeper, on the other hand, would actively entertain the guests, preside at his table, mingle in the common room, and permeate the establishment with a congenial personality. It can be certain that Devereaux Jarrett *was* a good representative of this other, more pleasant, extreme, as the only recorded impressions of Traveler's Rest are decidedly favorable.

The labor force at a roadside tavern was usually a disappointment to travelers such as Featherstonhaugh and Buckingham. Landlords used servants or slaves, and both served in this function at Traveler's Rest. At a particularly modest inn, however, the landlord's family might be the only help.

A professionally-minded tavern-keeper might advertise in local newspapers, and Yoder finds the typical advertisements to be simple and direct. For this study, an examination of several Georgia and South Carolina newspapers from 1807 to 1855 revealed no advertising for Traveler's Rest, although numerous other hotels around the state used the newspapers. A typical ad for a frontier inn appeared in the Pendleton, S.C. *Weekly Messenger* in 1823:

PENDLETON HOTEL

The subscriber begs leave to inform his friends and the public, that he has opened his new house at the sign of the RISING SUN, at the southwest corner of the public square, in the town of Pendleton, S.C., every attention in his power will be given to make those comfortable, who may honor him with a visit.

*Joseph Grisham*[29]

In northern Georgia in the 1830s, hotels also advertised their accessibility to the gold lands. Signs were often used to direct travelers to taverns on highways in the region. There may have been a sign at Traveler's Rest, but Buckingham was directed to Jarrett's farm as the only house on the road with glass windows.[30]

County tavern laws were designed to restrain the socially-irresponsible landlord, with these laws regulating prices and requiring licenses for lodging and liquor-dispensing. Sometimes such laws *were* intended to protect the public from "the impoverishment of many people and their families, and the ruin of the health and corruption of the manners of youth, who upon such occasions often fall in company with lewd, idle and dissolute persons..."[31] In Georgia, such laws provided for the establishment of tavern rates by the county inferior court, where taverns also secured their licenses. Unfortunately, the license records of Habersham County are apparently lost.

When traveling in those days, people found that "getting there" was a significant challenge in itself. Stagecoach travel, the most "civilized" mode of the time, was often an arduous, even hazardous, means of transportation. Buckingham reported American stages to be heavily built, so as not to fall apart on the atrocious roads. Under normal circumstances, stagecoaches jounced along, slowing the pace for hills, streams, and mud. Alice M. Earle describes a man's typical winter journey in *Stage Coach and Tavern Days*:

> It took seventeen hours to travel the sixty-six miles, and the coach stopped at ten taverns on the way. At each…passengers all got out and took a mint julep; perhaps he did likewise, which might account for the fact that he pronounced the trip a pleasant one, though it rained; "your feet get wet; your clothes become plastered with mud from the wheel; the trunks drink in half a gallon of water apiece: the gentlemen's boots and coats steamed in the confined air; the horses are draggled and chafed by the traces; the driver got his neckcloth saturated"—and yet, he adds, "the journey was performed pleasantly."[32]

Buckingham told a story of passengers outside Montgomery, Alabama, who were stranded when their stage broke down in the night and they had to stumble through the dark to town.[33]

Accidents were not unlikely, considering the habits of some of the drivers. Earle quotes this passage:

> "To the Public: The stage from New York to Albany was overset on the Highlands, on Friday last, with six passengers on board; one of them, a gentleman from Vermont, had his collar-bone broken, and the others were more or less injured, and all placed in the utmost jeopardy of their lives and limbs by the outrageous conduct of the driver. In descending a hill half a mile in length, an opposition stage being ahead, the driver put his horses in full speed to pass the forward stage, and in this situation the stage overset with a heavy crash which nearly destroyed it, and placed the wounded passengers in a dreadful dilemma, especially as the driver could not assist them, as it required all his efforts to restrain the frightened horses from dashing down the hill which must have destroyed them all. It was, therefore, with the greatest difficulty, and by repeated efforts, [that]

the wounded passengers extricated themselves from the wreck of the stage. Such repeated wanton and wilful [sic] acts of drivers to gratify their caprice, ambition, or passions, generally under the stimulus of ardent spirits, calls aloud on the community to expose and punish these shameful aggressions."

One particularly sado-masochistic aspect of stagecoach travel was what Earle called the almost universal practice of pre-dawn departures: "You had to rise in the dark, dress in the dark most feebly illumined, eat a hurriedly prepared breakfast in the dark, and start out in the blackness of night or the depressing chill of early morning." On one journey, "the way was very dark," said a traveler, "so that though I rode with the driver, it was some time before I discovered that we had six horses."[34]

The drivers themselves were a rugged, and all too often drunken, lot. Buckingham despised the Southern drivers, writing:

> The drivers on this road were very inferior to those of the Northern States in deportment and language; they were often insolent, always unaccommodating, and frequently most profligate in their oaths; while having no fee to expect from the passengers, they appeared to me to be studiously disrespectful, as if they sought that mode of displaying their independence. We sometimes hoped to get a better, by their frequent change, as each driver went only the one stage with his team, usually from ten to twelve miles, but there was a great uniformity in their worthlessness.[35]

Traveler's Rest benefited from the fact that the northeast Georgia area became well-noted for its great scenic beauty, and by the third decade of the nineteenth century, Habersham County was a considerable tourist attraction. The sites of Nacoochee Valley, Mount Currahee, Tallulah Falls, and Toccoa Falls were especially popular. Adiel Sherwood, in his 1827 *Gazetteer*, commented," The thick woods [at Tallulah], which stand on the precipice, and send their sombre shadows over the stream gives it a gloomy appearance, and strikes the beholder with awful feelings…[Each year] it attracts thousands."

Of Toccoa Falls, he wrote:

> [Toccoa Creek] is 20 feet wide, coming S. on one of the Southern extremities of the Allegheny Mountains, winding its way among the rocks, & without giving you a moments [sic] warning, all at once tumbles down a perpendicular rock 186½ feet! The quantum of water is so small, that it chiefly becomes spray before it reaches the

unfathomable basin below. Five miles from this it finds its way into the Tugalo near the head of boat navigation on that river…Parties of pleasure from the Madison Springs, frequently visit this cascade, taking the Curahee in their way, thence climbing the hills to catch a view of the awful Terrora [Tallulah]. The fatigue undergone in this jaunt is of great service to some invalids, who stand in greater need of profuse perspiration and vigorous exercise than the prescriptions from the shop. The party may not expect to find sumptuous fare after they leave the Toccoa Falls; but they may rest assured that there is something either in the mountain air which they inhale, or in the peculiar construction of the roads or the direction they run, which will produce a relish for even the coarsest food.[36]

This mid-1820s description of "the Grand Tour" of northeast Georgia conveys the impression that Devereaux Jarrett's lavish hospitality did not yet grace the stand at Walton's Ford, still deeded to James R. Wyly in county records.

If we imagine ourselves as tourists of the United States in the 1830s, already having encountered some of the horrors discussed above, let us now join Featherstonhaugh and the Buckinghams as they arrived at Traveler's Rest. Through their descriptions we can obtain a clear idea of their general pleasure at the people, premises, and fare at Jarrett's place.

Featherstonhaugh came to the Tugaloo by way of Clarkesville, the day after his adventure with the depressed landlord. First paying a visit to Toccoa Falls, which he called "one of the prettiest things I ever saw," the Englishman then reboarded the stage:

We now proceeded for eight miles at a rapid pace down the steep southern slope of the mountains, through beautiful woods and dales, to Jarrett's, on the Tugaloo, a main branch of the Savannah. Here I got an excellent breakfast of coffee, ham, chicken, good bread, butter, honey, and plenty of good new milk for a quarter of a dollar. The landlord cultivated an extensive farm, and there was a fine bottom of good land near the house; he was a quiet, intelligent, well-behaved man, a great admirer of Mr. C_____ [Calhoun], and seemed anxious to do what was obliging and proper, more from good feeling than for the poor return he chose to take for his good fare. [Perhaps Jarrett's attitude helps to account for his failure to advertise. He may have considered himself a prosperous farmer first and innkeeper second. In census schedules, he always referred to himself as a farmer.] What a charming country this would he to travel in, if one was sure of meeting with such clean nice quarters once a-day! The traveller does sometimes, but unfortunately they stand nearly in the same proportion to the dirty ones that the known planets do to the fixed stars. The driver of this stage coach was a very odd fellow, sometimes amusing, though upon the whole a great bore, full of conceit of himself, practising [*sic*] the most uncouth familiarity, and eternally making long speeches. When I refused to listen to him he talked to himself just with the same earnestness that he did to me. On going down the steepest hills, he drove so furiously as to make it almost impossible for me to sit in the coach, talking to himself all the time, and when at the bottom he would turn round and address me after the following manner:—"I say, stranger, do you see that are house? Last time I passed I bought a most splendid water million (they all pronounce melon thus) there for seven-pence, but it warn't ripe, that was the worst on it, and I had to throw it away jist a bit a-head here. Do you like water millions, stranger? There's a power of them in this country, it beats all. You beat all the chaps that goes this road for fixing the stones with your hammer. Do you find any thing you can sell in them? There ain't no gold on this side the mountains, that's what they say, I don't know much about it. I come from the low country in North Carolina. I han't much learning though I was two quarters at school. I was a schoolmaster though one winter in Buncombe up in the mountains, but it aint no go that; I like stage driving better, if they didn't give me sich horses on this line; this unackawntabul [unaccountable] sorrel won't back a bit going down hill, and the grey kicks like h_ll when he is going up, its next to onpossible to git along; but you'll have a splendid driver next stage, a reel splendid fellow that will take you twenty-nine miles to Picken's Court-house; and if I don't give it to this blasted grey when we go back and make him toe the mark, I'm no account." This was the sort of farrago I had to listen to without a possibility of avoiding it.

Upon leaving Jarrett's, Featherstonhaugh found "the country extremely wild, only here and there a settler, and abundance of small streams coming down from the mountains." Featherstonhaugh enjoyed his time at Jarrett's so much that when he came back through the area to see Tallulah Falls, he arranged to stay at Traveler's Rest again.[37]

While traveling through the southern part of Georgia, three years after Featherstonhaugh, the Buckinghams were told of the great beauty of the remote northern part of the state: "The roads are as yet so imperfect, and the houses of accommodations so few, that the district is rarely visited by mere tourists."[38] (Here, Buckingham contradicts the information in Sherwood's *Gazetteer*, which states that "thousands" of sightseers visited the area.) The Buckinghams resolved to pay a visit to north Georgia, and Buckingham wrote at length concerning the journey from Athens through the Tugaloo area, concluding with the following description of the family's stay at Traveler's Rest:

> Leaving Tukoa [Toccoa Falls], we proceeded by an excellent road—which seemed, indeed, by contrast with the one we had just passed over, to be perfection—and after a smooth and luxurious drive of eight miles, we arrived before sunset at a large farm-house and inn united, kept by a Mr. Jerritt [sic]: the directions by which we were enabled to distinguish it from other houses in the neighbourhood was this—that twas "the only house with glass windows in it on the road." While our luggage was unloading from the carriage, one of the white men assisting in this labour could not comprehend what our leather hat-boxes were; and when, in answer to his inquiry, he was told they contained hats, he asked whether we were carrying them about for sale, as he could not comprehend why a person should take with him any more than the hat he wore on his head. When he learnt, however, that my son and myself used cloth caps for travelling, and kept our hats in these two boxes to wear when we halted, he expressed himself surprised at such a piece of folly and extravagance as that of having more than one covering for the heat at a time!...
>
> Here, as in many other places of the interior, a great desire was manifested to examine the various articles of our dress, but especially those of Mrs. Buckingham. The ladies were constantly desirous of getting permission to take patterns of her gowns and caps, which was granted whenever our stay would admit of it, and always highly valued. The lady here, however, was astonished to find that they were not made in New York, but in London, for she had supposed that they were the latest New York modes; and said she had always understood that the French and English ladies invariably sent to New York for the fashions, and had their dresses made up in London and Paris, from the patterns sent there from the United States!
>
> On retiring to rest, we were put into a large room with four beds, but fortunately we had no companions to share the room with us. When passengers on this road are more numerous, it is quite common to have all the beds occupied at the same time in the same apartment. This is a custom of the country, which is very ill associated with the excessive prudishness and affectation of its inhabitants, in avoiding all ambiguous expressions. There were no drawers or trunks for clothes; so that the garments of all the family were ranged around the room, hanging on wooden pegs, to the number of forty

or fifty different articles of dress, including gowns, petticoats, and inner garments, of all sizes and materials, exposed to public view. The beds, as usual, were of three kinds; one of the softest down, another of cotton, and another of straw: the former being usually preferred by the people of this country, but the latter by strangers, as more nearly resembling moss or hair, which is too expensive to be found in any but the very best houses.

At daylight we were awakened by the sound of a common horn, with which it is the custom in the country districts to summon everybody to rise, instead of ringing a large bell, which is the custom in the towns; and as we did not intend to leave till nine o'clock, I took a walk around the farm, and conversed with the farmers before breakfast.

We left our station at nine o'clock on the morning of July 13th, and after less than a quarter of a mile, we crossed the Tugaloo river by a wooden bridge. We thus passed from the State of Georgia into that of South Carolina, the river being the dividing boundary between the two.[39]

Even by the time the Buckinghams visited Traveler's Rest in 1839, stagecoach lines elsewhere had begun to face serious competition from the railroad. One sensible wag pointed out: "You got upset in a coach—and there you were! You get upset in a rail car—and, damme [sic], where are you?" Despite this warning, however, the railroad was successful, and its acceptance signaled the demise of stagecoaches and stagecoach taverns. A "transportation revolution" occurred in the twenty-five years prior to the War Between the States, and historians agree that the "technological changes…rendered the wayside inn obsolete." Trains were much faster than coaches, but the change was more than one of speed: railroad cars, it was felt, were much more suited for all-night travel. "The displacement of inns was abrupt. The opening of a railroad line could take most of the freight wagons, stages, and private vehicles off of a given road almost overnight."[40]

Little is known about the fading of Traveler's Rest as an inn. The surviving ledgers cover the store business, and almost no passages deal with the hotel. Consequently, figures on the numbers of guests are lacking for almost every period. Evidently the stagecoach inn was still thriving sufficiently to be the first stopping-place on the sumptuous honeymoon of Joseph E. Brown and Elizabeth Grisham in July of 1847, however. No description of their wedding-night stay at Traveler's Rest survives, but the blissful couple definitely spent a night there en route in buggy from West Union, South Carolina, to Tallulah Falls and Clarkesville.[41]

Perhaps the hotel had already begun to fade in the 1850s, when it was taken over by Charles Kennedy Jarrett, who may have preferred to be a planter like his older brothers rather than an innkeeper, but there is no way to ascertain this. Then and afterwards, the prostrate Southern economy must have been reflected in the tavern's business, however, and Traveler's Rest may have been defunct as an inn by the time the Atlanta and Richmond Air Line Railroad was completed (giving birth to Toccoa) in 1873. Yoder quotes a poem on the demise of the stagecoach tavern:

> So…a day came at last when the stage had no load
> To the gate, as it rolled up the long, dusty road.
> And lo! at the sunrise a shrill whistle blew
> O'er the hills—and the old yielded place to the new
> -And a merciless age with its discord and din
> Made a wreck, as it passed, of the pioneer inn.[42]

## NOTES

[1] Lane, *Rambler in Georgia* p. x; George W. Featherstonhaugh, *A Canoe Voyage Up the Minnay-Sotor* (St. Paul: Minnesota Historical Society, 1970), introduction.

[2] All quotes from Paton Yoder, *Taverns and Travelers: Inns of the Early Midwest* (Bloomington, Ind.: Indiana University Press, 1969), pp. 2, 32.

[3] Ibid., p. 2.

[4] Ibid., p. 9.

[5] James Silk Buckingham, *The Slave States of America* (London: Fisher, Son & Co., 1842), Vol. II, p. 195.

[6] Taverns" file, Historic Preservation Section, Georgia Department of Natural Resources.

[7] Buckingham, *Slave States,* Vol. I, p. 189.

[8] Yoder, *Taverns and Travelers,* p. 140.

[9] Ibid., p. 148.

[10] Ibid., pp. 153-54.

[11] Ibid., pp. 155-56; Buckingham, *Slave States,* Vol. II, pp. 128-29.

[12] Buckingham, *Slave States*, Vol. II, pp. 46-47, 129.

[13] Yoder, *Taverns and Travelers*, pp. 157, 159.

[14] Ibid., p. 159.

[15] Ibid., p. 161.

[16] Ibid., p. 127.

[17] Ibid., p. 107.

[18] Ibid., p. 104.

[19] Ibid., p. 126.

[20] "Taverns" file, Historic Preservation Section, p. 2.

[21] Featherstonhaugh, *A Canoe Voyage* , Vol. II, pp. 196-97.

[22] Ibid., p. 226.

[23] Rouse, *Great Wagon Road*, p. 98.

[24] Featherstonhaugh, *A Canoe Voyage*, Vol. II, pp. 261-62.

[25] Yoder, *Taverns and Travelers*, p. 32.

[26] Ibid., p. 35.

[27] Ibid., p. 35.

[28] Devereaux Jarrett as justice of the peace, *Stephens County History; Franklin County Deeds*, p. 341; and Featherstonhaugh, *A Canoe Voyage*, Vol. II, p. 266.

[29] Yoder, *Taverns and Travelers*, p. 55; Pendleton, S.C., *Weekly Messenger*, March 19, 1823.

[30] Ibid., p. 54; Buckingham, *Slave States*, p. 162.

[31] Yoder, *Taverns and Travelers*, pp. 165-71.

[32] Thomas R.R. Cobb, *A Digest of the Statute Laws of the State of Georgia* (Athens, Ga.: Christy, Kelsea, and Burke, 1851), pp. 1037-38; Alice Morse Earle, *Stage Coach and Tavern Days* (New York: Dover Publications, Inc., 1900; reprinted 1969), pp. 364-65.

[33] Buckingham, *Slave States*, Vol. I, p. 261.

[34] Earle, *Stage Coach and Tavern Days*, pp. 369-71.

[35] Buckingham, *Slave States*, Vol. I, p. 234.

[36] Adiel Sherwood, *A Gazetteer of the State of Georgia* (Athens, Ga.: University of Georgia Press, 1939 [1827]), pp. 105-06.

[37] Featherstonhaugh, *A Canoe Voyage,* Vol. II, pp. 264-66, 306-07.

[38] Buckingham, *Slave States*, Vol.. I, pp. 219-20.

[39] Ibid., pp. 162-66.

[40] Earle, *Stage Coach and Tavern Days*, p. 287; Yoder, *Taverns and Travelers*, pp. 174-76; Trogdon, *Stephens County History*, p. 77.

[41] Dorothy Cable, "Oconee Wedding in 1847 Recalled," Traveler's Rest Papers, Historic Preservation Section.

[42] Yoder, *Taverns and Travelers,* p. 178.

Image 1: Traveler's Rest: South View, 1977

Image 2: Traveler's Rest: Northeast View, 1977

Image 3: Traveler's Rest, Early Spring, 1977

Image 4: Devereaux Jarrett, proprietor of Traveler's Rest, in a photograph obtained from Jarrett descendants, date unknown.

Image 5: House of Robert Jarrett, 1977

Image 6: House of Thomas Patton Jarrett, 1977 (House has since been destroyed by fire.)

Image 7: Toccoa Falls, 1977

Image 8: House of Joseph Prather and Sally Jarrett, 1977

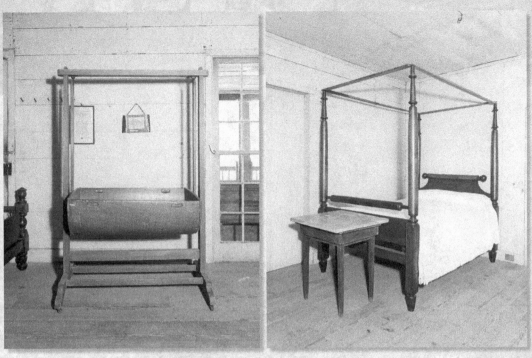

Image 9: Cradle

Image 10: Bed brought to Traveler's Rest by Lizzie Lucas Jarrett around 1852.

Image 11: "Indian Rock"

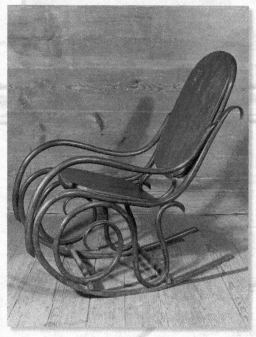

Image 12: Bent-wood Rocking Chair

Image 13: Corner Cupboard

Image 14: Detail of Main Stairway

Image 15: Traveler's Rest. Photo taken near the turn of the twentieth century.

Image 16: The Jarretts' Tugaloo River "bottom lands," facing northward toward the Appalachian Mountains. Photo taken about 1900.

Image 17: Sally Grace, date unknown.

Image 18: Mary Lizzie, 1890s

Image 19-Lizzie Lucas Jarrett and family, about 1898.

Left to right: Charles Patton Jarrett, Mary Lizzie Jarrett, Lizzie Lucas Jarrett, Sally Grace Jarrett, George Devereaux Jarrett.

Image 20: Charles P. Jarrett and friends "camping in the Mountains of NE Georgia, 1894." Charles Jarrett is in the center in the vest.

Image 21. Charles P. Jarrett, camping in northeast Georgia, 1894. Charles, wearing a vest, is in the center.

Image 22: Charles Patton Jarrett with unknown women and girls, about 1898.

Image 23: Charles Patton Jarrett and an unknown woman, perhaps at Tallulah Falls, about 1898. The back of the photograph reads, "He and his girl all alone. Gloom and splendor crowned their comely faces."

Image 24: Left to right: Unidentified woman with dogs, Sally Grace Jarrett, and Lizzie Lucas Jarrett at Traveler's Rest in the early 1900s.

Image 25: Charles Patton Jarrett in New Mexico for his "consumption" in 1898.

Image 26: Victorine Faillett Jarrett, wife of Lt. George Devereaux Jarrett, location unknown. Photo taken in early 1900s.

Image 27: Neeley Jarrett, former slave. Date unknown. "Taken in front of her little cabin."

Image 28: Lt. George Devereaux Jarrett and Sally Grace Jarrett at smokehouse in early 1900s.

Image 29: Lizzie Lucas Jarrett and son, Lt. George Devereaux Jarrett, on front porch at Traveler's Rest in early 1900s.

Image 30: Lizzie Lucas Jarrett on front porch at Traveler's Rest in early 1900s.

Image 32: Lt. George Devereaux Jarrett at home in the Philippines in early 1900s.

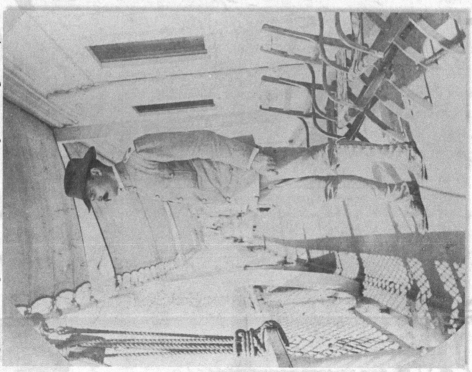

Image 31: Lt. George Devereaux Jarrett on transport *Rawlings* in early 1900s.

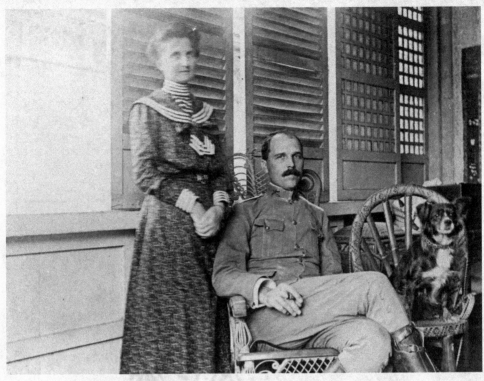

Image 33: Lt. George and Victorine in the Philippines, about 1903.

Image 34: Lt. George and Victorine in Cuba, about 1901

Image 35: Steamboat on the Tugaloo River, date unknown.

Image 36: Unknown woman at small house near Traveler's Rest in early 1900s.

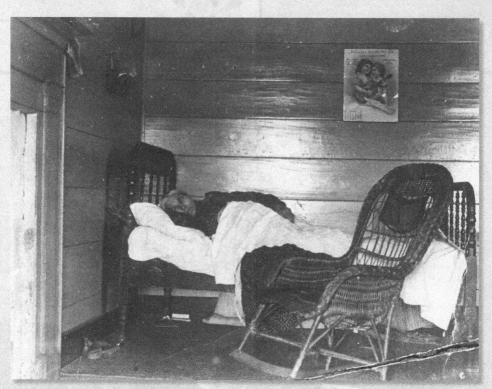

Image 37: Lizzie Lucas Jarrett in a small room at south end of Traveler's Rest in early 1900s.

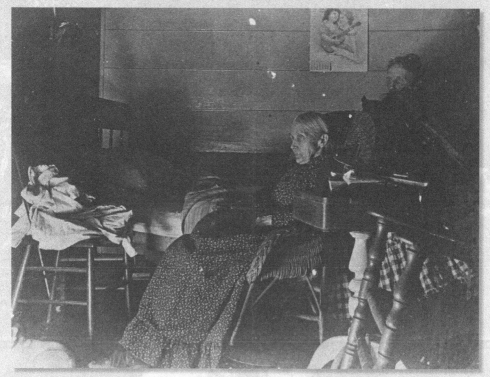

Image 38: Lizzie Lucas and Sally Grace Jarrett in a small room in early 1900s.

Image 39: Family picture before the front porch at Traveler's Rest in early 1900s.

Left to right: Mary Lucas Jarrett White, V. A. White, unknown woman, children, Sally Grace with child, Victorine P. Jarrett, Lizzie Lucas Jarrett, and other unknown people.

Image 40: Front view of unrestored Travelers Rest. Photo taken in 1953.

Image 41: Rear view of unrestored Traveler's Rest in 1953.

Image 42: Basement Kitchen

Image 43: Upstairs "Common" Bedroom

# Chapter 7

## Devereaux Jarrett's Little Empire

In addition to his stagecoach inn, Devereaux Jarrett operated several other enterprises. First and foremost, he was master of a large, slave-worked farm; he also maintained a toll bridge, country store, post office, cash-lending business, cotton gin, blacksmithy, tanyard, gristmill and sawmill, and at least one gold mine (see Map 12).

Both Buckingham and Featherstonhaugh refer to Jarrett as a farmer. While Featherstonhaugh mentions "an extensive farm…a fine bottom of good land near the house," Buckingham gives the impression of a conglomeration of farms growing wheat, oats, and maize, but little cotton.[1]

Ledgers support the hypothesis that much of Jarrett's vast acreage was cultivated by tenant farmers. Other records broaden our impression of Jarrett's prosperous farm. When Buckingham took a morning stroll at Jarrett's place, he reported the following information from his conversations with the farmers in 1839:

> The climate of this elevated region not being sufficiently warm for the cultivation of cotton, the soil is devoted to the growth of wheat, oats, and maize, or Indian corn. The former is said to have yielded a larger harvest in the present year, than in any preceding one within the memory of man; arising from the fact, that the high prices of wheat in the last year, induced the farmers to turn every acre of land to the growth of this. The fluctuation in price, in consequence of this increased quantity, was supposed to be as much as from two dollars, or eight shillings a bushel, the price it bore last year–down to fifty cents, or two shillings a bushel, which it was expected to be this year, when the harvest, now nearly completed, should be fully gathered in. One of the farmers, who was upwards of sixty-five years of age, told me that he had made up his mind to emigrate next year, to the valley of the Mississippi: and when I asked him what could induce

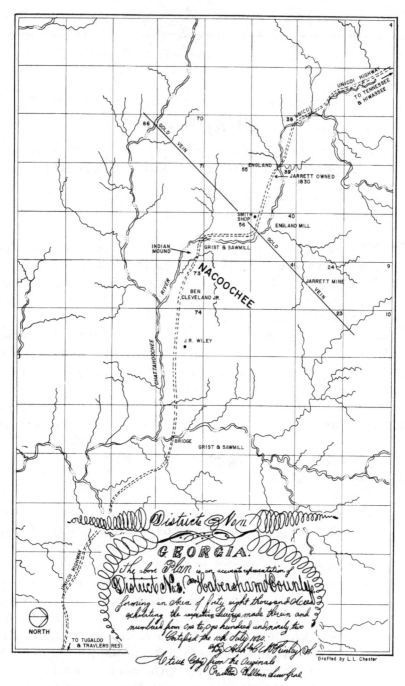

Habersham County Gold Mines, Nacoochee, and Unicoi Turnpike, also showing land lots in part of District 3, Habersham County.

## Map 12: Habersham County Gold Mines

him, now so far advanced in life, and with a large family, to move so far from his home, he replied, that there was too much aristocracy here for him! I asked him who or what constituted the aristocracy of which he spoke. He said they were the rich men of these parts, who bought up all the land at extravagant prices, and left none for the poorer citizens to purchase [as did Devereaux Jarrett?], the prices which he deemed so extravagant being from ten dollars an acre for the freehold property. I asked him whether he could not rent land from these proprietors, and live by farming in this way. He said, yes; but added, that the rent demanded was extravagant also, amounting to ten barrels of corn for a small farm of twenty acres; which, in sterling money would be about one dollar per acre for annual rent, without tithes or other imposts, and no expense of manure or draining. I asked him what he would think of paying ten dollars an acre rent, and a tenth of all the produce of the farm besides, which was the rate paid by many English farmers. He replied that "no land in the world could stand such a rent;" and he evidently doubted the fact of its ever being paid. Among the peculiar expressions used here, travelling rapidly is called "moving peert;" and to provide a family with food, or to feed them is expressed thus–"He always grows enough to bread his own people for a year at least, and sells the balance." The white men looked healthy, but were all slender, and the growing youths of both sexes were peculiarly tall and thin, with long features, light hair, and wholly without the fine ruddy complexions of the English peasantry.[2]

Throughout his life, Devereaux Jarrett accumulated acreage, and the U.S. Census 1850 Agricultural Schedule lists him with 14,400 acres (1,000 "improved"), not all of which was at Traveler's Rest. Two of his sons, Robert and Thomas Patton, are shown in the census as owning 900 acres each. Jarrett land included acreage on Toccoa, Walton's, and Ward's creeks, as well as acreage at Dry Pond, the present site of Toccoa. For a brief period in the 1830s, Devereaux also owned Toccoa Falls.[3]

The agricultural schedules also provide other information concerning the farms. Devereaux owned livestock–horses, mules, "milch" cows, oxen, cattle, sheep, and hogs–valued at $1,865. Robert's stock was worth $1,120, and Thomas Patton's was worth $750. The farms produced butter, hay, peas and beans, cotton, plentiful corn, oats, wheat, potatoes, and some rye and honey. All three farms produced between forty and eighty pounds of wool each, and Devereaux's farm also listed $500 in home manufactures.[4]

Most of the work at the farms was done undoubtedly by the Jarretts' many slaves. Even before he owned land, young Devereaux possessed from ten to seventeen slaves, and in 1820, he owned twenty-one slaves. (By comparison James R. Wyly, previous owner of Traveler's Rest, owned four slaves.) By 1830, Jarrett had forty-five slaves, and ten years later, he owned seventy-four in Habersham County, including four persons "engaged in mining."[5]

In the early nineteenth century, the Tugaloo area continued to be one with relatively few slaves. Devereaux Jarrett was by far the greatest slaveowner of Habersham County, where there were only 954 slaves in 1840 and 1,218 in 1850. The 1850 Slave Census reveals that Robert Jarrett possessed twenty-four slaves; Thomas Patton Jarrett had twenty-seven; and Devereaux Jarrett's sixty-eight remained an extremely high total for the region. One might well wonder what use he had for so many slaves, for his was not a cotton plantation. Some certainly worked at the house, the smithy, the tanyard, and the mills. Most must have been field hands, but several women were no doubt utilized in weaving. Jarrett found it quite profitable to use his good farm land for maximum food production. A great many of the cotton plantations in southern Georgia were not self-sufficient, and these provided a ready market for as much bacon, beef, ham, wheat, corn, oats, and other goods as the farm at Traveler's Rest could produce.[6]

Almost nothing is known concerning the lives of these slaves. It is unfortunate that people so important for life at the Tugaloo Crossroads enter the historical record almost entirely as human property. Family legends give the impression that they were well-treated, and certainly this is in accord with what is known of Jarrett's character. It is probable that his slaves received the simple fare mentioned in Basil Hall's account of life on a Georgia cotton plantation in 1828:

> The stated allowance of food to every slave, over fourteen years of age, is nine quarts of Indian corn per week, and for children from five to eight quarts. This is said to be more than they can eat, and the surplus is either sold, or is given to the hogs and poultry which they are always allowed to rear on their own account. A quarter of salt monthly is also allowed, and salt fish, as well as salt beef occasionally, but only as a flavour, and can never be claimed as a right. A heaped-up bushel of sweet potatoes is considered equal to the above allowance, and so are two pecks of rough, that is unhusked, rice or paddy. But this is not thought so substantial a food as the Indian corn...
>
> The slaves are generally dressed in what is called White Welsh plains, for winter clothing. They prefer white cloth, and afterwards dye it of a purple colour to suit their own fancy. Each man gets seven yards of this, and the women six yards,–and the children in proportion. Each grown-up negro gets a new blanket every second year, and every two children in like manner one blanket. The men receive also a cap, and the women a handkerchief, together with a strong

pair of shoes, every winter. A suit of homespun cotton, of the stuff called Osnaburgs, is allowed to each person for summer dress.

A more vivid picture of the slave's costume can be found in an 1810 *Miller's Weekly Messenger*, which describes Anthony, a "remarkably *heavy made*" runaway, as wearing "a pair of coperas coloured, striped pantaloons, a mixed blue, red, and white homespun jacket, a blue and white hunting shirt, a large hat with a high crown…will attempt to pass for a freeman."[7]

It is not known whether Jarrett worked his hands on the "task" system, in which each slave was allotted a daily assignment; or the "gang" system, in which a team of slaves worked all day with no necessarily predetermined stopping place; or some variation of these. The slaves usually preferred the "task" system, because after the completion of the day's chores, their time was "their own," to relax or work in their private gardens. The "gang" method was used on most tobacco, cotton, and sugar plantations. Since Jarrett did not concentrate on these crops, it appears likely that his slaves were worked on the "task" system. Legend has it that he addressed "his people" from the second-story porch each morning, assigning the day's duties.[8] According to Flanders' *Plantation Slavery in Georgia*, "It was the universal custom in Georgia to allow the slaves the privilege of raising small crops of their own," which could be sold for cash or traded for store goods. It was also possible for the slaves to raise poultry for food and sale. The Jarretts quite likely allowed their slaves some private enterprise, for 1850s ledgers show C. K. Jarrett's slaves buying goods at the store.[9]

The slaves lived in cabins; apparently some of them were just across the river from Jarrett's bridge. Wise masters made these slave quarters as comfortable as simple cabins could be, and in north Georgia, the slaves' good health required that their cabins have some kind of floor. Experts advised the slaveowners: "The popular idea that the cheapest style of Negro houses is the cheapest in reality is fallacious…Small, smokey cabins, built flat upon the ground, with no windows or aperture for ventilation, is the style that is too common."[10] Although it is not known exactly what the slave cabins at Traveler's Rest were like, it is true that their hypothetical location was a good one, on high ground. No doubt, furniture in the slave cabins was "scant and simple," and most likely homemade.

For amusement, slaves were allowed to participate in Jarrett family holidays, feasting, dancing, and so forth. Some masters encouraged the slaves to take a festive approach to projects such as log-rolling and corn-shucking, and marriages were also an "occasion of great frolic." Religion was another distraction available to the slaves, and the Jarrett African Americans participated in services at the Providence Methodist Church.[11]

As a slaveowner of such caliber, Jarrett must have approved of the traditional system. Being a Methodist, he probably supported the Southern Methodists' withdrawal from the national Methodist organization in 1844, over the slavery issue. If asked, Jarrett might well have agreed with his political idol and South Carolinian neighbor, John C. Calhoun, who wrote in 1837, "I hold slavery to be a good…moreover, there never has existed a wealthy and civilized society in which one portion of the community did not in point of fact live on the labor of the other."[12]

Buckingham noted that the average farmer of the area, once having acquired a few slaves, turned the work over to them and became exceedingly lazy. This may have been true of the neighborhood in general, but it is probably not true of the antebellum Jarretts.[13]

Buckingham also reported the presence of a silk-producing operation at Traveler's Rest. The English traveler was amused by a Jarrett boarder who produced expensive silk with worms and Chinese Mulberry trees at Jarrett's farm. This unnamed woman gave the Buckinghams

> a narrative of her success in raising the silkworm on the leaves of the morus multicaulis, of which she had several plants in her garden; and having purchased a quart of the eggs of the silkworm, she hoped to produce, from these, a million of workers, by whose labour she would be soon made rich. She showed us some of the cocoons, the silk thread she had spun from her wheel, and though coarse, was strong and even in texture. She added, that she could find a ready sale for as much as she could weave of this, at five dollars, or twenty shillings a yard, while English and French silks could be had for half the price. When asked the grounds of this extravagant expectation, she said that the people of South Carolina were all for living on their own resources, and having no dependence on other countries; they, therefore, readily paid double prices for silks grown and manufactured at home, because it shut out the foreign trader, and kept all the money in the country! I could not, of course, dispute the fact about the relative rates, though I ventured to doubt the accuracy of her supposition as to the willingness of the Carolinians to pay such high prices from pure patriotism.[14]

Buckingham had already been surprised to discover a silk mania of considerable proportions sweeping Georgia, and he wrote that "the recent introduction of *morus multicaulis*, with its wonderful powers of re-production and multiplication, has, however, given an entirely new stimulus to this subject." In Macon, he found being circulated two publications concerned with the subject of silk, and Chinese mulberry cuttings were apparently much in demand. The Macon newspapers were full of passages on silk, denying that zeal for silk was a "mania." So prolific was *morus*, the paper confidently predicted, that within ten years the Southern states would rival China for the silk market of the world. "Great efforts" were being made to "determine...how far the cultivation may be carried on to the general advantage." Premiums were being offered by the American Silk Society for the best and greatest quality and quantity of silk. (See note 15.)

The furor that Buckingham observed in Georgia, however, was merely a manifestation of a "strange frenzy" for silk that swept the entire nation in the 1830s. William Leggett and L.P. Brockett, historians of silk in America, recounted the story of a wave of "unbridled speculation" indulged in by Americans after the introduction of *morus multicaulis*, a Chinese mulberry tree which "grew so rapidly" that it could produce silkworm feeding leaves in just three months. In the 1830s, the United States was frequently caught up in speculative paroxysms, as ambitious citizens grasped for the fortunes that a rapidly expanding national economy rendered available. The onset of the Industrial Revolution made just about any economic development seem possible, including a massive burgeoning of the silk industry. In 1826, *morus multicaulis* was imported to America from France, coming into the possession of a Gideon B. Smith of Baltimore. The Chinese mulberry grew so much faster than *morus alba*, the white mulberry, that hopes were soon aroused for widespread silk production in the United States.

Pamphlets were circulated, claiming that *morus multicaulus* could nourish two crops of silkworms per year, and state governments were soon persuaded to offer bounties for silk production. In 1832, a New York capitalist named Samuel Whitmarsh started a silk factory at Florence, Massachusetts, and began cultivation of considerable numbers of Chinese mulberries. Daniel Webster and Henry Clay, leading national politicians, were presented with fine vests, and expressed great hopes for American silk. Unfortunately, the supply of raw silk produced by Marsh's worms was "always deficient for the factory," and by 1838 the project had collapsed, leaving the incipient industrialist with an overplentiful supply of mulberry trees. Despite this setback, however, Whitmarsh had outrun "all his compeers in enthusiasm concerning silk culture and manufacture," and apparently he believed there was no turning back. When he encountered difficulty selling his trees, he publicly offered to buy back some he had already sold, at higher prices, hinting that he expected prices to escalate dramatically and soon. Somehow this stratagem touched off the nationwide wave of speculation encountered by Buckingham in Georgia in the summer of 1839.

Mulberry sprouts, which had sold for $3 to $5 per hundred in 1834 and 1835, rose in price to $25, $50, $100, and even $500 per hundred in 1839. Whitmarsh promoted American silk as the solution to the national depression of 1837 (caused by just this sort of rampant speculation). Imaginative people began to envision American farmers and their families cultivating silk until it became as cheap and common as cotton. "Every state caught the infection," overlooking the North American continent's bad production record for silk. A great many people became enthusiastically involved, as did the woman Buckingham met at Traveler's Rest, without any expertise for producing silk.

In Georgia, the mania caused people to entertain hopes that silk production would "bring into utility [Georgia's] exhausted soils and greatly increase the wealth and capital of our state." But the speculative bubble burst in the fall of 1839. Inexpert cultivators could not produce high quantities of silk in North America, and thousands who tried were "ruined." This fiasco was not quite the "final blow" to the silk industry in Georgia, but silk production was never again attempted on such a large scale.[15]

The Jarrett ledger books made it clear that Devereaux Jarrett had operated a blacksmithy somewhere near his home for decades. Entries for horses shod and farm equipment repaired appear in most of the ledgers after 1806. At Jarrett's smithy, prices did not vary greatly over the years. In the 1830s, local farmers could get horses shod for 50¢ to $1.25. A belt buckle could be purchased for 12½¢. Twenty years later, the same services could be obtained at the same rates.[16]

The 1830s ledgers appear on scattered sheets in various places, but most are in the back of the book which begins in 1818. A perusal of these ledgers reveals that the Jarrett store had not changed greatly in prices or stock in thirty years. The major changes for earlier stores were a vast increase in tobacco sales, a smaller increase in the sale of food and grain, and a great decline in the sale of yardgoods. As yet, little soap was being sold, for most of Jarrett's neighbors continued to make their own.[17]

Entries concerning other of Jarrett's enterprises also appear in the ledgers, such as the blacksmithy accounts, and the entries contain occasional, mysterious clues about the Jarrett business operations, as well. Some of the customers paid by working for Jarrett; a handful of men appear to have worked for periods of several months, but most performed more limited tasks. Among the jobs mentioned were: on the bridge (1834 and 1836), on the cupboard, at the sawmill, mending the steeple, making forty-two pairs of shoes, selling plank, "mending house & plating [sic] chimney and firepases [sic]," working on the barn, working on the mountain, or payment by schooling.[18]

Dates on some loose ledger pages range from 1842 to 1856, but these are disorganized. Several kinds of accounts appear, some pages containing regular country store items interspersed with occasional sales of considerable yards of osnaburgs (cloth used in the making of garments for slaves) to the "Pendleton Factory." For a large number of pages, the names of Devereaux Jarrett, William Hackett, William Gray, and Martial "Woolbanks" appear, as if they were taking turns minding the store,[19]

More mysteries and clues included in the ledgers are lists of hogs' weights, references to Joseph Prather's sawmill (1855), and a couple of pages of the "House Bill," which include some rare clues about guests and prices at the time. These are apparently from Charles Kennedy Jarrett's inn of the mid-1850s, so it is known that the inn lasted at least until that time. Other entries in the ledgers include some "Hackett & Jarrett" pages from the early 1840s which list "Franklin notes, Habersham notes, and South Carolina notes" of those who owed money to the firm.[20]

All the ledgers are most useful for showing the continuity of Jarrett's store and the types of items sold there. Occasional references indicate that Jarrett operated a cotton gin, sawmill, and a gristmill, and deeds reveal that these were located on Ward's Creek. Unfortunately, however, no clues have been discovered which would indicate the origins, or the waxings and wanings of these ventures. In the 1830s, Jarrett was also quite likely still connected with a tanyard, his partner in this enterprise being William Gray, who appears in the 1840 census as a tanner. The accounts for the tanyard of the 1840s and 1830s are lost, but the yard is occasionally mentioned in other ledgers.[21]

Another enterprise of which we have few clues is Devereaux Jarrett's cash-lending transactions. Mary Elizabeth Jarrett White referred to her grandfather as "the greatest financier in Georgia history," but she was undoubtedly indulging in her habit of elaboration. The ledger entries do show scores of small cash loans, occasional lists of accountsoutstanding, but most of these were for a few cents or dollars. Nonetheless, Jarrett must have derived some profit from them, as he continued loaning money for decades.[22]

Before the construction of Jarrett's covered bridge, travelers at Walton's Ford crossed the Tugaloo by means of a ferry. Although the Georgia legislature was supposed to authorize all ferries and bridges, the act licensing the ferry at the Tugaloo Crossroads has not been discovered. The earliest evidence of its existence is a loose page from an 1831 ledger headed "Wily's Ferry." The operation of a ferry could date as far back as the opening of the Unicoi turnpike, ca. 1816, or even earlier. In an 1818 issue of the *Pendleton Messenger*, William Cleveland's ferry was advertised as having a new flat, "14 feet long and between 9 and 10 feet wide." The ferry at Walton's Ford was probably similar.

In 1834, the Georgia legislature authorized Devereaux Jarrett to build a bridge "at or near the place now known as Willies Ferry." The legal rates were:

  50 ct. loaded wagon & driver
  37½ ct empty wagon
  25 ct pleasure carriage
  12½ ct two wheel pleasure carriage
  25 ct cart, team & driver
  6¼ man & horse

2 ct herd of meat cattle

1 ct herd of hogs, sheep or goats

Jarrett's license was "indefinitely" extended in 1843.[23]

As an old man, Jarrett became postmaster for the Tugaloo area. The first post office at Walton's Ford was created in 1817 on the South Carolina side of the river. On February 2 of that year, Robert Stribling was appointed postmaster, and in November of 1828, James R. Wyly was named postmaster at Walton's Ford, Georgia, but his post was discontinued in 1830. In 1833, South Carolina once again was the site of the Walton's Ford office, with Allen Elston as postmaster, and Robert Ballew succeeded him in 1835. Five years later, the post office name was changed to Davis Ferry, South Carolina, with Young Davis serving as postmaster. In 1842, it became Walton's Ford, South Carolina, once more, and Harvey Davis was the new postmaster. Then, at the age of fifty-nine, Devereaux Jarrett got his hands on the job, not to relinquish it during his lifetime. He was named postmaster of Walton's Ford, Georgia, in October of 1844, and the office was not moved again for over twenty years.[24]

James S. Buckingham reported that most Southern post offices were "very humble buildings," and he believed that far more than the country needed had been established due to the fact that the position of postmaster was utilized for political patronage.

> Since the days of General Jackson, it is well known that the only qualification required for such appointment, has been the advocacy of the politics of the ruling party; there is thus an army of political postmasters arrayed on the side of the Administration. The post-offices in the country and districts here are like the old barbers' shops in English villages a century ago–places for the idle and the gossiping to assemble and discuss the news. To add to the attractions of the post-offices here, many of them are also "confectionaries," at which liquors of all kinds are freely sold; and the class of persons usually assembled to hear the news on the arrival of the mail, were among the most dirty, dissipated, and reckless in their appearance.[25]

There can be little doubt that Jarrett's appointment as postmaster was a political "plum" of some sort, but his retention of it was probably not dependent on any party-groveling. The early fluctuations of the postmastership do not appear to correspond to party-Presidential fortunes. After Jarrett obtained the position, he held it during the sway of both major parties.

Another major portion of Devereaux Jarrett's attention was devoted to the pursuit of gold. Gold was discovered in northeastern Georgia in the summer of 1829 in two locations–on Duke's Creek in the Nacoochee Valley and near Dahlonega. The Nacoochee region had been ceded to Georgia by the Cherokees in 1819, divided in a lottery in 1820; but the Dahlonega region was still in the hands of the American Indians, and the State rapidly became inflamed with enthusiasm to acquire the long-coveted Cherokee lands. As E. Merton Coulter states it, "a stampede set in which filled the diggings [mostly in Indian territory] with a wild and lawless population." Governor George Gilmer combined the jobs of controlling the gold-seekers and removing the Cherokees. In December of 1829, the Georgia legislature confiscated a large section of Cherokee land promised to the state by the United States government in 1802, nullified all Cherokee laws within the seized territory, prohibited further actions of the Cherokee government within Georgia's boundaries, and provided for the arrest of any Cherokee who agitated against removal. The Georgia laws also voided all contracts between American Indians and whites, made it illegal for an Indian to testify against a white, and forbade the Cherokees to dig for gold or anything else on their land. The stage was thus set for the removal of the Cherokees, although completion of the usurpation took some eight years.[26]

Having dealt with the "savages," Gilmer and Georgia now turned their attention to the "stampede" of gold-seekers, who proved difficult to control. By the summer of 1830, between 4,000 and 5,000 of these people were "digging and searching for gold" in the Cherokee territory. Fighting erupted among the treasure-hunters and the outraged American Indians. Federal troops were sent in, but President Andrew Jackson removed them at Georgia's request. Gilmer ordered the intruders out of the territory, but the Georgia Guard was required to "muscle" them out. Yelverton King, an agent of Gilmer's, reported the following:

> As I approached the territory I met a vast number of persons citizens from different parts of this State returning to their respective homes. So great was the number of persons that I met, that I was led to believe I should not find any persons at the mines, but in this I was sadly disappointed–There were at Reubin Daniels (the place where I put up) and in its vicinity together, at least one thousand persons principally Tennesseeians [sic] whose conduct (notwithstanding it was the Sabbath day) beggars all description–There was much excitement prevailing, the troops had been engaged in burning their houses and tents and destroying their tools and implements for digging gold.

The anarchistic gold-diggers were driven out, and the Cherokees "rescued" by the slovenly, brutal Georgia Guard.[27]

While the horde of gold-rushers was scrapping over the Cherokee lands near Dahlonega, a more orderly scramble to acquire gold lands was taking place at Nacoochee. There, Devereaux Jarrett must have been one of the first into the field, choosing a likely place to mine, but he was not the typical irresponsible gold seeker. In August of 1830, Jarrett paid Joseph England $450 for the mining rights to Lot 38, Third District, Habersham County. Later that year, he bought this lot from "David England of the Cherokee nation" for $1,000, the lot being identified as a "gold mine lot." Years earlier, Jarrett had acquired Lot 39, formerly the property of Thomas Moore, from the Habersham County Superior Court (in 1825 for $301). These lots were both on the Unicoi Turnpike but for some unknown reason, Jarrett apparently chose not to hold the valuable lots for long. In 1832, he negotiated to sell Lot 39, which comprised 250 acres, to Joseph England for $800. Although fifteen copies of early deeds show Jarrett's interest in Lot 38, these deeds were never recorded (see Map 13).[28]

Georgia prepared to survey the Cherokee land in 1831, whereupon it was divided into 40- and 160-acre lots, to be distributed in a lottery the following year. All "free, white" adult males in Georgia could register for the lottery if they had not already received land in a previous lottery. Jarrett was quite active in buying the rights to peoples' draws in the lottery. In 1834, Georgia allowed whites to prepare to move onto their new lands, and the Cherokees were allowed two more years to leave.[29]

The American Indians were fighting in the courts and winning some recognition of their rights. Unfortunately, they had a determined enemy in President Jackson, who acted along with Georgia and a Cherokee minority faction to remove the American Indians and ignore the Supreme Court. Finally, the American Indians were rounded up in 1838 and herded down the "Trail of Tears,"[30] to their unwanted, federally-Promised Land in what was to be Oklahoma.

Jarrett chose his gold mine in 1837; for a bargain ($362), he bought part of Lots 23 and 24 in the Third District, Habersham County, from James R. Wyly, administrator for the Burnetts' estate. The other owners were members of his wife's family, William and Fidelio Patton. These were then known as the "Burnett Mines," but they came to be called the "Jarrett Mines,"[31] and it was from these that Jarrett's gold came (see Map 13).

Devereaux's interest in gold was the springboard for his relationship with John C. Calhoun. His admiration for the South Carolina politician derived from their business and personal relationship. Traveler's Rest was on Calhoun's route from his South Carolina home to his mine near Dahlonega. From the Clemson and Calhoun papers, it is known that Thomas Clemson, Calhoun's son-in-law and mine manager, bought bacon for the mine workers from Jarrett. A January 6, 1843, letter from Clemson to Calhoun states:

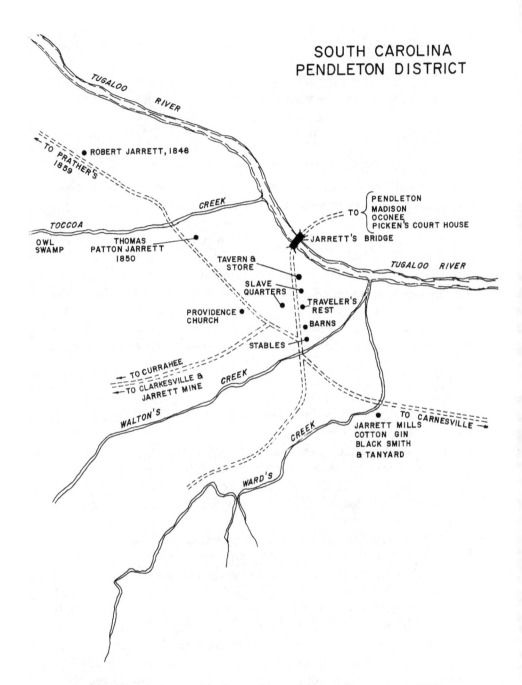

TRAVELER'S REST AND JARRETT ENTERPRISES 1850

**Map 13:** Traveler's Rest and Jarrett Enterprises, 1850

When I came by Mr. Jarratt's [sic] he made application to me for a lease to work a Surface which he thinks will pay & [some]where without direction. I told him that I would grant no lease on the surface or up land without first consulting you which I promised him I would do & give him your answer as soon as I heard from you on the subject.

Calhoun refused to grant any leases, and in February, he replied to Clemson's query: "As to what you say in reference to Mr. Jarratt's [sic] desire to lease to surface mine on the Obar [Calhoun's mine], to which you refer, you may say to him that I have concluded to decline giving any lease till I return." This matter was not mentioned again.

Clemson and Calhoun also had a business relationship with Traveler's Rest former owner, James R. Wyly. Calhoun purchased the "Habersham Iron Works" from him on July 9, 1842, in a deed mentioning a forge, furnace, and mills. One of Wyly's sons was hired to manage the works, apparently with unfortunate results. In January of 1843, Clemson wrote to his father-in-law: "We placed Gen. Wyly at the Furnace (where he is to work up all the pig or cast metal into bar iron) for the coming year...One of Wyly's own sons who we placed there to protect our property turned to swindling & cheating us & with us his own father."[32]

Pages from ledger books, with faint writing, exist on microfilm at the Historic Preservation office concerning a Jarrett gold mine in 1848-49. One page indicates, "commenced work for Jarrett and Smith on the 11th Sept., 1848." The ledger was kept by Sorrow Shaw, who managed the mine for Jarrett and Thomas Smith, Jarrett's financial partner and a fellow dweller by the Tugaloo. The entries state: "Sept. 12 7 hands made 7.06; Sept 13 7 hands made 3.11; Sept 14 7 hands made 6.07," and so forth. Some days, part of the crew would be absent, and usually, no work was done in the rain. On September 19th, the crew "raised houses."

Many entries in these ledgers are quite mysterious. For instance, on "boys day," a frequent occurrence, the crew would work. The quantities represented by the daily figures are also difficult to decipher, but they probably refer to the weight, in ounces, of gold mined. In September, the mine produced 62.15 ounces; in October, 74.14; in November, 45.07; December, 59.00. Both Charles Kennedy Jarrett and Devereaux Jarrett came to collect the "clean goald [sic]." The record recommenced in February, and then carried through the summer of the following year. Presumably, the mine was profitable into the 1850s, but the next records of it come after Devereaux Jarrett's death.[33]

Jarrett was sixty-five years of age in 1850. During the following year, he decided to divide most of his property among his children, and this was accomplished on November 23rd. To the oldest son, Thomas Patton Jarrett, he deeded about 800 acres in the area of Old Owl Swamp, this land being located on Toccoa Creek and embracing the site of Old Tugaloo Town, the latter now under Lake Hartwell. This was Devereaux Jarrett's first homestead in then-Franklin County, now known as the Turnbull Place. Already about thirty-eight years old, Thomas P. was probably established there well before 1851, as he claimed his own farm of 900 acres in the 1850 Census. According to the November 23rd deed, the farm was on the river and on the "ridge road." The deed also indicated twenty-four slaves, who are named in it.[34]

To Robert Jarrett, who was then thirty-five years of age, Devereaux gave 900 acres adjacent to Thomas' land, "lying on Tugalo River...." According to the deed, the land had been originally granted to N.B. Hunter, Ben Cleveland, and Blake Denman. To Robert went twenty-six slaves.[35]

Charles Kennedy Jarrett, at age thirty-one, received the largest plot of land, his being over 4,000 acres at Traveler's Rest. The line proceeded "with the meanders of the river to the Island, including the Bridge across Tugalo River." Charles Kennedy received seventeen slaves.[36]

Sarah Ann Jarrett, twenty-seven years old, received land originally granted to Young, next to the Currahee place, and also "the place on which C. Mills now lives," as well as three other lots of land adjoining this. In addition, she was deeded one tract of 150 acres adjoining the Blair place on Toccoa Creek and fourteen slaves.[37] On January 28, 1852, five more slaves were given to Charles Kennedy Jarrett, and in an undated gift, Devereaux Jarrett bestowed three slaves and his new carriage–with two horses, John and James–on his second wife, Elizabeth.[38]

Devereaux Jarrett died on February 9, 1852. His will disposed of two slaves, $500, six horses, eight cows and calves, and two and one-half tons of pork. He willed that all other property be sold, put against his debts, and the remainder divided among his four children.[39]

## NOTES

[1] Featherstonhaugh, *A Canoe Voyage*, Vol. II, p. 26; Buckingham, *Slave States*, Vol. II, p. 166.

[2] Buckingham, *Slave States*, Vol. II, p. 166.

[3] See Franklin and Habersham counties, Superior Court Deeds, 1814-1851; on the site of Toccoa, see Traveler's Rest papers on microfilm, Historic *Preservation* Section, and Deed Book s, p. 42; on Jarrett's ownership of Toccoa Falls, see Habersham County *Deed Books F*, p. 112, and Q, p. 146.

[4] U.S. Census 1850 Agricultural Schedules, Habersham County, p. 643.

[5] U.S. Census 1820 Population Schedules, Habersham County, p. 114; 1830, pp. 19, 35; 1840, pp. 137, 155.

[6] Ralph Flanders, *Plantation Slavery in Georgia* (Chapel Hill: University of North Carolina Press, 1933), pp.76, 123; U.S. Slave Census for 1850, Habersham County.

[7] Captain Basil Hall, *Travels in North America, 1827 and 1828* (Philadelphia: Carey, Lea & Carey, 1929), Vol. II, pp. 232-33; *Miller's Weekly Messenger*, July 7, 1810.

[8] Flanders, *Plantation Slavery*, pp. 154-55.

[9] Ibid.; Jarrett ledger books, Historic Preservation Section.

[10] Flanders, *Plantation Slavery*, pp. 154-55.

[11] Ibid., p.172; Traveler's Rest papers, Historic Preservation Section.

[12] Coulter, *Georgia, A Short History*, pp.301-02; Flanders, *Plantation Slavery*, p. 284.

[13] Buckingham, *Slave States*, Vol. II, pp.155-56.

[14] Ibid., pp.163-64. Perhaps this silk project was the derivation of the mulberry trees east of the house.

[15] Ibid., Vol. I, pp. 205-06, for the sources of the paragraphs on Silly; Allen U. Candler and Clement A. Evans (eds.), *Cylopedia of Georgia* (Atlanta: State Historical Association, 1906), Vol. III, p. 290; L.P. Brockett, *The Silk Industry in America* (New York: George F. Nesbitt & Co., 1876), pp. 38-39, 54-55; William F. Leggett, *The Story of Silk* (New York: Life-Time Editions, 1949), pp. 332-36.

[16] Jarrett ledger books, Historic Preservation Section.

[17] Ibid.

[18] Ibid., back of 1818 ledger books. The teacher was Burges Smith.

[19] Ibid.; on the Pendleton Factory, see Beth Ann Klosky, *The Pendleton Legacy* (Columbia, S.C.: Sandlapper Press, Inc., 1971), pp. 75-76, who says that the factory was established in 1836 as a cotton mill.

[20] Jarrett ledger books, Historic Preservation Section.

[21] Ibid.

[22] Ibid.; Traveler's Rest papers, Historic Preservation Section.

[23] Louise A. Vandiver, *Traditions and History of Anderson County* (Atlanta: Ruralist Press, Publishers, 1929), p. 199. The page in the 1831 ledger book includes a typical list of food, clothing, and equipment, raising some interesting questions: Did James R. Wyly have a store? Or was the "Wyly's Ferry" heading merely an indication that Jarrett's store was near the ferry? Perhaps Jarrett and Wyly were partners at one time. We also have 1831 ledgers clearly pertaining to Jarrett's store. On the bridge, see *Georgia Laws, Acts of the General Assembly of the State of Georgia,* 1834 (Milledgeville: P.L. & B.H. Robinson), p. 126; 1843, pp. 64-65.

[24] National Archives and Records Service, U.S. Post Office Records, Appointment of Postmasters, Vol. 2, p. 174; Vol. 5, p. 207; Vol. 7, p. 177; Vol. 10, October 12, 1833; December 11, 1835; July 23, 1840; November 9, 1842; October 4, 1844; March 24, 1852 (Vol. 17).

[25] Buckingham, *Slave States,* Vol. II, p. 234.

[26] Coulter, *Old Petersburg,* p. 233; Woodward, *Cherokees,* p. 159.

[27] Sherry Boatright, *The John C. Calhoun Gold Mine* (Atlanta: Department of Natural Resources, Historic Preservation Section, 1974), pp. 6e7; on the Georgia Guard, see Woodward, *Cherokees,* p. 190; Featherstonhaugh, A *Canoe Voyage,* Vol. II, p. 251.

[28] See Microfilm, Traveler's Rest papers, Historic Preservation Section; the Jarrett-England deeds were never recorded; on Moore, see Habersham County *Deed Book G,* p. 151.

[29] Coulter, *A Short History,* p. 233. For the outcome of Jarrett's many purchases of mining rights to these lots, see microfilmed Traveler's Rest papers, Historic Preservation Section.

[30] Ibid.; Boatright, *Calhoun Gold Mine*, pp. 7-9; Woodward, *Cherokees*, pp. 157-82; Traveler's Rest papers on microfilm, Historic Preservation Section.

[31] Traveler's Rest papers, Historic Preservation Section.

[32] Calhoun-Clemson papers at Clemson University; Calhoun to Clemson, February 6, 1843; Clemson to Calhoun, January, 1843. Wyly was a general of the Habersham County militia. Traveler's Rest papers, Historic Preservation Section.

[33] Traveler's Rest papers on microfilm, Historic Preservation Section.

[34] Traveler's Rest papers, Historic Preservation Section; Habersham County *Deed Book RR*, p. 454.

[35] Ibid., p. 457.

[36] Ibid., p. 458.

[37] Ibid., p. 459.

[38] Traveler's Rest papers, Historic Preservation Section. After Sarah Patton Jarrett died in 1842, Devereaux Jarrett married her sister, Elizabeth.

[39] Traveler's Rest papers, Historic Preservation Section.

# Chapter 8

## Jarrett Plantations in the 1850s

The 1850s found Devereaux Jarrett's four children prospering at adjacent plantations on the Tugaloo. Thomas Patton Jarrett married Elizabeth Hackett in 1846, and they moved into her father's former residence, a ten-room log house on Toccoa Creek. His inherited slaves made bricks and subsequently built another house for the family sometime in the 1850s. Thomas set his mind to family and farming then, and was not an executor of his father's estate, as were Robert and Charles Kennedy.

By 1860, Thomas (often known as "Patton") and Elizabeth had five young children; their farm was worth $10,000, and their property, $22,000, consisting mostly of slaves. The census for that year indicates that Thomas grew 130 bushels of peas and beans, 3,500 bushels of corn, forty of oats, 140 of wheat, forty of Irish potatoes, and 150 pounds of tobacco. The farm also produced 135 gallons of molasses, three bales of cotton, and 500 pounds of butter, and the family had four horses, four mules, fifteen milk cows, two oxen, ten cattle, seventy hogs, and ten sheep, from which Thomas produced ten pounds of wool.

This plantation was operated with the labor of thirty-five slaves. When the brick house was completed, Thomas and his family moved from the "10 room log cabin," dividing his father's old place into slave quarters, and he also bought a fancy German-made piano with profits from a gold-mining operation. His children were taught by tutors, and as teenagers; some of his daughters attended Madame Sosnowski's and Lucy Cobb's schools in Athens, Georgia.[1]

Little is known of Robert Jarrett, Thomas's brother. As a young man, he found adventure by joining the Georgia Volunteers in the Creek War of 1836 and 1837. This short, but bloody, war did not engage Robert long, but perhaps he found excitement in the Battle of Pea River Swamp, described somewhat ironically in White's *Collections of Georgia*:

A company of volunteers from this county [Franklin], commanded by Captain Morris, was engaged in a battle with the Creeks in Pea River Swamp, in Alabama, March 25, 1837. They won for themselves a reputation that may be envied by the victors of any field. Their deeds of noble daring were the theme of their associates in arms, and they were not behind the rest of the brave fellows, either in the march, the swimming, or the charge. An incident that occurred during the charge is worthy of note. One of the Franklin Volunteers was in hot pursuit of an Indian, who, finding that he must fall into the hands of his pursuer, attempted to save himself by running in the midst of the women, two of whom seized the volunteer; he used every exertion to disengage himself from them, but they made furious and deadly assault upon him with their knives, and in self-defence he drew his bowie, and with two blows killed them both.

This section of the State was for a long time exposed to the ravages of the Indians. In almost every part it was found necessary to erect forts and block-houses to protect the inhabitants against the savages. Cruelties were inflicted upon the helpless women and children, the record of which would chill the blood.[2]

Robert married Elizabeth by 1853, and by 1860 the couple had four children. The census for that year indicates that Robert was a bit more prosperous than Thomas in the value of his slaves, which was $25,000. On his farm were grown 200 bushels of peas and beans, 3,000 bushels of corn, 200 of oats, 240 of wheat, fifteen of Irish potatoes, and 500 of sweet potatoes. Also produced were ten gallons of wine, 225 gallons of molasses, one bale of cotton, and 1,000 pounds of butter. Robert and Elizabeth owned one horse, five mules, eighteen milk cows, two oxen, ten cattle, sixty hogs, and fifty sheep, which produced 100 pounds of wool. Living in a brick plantation house much like the one built by Thomas, they owned forty-three slaves.[3]

Sarah Ann Jarrett married an up-and-coming young farmer, Joseph J. Prather, in 1852, and by 1860, the couple had two children. The census taker that year recorded that the family had $15,000 in real estate and $39,300 in personal estate. Sarah Ann so impressed him that he wrote "a lady of the first quality" next to her name in the census. The census agricultural schedules show that the Prathers' farm was quite similar to the Jarrett brothers' in production and livestock, although Prather did grow considerably more cotton than his brothers-in-law.[4]

Charles Kennedy Jarrett, known as "Kennedy," was apparently the most ambitious of his father's children, undertaking to carry on the family businesses. Far more material has been discovered regarding Charles Kennedy than any previous Jarrett. In 1860, he had a family of five, including his mother-in-law, living on his $15,000 plantation at Traveler's Rest. He and his wife, the former Elizabeth Lucas, were married by 1855 and had two children—Sally Grace, who was four years old in 1860, and Charles Patton, who was two years old. Their farm produced 150 bushels of peas and beans in that year, as well as 4,000 bushels of corn, fifty of oats, 1,300 of wheat, fifty of Irish potatoes, 800 of sweet potatoes, and two bales of cotton. Also produced were 1,000 pounds of butter, $1,300 of home manufactures, $200 of garden produce, eight gallons of wine, 200 pounds of honey, ten pounds of wax, and 350 gallons of molasses. The family owned nine horses, eleven mules, twenty milk cows, six work oxen, fifteen cattle, 150 hogs, and 112 sheep, which were shorn of 250 pounds of wool. In addition to this sumptuous farm, Kennedy also maintained as well as he could the gold mine, the inn, the store, the post office, the mills, and the blacksmithy, and he even bought a bridge in Clarkesville.[5] Kennedy had thirty-five slaves in 1860.

The detailed biography of Kennedy Jarrett can begin when he was about thirty years of age. There is slim evidence that Devereaux Jarrett groomed Kennedy to take over the family enterprises, sending him to pick up the gold at the mine in 1849, and two years later, he deeded Traveler's Rest to his son and returned "to rest with God." Soon after the death of his father, the wealthy young bachelor visited Atlanta, where he met Lizzie Lucas, a beautiful "Southern belle" from Athens, Georgia.[6] This was an important incident in the Jarrett family history, deemed worthy of immortalization by the great elaborator of Traveler's Rest history, Mary Jarrett White, the couple's daughter. According to Mary, whose nickname was "Baby," the courtship began as follows:

> In the early days of the history of Atlanta (then called Marthasville in honor of Gov. Lumpkin's daughter Martha who was a friend of the beautiful Miss Elizabeth Lucas of Athens), Miss Lucas was walking down the street with some cousin who cast sly glances at the few beaux who lived in this little village at that time. Among them was Mr. Charles K. Jarrett a bachelor of about 28 years of age. He and his friend Judge Logan Bleckley were discussing the current events when all of a sudden Judge Bleckley was startled by the abrupt manner of his friend Jarrett who in an excited voice said, "Look at the beauty! I never saw anything as supremely lovely as she is. Who is she?" Judge Bleckley laughed and said, "That is Miss Lizzie Lucas of Athens, the belle and beauty of Georgia. She wouldn't even look at you." Mr. Jarrett responded "I don't care where she lives or who she is, I'm going to marry her." He knew he was a man of importance, owning ten thousand acres of land and fifty negro slaves, twenty-two Kentucky thoroughbred horses and a lovely home situated in Haber-

sham County in the foot hills of the beautiful Blue Ridge Mountains. In about a year he brought his bride to his home, Travelers Rest, driving from Athens in a coach of "ye olden tyme" driven by his negro "Harry" who was a faithful slave and was proud of the honor of bringing young "Miss" and young "Master" home to the big house where the brothers and sister and other relatives awaited them with the happy slaves who prepared the wonderful wedding supper which consisted of whole roasted pigs with apples in their mouths, turkeys, fruit cakes, boiled custard, "syllabab" [syllabub, a dessert or punch made with cream and wine or cider] and other good things. After this sumtuous [sic] retart [repast] the minuet and Virginia reel was danced to the music of "de fiddle and de bow" till the "wee small hours."[7]

Life was more than courtship and parties at Traveler's Rest in the 1850s, however. Occasionally, Kennedy had to neglect his beautiful wife and tend to the store, the gold mine, or one of the other enterprises. In March of 1852, he succeeded his father as postmaster at Walton's Ford, Georgia, a job which he held until 1866, when he gave it up for the following ten years.[8]

Kennedy greatly expanded the scope of the Jarrett store. The ledgers from the 1850s are the most extensive yet found, running from 1853 through 1859 and including accounts from the blacksmithy and the tollbridge. The pages are headed "C. K. Jarrett—Walton's Ford." By this time, the operation genuinely qualified as a "general store," medicine being added to a stock of yard-goods, food, tools, kitchen merchandise, and clothing. The store began to sell soap occasionally, and other items sold at the time were "spectacles," candy, locks, violins, and oranges. Like his father, Kennedy was available for small cash loans, and there were also occasional entries for a drink of brandy or a bottle of wine. Very little liquor was sold, however, compared to the earlier days, but in 1855, the trade in alcoholic beverages, especially whiskey, picked up again. Entries for shoeing horses, laying plows, and similar items, indicate that the Jarrett blacksmithy also survived.

Jarrett family tradition maintains that much of the furniture at Traveler's Rest today was made by a man named Shaw, and the surviving records support this claim. A Caleb T. Shaw lived in Franklin County, near the Habersham County line, throughout the 1850s. What is known of Shaw comes from United States Census records and the Traveler's Rest ledgers. In 1850, Shaw was listed as a 46-year-old mechanic from Massachusetts, a man with a small family. Sometime before 1852, Shaw probably made the large bed which has since become known as that of Devereaux Jarrett. During the 1850s, Shaw made furniture for the four Jarrett plantations. This is partially proven by entries in C. K. Jarrett's ledgers for the late 1850s, which show C. T. Shaw settling his store account as a relatively well-paid

Jarrett employee. The 1860 census records show Shaw as a "cabinet maker." Little else about him has been discovered.[9]

The bridge does not seem to have been used much. Many people may have been allowed to cross without paying, but in yearly subscriptions and daily tolls, the bridge had surprisingly little business—sometimes days would pass without a toll being collected. Crossing the bridge cost twenty cents, and a year's privilege was a dollar. Perhaps the road passing Traveler's Rest was no longer well-traveled.[10]

Two of the surviving ledgers deal with matters pertaining to the Jarrett slaves. A slim one, headed "Negro book, 1855," contains a few accounts of purchases made by the slaves, whose names appear as "Robt's Noboru, "CKJ's Dicy," "Prather's Alford," and so forth. For a few dollars, the slaves bought such items as knives and forks, muslin and calico, shoes, ribbon, caps, "sirup," tobacco, and other small items. This material indicates that the Jarretts did indeed make it possible for their slaves to earn petty cash, probably through their private gardens, poultry, and animals. Another ledger, the "Book of Prompt Payments," records numerous similar purchases by the slaves. On occasion, the Jarrett slaves even enjoyed, could they obtain the funds, such luxuries as cinnamon, mirrors, silk, cologne, and fishhooks. In the back of this ledger are several lists which give the "Names of the Negroes who has had shoes," "Those who got socks," and "who got wool."[11]

Scattered entries in the pages of a ledger recently discovered show that Traveler's Rest survived as a stopping-place throughout the 1850s and the Civil War. A couple could stay at the inn for one night for a dollar, though some people managed to spend as much as $3.25 during their stay. There are clues in these pages that stagecoaches still passed the inn, but during the war years, most of the travelers stopping at Jarrett's were soldiers.[12]

In 1854, Kennedy Jarrett formed a partnership with Archibald, John, and Edmund Patton (uncles or cousins of his) to work the Burnett Gold Mine. The scarcely-legible document drawn up in forming this partnership indicates that the Pattons and Jarrett, "who has obtained on his part a lease from two of the owners," agreed to split expenses and profits, fifty percent for Jarrett and fifty percent for the Pattons. On a contract to run for twelve years, Archibald Patton was chosen to manage the mine. Things apparently did not run smoothly, however, for in 1855, the partners were called into court by a John Dobbins, who sued them for $276 he claimed they owed him for hired slaves. They had promised not "to work them in pits, tunnels, or any dangerous work," Dobbins said, and they used the slaves for a full year without paying him. From this it may be inferred that the mine was not producing as much gold as had been hoped.[13]

Most of the rest of the information known about the antebellum Jarretts comes from the personal papers of Elizabeth Lucas Jarrett, and in fact, her correspondence and that of her children is the only personally intimate material available. With the exception of letters written among members of the family, most of the correspondence consists of letters written to the Jarretts, and this makes for a frustrating situation, only partially alleviated by the presence in this material of a lock of Lizzie Lucas's blonde hair.[14]

Lizzie's correspondence, especially that of her single days, conforms to the traditional image of the "Southern belle." Letters from both girlfriends and boyfriends are full of romance and gossip—and seldom touch on other aspects of life. Lizzie's friends always tell her that life is never so gay as it was before or should be, but nonetheless contains a round of "rich and racy" parties, concerts, theatrical exhibitions, and courtship. An 1852 letter from Cousin F.G.A. Johns in Macon, Georgia, tells of a *"Fancy Dress Party"* attended by the guests in costume:

> I was one of the Kossuth aids [*sic*] on the occasion and Judge A.P. Powers was Kossuth [a Hungarian revolutionary hero who led a struggle against the Hapsburg Empire]. This suite was composed of seven gentlemen all dressed in the hungarian officer style and our military appearance looked quite foreign and appropriate to the occasion...We had quite a No [number] of Kings Queens Turks Pages Spanish noblemen and all sorts of foreign characters.[15]

Cousin Johns takes "knightly" pride in telling Lizzie of all his military activities—Macon, he reported in the letter, had "a great deal of military pride for a small town & can show two of the prettiest companies in seven adjoining states." When the company had trained recently, Johns caught a severe cold from exposure, although the soldiers had a "grand collation & a variety of Picnics etc...and beautiful weather all the time." Lizzie was quite a seamstress, it seems, for she had made Johns several fine shirts. In the letter, Johns indulges in some flattery, quoting "old man davy" that "Lizzy_____ is a great gal!"[16]

Lizzie also carried on an extensive correspondence with "Cousin" George Dews, whose letters are frivolous, but fine examples of the antebellum Southerners' aspirations to gentility. Dews was something of a stylist who liked passages such as the following, which he wrote while traveling across Georgia by buggy: "All animal nature seemed to be quiet and the piercing wind moaning through the trees seemed to be singing the requiem of the falling leaves. We had to get out and walk very often to keep the blood circulating in our bodies."

In the same letter, dated February 14, 1851, George wrote of how he longed for Lizzie's company on his visit to "Towellagre [Towaliga] Falls" [High Falls, Butts County, thirty-five miles north of Macon]:

I love to look at such places. It seemed to be made for lovers. The sublimity of the scene would cause their love to burn more intensely; the soarings of the waters making them feel dependent, would cause them to draw nearer each other and then their voices could not be heard by the listener. They could sit there and feel they had a world entirely to themselves…

Back at college at Penfield [Mercer], Dews' heart felt a void in his life, yet, he said, "I am willing to sacrifice all on the altar of learning." Lizzie was sick—as she often seems to have been—so George implored and philosophized:

Could my exertions avail anything, one pang of sorrow or pain should never cross your bosom: but it is a blessed thing, that we are not always freed from sickness; otherwise, we could not appreciate the blessings of health: "We would never feel our dependence upon our Creator; thoughts of heaven would be forgotten in the pleasures of the world; and all spirituality would wither in our hearts." I always regard afflictions as messengers of God sent to warn us of our duty and to wean our affections more & more from the world.

Dews then noted:

This is St. Valentine's day. Hundreds [of Valentines] have been written here. I would have written you one in a disguised hand, had it not been, that I was owing you a letter and I supposed you would prefer that, where every sentiment expressed you would know was sincere, to a Valentine where nothing said could be relied on.

Dews wrote Lizzie of courtship and love, gossip and insults, health and predestination. He went to parties where the guests consumed lemonade, cakes, candy, almonds, and raisins, and then exchanged orations. In August of 1851, Lizzie sent Dews a Bible, and overcome with ecstasy, he effused: "It shall always be my companion, and when the Angel of Death shall flap his wings over the ocean of my heart and its waters are ceasing its ebbing and flowing then it will be clasp [sic] to my bosom, I trust and laid by my side in the cold grave."

In spite of such ardent passages, however, Dews apparently found room in his heart for someone else. He proposed to this unnamed "belle," but his love proved unrequited. On learning of Lizzie's forthcoming marriage to Kennedy Jarrett, Dews confided, "My hearts first love has already been crushed." Perhaps as a consequence of losing both women, he then decided to take a course opposite that pursued by most scorned bachelors and joined the "Sons of Temperance." After this fairly brief flurry of correspondence, Dews then faded from the scene.[17]

One of Lizzie Lucas's most interesting friends seems to have been a young woman known now only as Fannie, from whom a few letters have survived. Fannie's assessment of the opposite sex was ambiguous, as seen in the following passage, written May 12, 1852:

> I know "them mens" too well—deceiving worthless scamps! I feel sometimes that I despise the whole sex. Then I begin to select those I do not despise, and lo! I find that I do not really despise a single one. They certainly have a mighty influence on our sex. And I presume the influence exerted by us is equally as great.
>
> *Your own loving Fannie*

Fannie was apparently "confined" to Dahlonega, where life was never as exciting as she felt it should be:

> Dahlonega is such a moral place that news is not permitted to enter its portals…We have had a spiritual rapper—(I should have said, a Psychologist, excusie moi) a real live animal of that species—but let me tell you the truth Bettie the people up here were so green; so completely knocked out of the world, that when he came and informed them what he designed doing, they had not sense enough to believe him, consequently not enough to permit him to craze them. The poor fellow, Prof Estes left, no doubt thoroughly disgusted at the idea of the existence of such ignoramuses.[18]

One carefully-saved piece of paper is a final testimony to Lizzie Lucas's "Southern belleness." It is headed, "For the Dahlonega Journal":

> Mr. Editor—Being often in the group of the young Gentlemen of this place who are in the die-away state called Love and who gather themselves together for mutual consolation—I frequently hear a name softly and tremulously pronounced in syllables like these Lizzie Lucas—she is numbered among the many mischievous instruments through which Cupid lacerates the hearts of men—Her abscence [sic] is very much regretted—and her revisitation to the romantic hills and poetic vales of Lumpkin County would be hailed by all particularly by a few with demonstrations of joy—One heart is forever sighing out her description in strains like the following:
>> Her looks How lovely! and her face
>> So eloquent with mental grace!

She is, in truth, a wayward child,
Her words so gay, her steps so wild;
And never can she speak or move
Without some glow akin to Love!

The aforesaid Miss Lucas will sooner or later be bound to respond at some tribunal for having wounded mortally our boys and
left them wounded suffering victims of Love.

*A Young Contributor*[19]

Kennedy Jarrett proved to be just the man to sweep Lizzie away from all
her beaux. She gave up her Scarlett O'Hara life to live at the Tugaloo with
him, and subsequently had three children before the Civil War. According
to her romantic younger daughter,

> The beautiful young mistress was a queen in her home and in her
> community. She was loved by rich and poor...A daughter Sarah
> Grace and two sons Charles Patton, and Fred Lucas, came to make
> their happiness complete. Then the dark war clouds began to hover
> over the South, bringing desolation to all classes.[20]

Unfortunately, few clues remain to indicate how these gathering "clouds"
affected the Jarretts. An interesting letter from Helen, another one of Lizzie's correspondents whose last name is unknown, to "Dear Auntie" (probably Lizzie) is one of the rare pieces of Jarrett evidence related to the coming
of the war. Writing in 1860, Helen mentioned that she went to a fair in
Atlanta, where she "met up with a number of friends and I enjoyed myself
finely about 20 of us eat a dinner on the ground together." Helen visited the
fair several times, especially impressed by "3 fire cos. 1 hook and ladder
and 3 Military cos. of Atlanta and the Marietta Cadets." She also noted that
some "patriotic" Southern women were wearing homespun, and a school
from Cassville appeared dressed in homespun to show that the South was
independent of Northern textile manufacturers. "Miss Helen" was not concerned enough to worry about the ominous, imminent Presidential election,
and she commented casually, "We did not exhibit anything but ourselves."[21]

Far more serious than such "exhibitions," however, was the subject of
slavery, over which the nation was on the verge of dividing and fighting a
bloody wax. As historians such as John Hope Franklin and Clement Eaton
have shown, slavery was a terrible trap which had gone far toward destroying free expression and democracy in the South.[22]

Above all, white Southerners feared slave revolt. Slave plots were ruth-
lessly suppressed; slaveowners went to great lengths to keep ideas of freedom from circulating among the slave population. Ulrich B. Phillips, a his-

torian inclined to view slavery through rose-tinted glasses, wrote on slave conspiracies: "The revolts which occurred and the plots which were discovered were sufficiently serious to produce a very palpable disquiet from time to time, and the rumors were frequent enough to maintain a fairly constant undertone of uneasiness."[23]

No amount of repression and patrolling, however, was sufficient to totally "protect" slaves from the idea of freedom. Small conspiracies were more frequent after John Brown's abortive raid of 1859 and the excitement of the Presidential election of 1860.[24] In the fall of the election year, a relatively unknown slave conspiracy was exposed at Walton's Ford. The details of this plot are almost entirely unknown, for only a few newspaper notices have survived to tell of it. Two were reprinted from an October, 1860, edition of the *Clarkesville Herald*. The most detailed description, reprinted in the Athens *Southern Banner*, follows:

### ALARM

The people in the lower portion of this county [Habersham], in the neighborhood of Walton's Ford, have been greatly alarmed for several days past by the discovery of a hellish plot among the negroes. Mrs. Philip Martin first overheard the talking of the arrangements—heard them say, they were going to pitch her into the well—Then how they were going to dispose of others in the neighborhood.

The negroes have been taken up and severely whipped, a free negro among them seems to have been the head leader who was made to confess the whole of it. They were instigated to it, by one John K. Wilson, who was employed as a gardner [*sic*] by Mr. J.J. Prather [husband of Sally Jarrett]. He [Wilson] had been talking and reading to them for sometime. The scamp was given five hours to get away. The citizens did entirely wrong in letting him escape. If he were innocent it was cruel to drive him off.—if he were guilty (of which they had evidence) it was wrong to let him escape punishment. Clarkesville Herald. [25]

Such emotional prose conveys an indication of the seriousness with which white Southerners viewed the problem of slave revolt, but it can only provide a paltry impression of the excitement which discovery of the "hellish plot" must have brought to Walton's Ford. Unfortunately, the details of the African Americans' "arrangements" for the Prathers and the Jarretts, the grievances and hopes that inspired their desire for liberty, and even the names of the individuals, have been lost. Barring an unexpected discovery of valuable primary documents, the details of the Walton's Ford conspiracy will remain unknown. The plot foreshadowed the years of upheaval and confusion which began at the Tugaloo Crossroads in the fall of 1860.

## NOTES

[1] Traveler's Rest papers, Historic Preservation Section; U.S. Census 1860 Population Schedule, Habersham County, p. 894; U.S. Census 1860 Agricultural Schedule, Habersham County, p. 13; U.S. Slave Census, 1860, Habersham County; "Jarrett Descendants Occupy Historic Homes," *Toccoa* [Georgia] *Record*, March 25, 1976, p. 6-B.

[2] George White, *Historical Collections of Georgia* (New York: Pudney and Russell, Pub., 1854), P. 460.

[3] Traveler's Rest papers, Historic Preservation Section and in the possession of the Henry and Elizabeth Hayes family, Habersham County; U.S. Census 1860 Population Schedule, p. 894; U.S. Census 1850 Agricultural Schedule, p. 13; U.S. Slave Census; George White, *Statistics of Georgia* (Savannah: W. Thorne Williams, 1849), reported that Habersham County farmers grew an average of 15 bushels of corn per acre, five bushels of wheat. The county produced a total of 50 bales of cotton in 1849, p. 299.

[4] Traveler's Rest papers, Historic Preservation Section; U.S. Census 1860 Population Schedule, P. 893; U.S. Census Agricultural Schedule, p. 13.

[5] U.S. Census 1860 Population Schedule, p. 896; U.S. Census 1860 Agricultural Schedule, p. 13.

[6] Traveler's Rest papers (some on microfilm), Historic Preservation Section.

[7] Ibid.

[8] National Archives and Records Service, U.S. Post Office Records, Appointments of Postmasters, Vol. 17, March 24, 1852, p. 36; Vol. 26, pp. 92-93.

[9] Jarrett ledgers, Historic Preservation Section. U.S. Census records 1850, 1860, Franklin County, pp. 315, 675.

[10] Jarrett Ledgers, Historic Preservation Section.

[11] Ibid.

[12] Ibid.

[13] Ibid.

[14] Ibid.

[15] Ibid.

[16] Ibid.

[17] Ibid.

[18] Ibid.

[19] Ibid.

[20] Ibid.

[21] Ibid.

[22] See John Hope Franklin, *The Militant* South (no publishing place, Beacon Press, 1956); Clement Eaton, *Freedom of Thought in the Old South* (Durham, N.C., 1940).

[23] Ulrich B. Phillips, *American Negro Slavery* (Baton Rouge: Louisiana State University Press, 1969 [19181), p. 488.

[24] Ibid., pp. 487-88; see also Joseph Cephas Carroll, *Slave Insurrections in the United States, 1800-1865* (New York: Negro Universities Press, 1938) and Nicholas Halasz, *The Rattling Chains, Slave Unrest and Revolt in the Ante-bellum South* (New York: David McKay Company, Inc., 1966).

[25] "Alarm," Athens *Southern Banner*, November 1, 1860, p. 2; *Macon Telegraph*, November 21, 1860; Flanders, *Plantation Slavery in Georgia*, p. 179.

# Chapter 9

## The Civil War on the Tugaloo

No diaries or journals have been found, and but little correspondence to and from the front tells of the Jarretts during the Civil War. Most of the details of their lives during those four tragic years remains unknown or at least undocumented. Devereaux Jarrett's sons were all a bit old for arduous military service, and while one might expect a wealthy man of forty years of age such as Kennedy Jarrett to be an officer, this apparently was not the case. Few Civil War records relating to the Jarretts during this period are extant, and the Confederate records at the Georgia Archives show only that C. K. Jarrett enlisted as a private on March 3, 1862, in Cherokee County. He received a $50 bounty, having signed up for three years, or the duration of the war, but soon, however, Kennedy became an "absent enlisted man, accounted for–" in July of 1862. The explanation for this short-term service can be found in *The Roster of the Confederate Soldiers of Georgia*, which provides the information that Kennedy Jarrett was "discharged on account of weak eyes" in 1862.[1]

C. K. Jarrett's post-war letter requesting a federal pardon reveals that he served as purchasing agent for the Confederate Army, his work in that capacity perhaps resulting in one of the interesting documents in the Jarrett family papers, a receipt for $20,000 (Confederate) worth of beef.[2] A handful of letters have also survived to offer glimpses of the Jarretts' lives, one being undated and probably written April 18, 1861, by James W. Wrenn of Gainesville, Alabama, to "Dear Brother," who could be a neighbor, a guest, a tenant farmer, or even a Jarrett. The letter can be dated 1861 because it apparently refers to the secession of Virginia, which occurred on April 17 of that year. The letter's text shows the carefree spirit with which many Southerners entered the fray:

> I am in Gainesville now, the guns are firing, drums are beating, fifes are playing, bells are ringing & the town in an uproar generally. So

am I. We have a meeting here tomorrow to organize a volunteer company & I have almost concluded to join & will immediately if you can find someone to stay on your farm & come home. Let me know immediately what you can do I am in earnest. We are all well & looking for you tomorrow.

Your Brother
*Jas. W. Wrenn*

N.B. The noise is for old Virginia.[3]

What this letter had to do with the Jarretts or Traveler's Rest is not known; nor is it known if the Jarretts entered the war in the same ebullient mood as did Wrenn.

Early in the war, one of Lizzie Jarrett's correspondents, known only as Sue, was already expressing regrets. Writing from Penfield, Georgia, she lamented: "I wish it were possible this bitter cup of war that we have had to and are drinking could pass from us & we could have peace again–we will not have scarcly [sic] a young man left to us…If you have any brandy made this year–keep some for me as I am going to hard drinking."[4]

One letter from the front to "My Dear Friend" has been found at Traveler's Rest. On May 17, 1863, J.W. Wyly wrote to his unnamed friend from a camp near Fredericksburg, Virginia, as follows:

I have been studying for the last day or two wheather [sic] I owe you a letter or not, and I still cant [sic] tell, and for fear I did not answer your last letter I take this opportunity to write you a short letter.

This is a beautiful Sabbath Morning in May and the trees are in full bloom. It resembles very much the beautiful May days which in bygone days of peace, we have seen so many fine enjoyments but those times for a while have ceased to exist but I do hope before another May month shall make its appearance we will all be at our lovely homes in peace, and prepared to see those enjoyments that we once saw again. On the first of this month we was engaged in Battle, and on the third and fourth one of the most terrible battals [sic] of the war was fought [Chancellorsville]. The fighting commenced on the thirtieth of last month (April) and continued for eight days but on the second third & fourth was the days of the hard fighting and many of the noble sons of the South was caused to leave this world of sorrow and troubles. The night of the Second instant our Loard [sic] & lost hero Genl. Jackson faught [sic] very near all night. Twas in that grate [sic] and hard fought battle that he was wounded. he and his staff rode out in advance of our Skirmishers and just before he went out (it was night) he instructed his men to fire at any one coming up in front of them. Soon on his return he missed the road and came up in front of his pickett [*sic*] and they doing their duty hit him in the left wrist one in the left hand and another in the right hand his left arm was taken off near his elbow, but he was doing very well untill [*sic*] he was taken with a very severe attack of Pneumonia of which he died. Our casualties in our company was very light in this engagement we lost but one man killed it was Pate Fuller no doubt you have heard of his sad fate long ago he was shot in the head and died instantly he was a brave & Gallant Lou[isian]ian. We had six or seven wounded. None of which you know.

Genl. Lee says that this victory won here was the greatest of the war. the Yankees chose the battle ground had two men to our one and we completely routed them across the river. The Yankees acknowledge themselves that we out General them and our men fought better and they say we can whip them any time with anything like an equal number.

So I have written you such an uninteresting [letter] I will close there is no news in camp at all. I see by yesterdays [*sic*] papers the the [*sic*] Yankees have taken possession of Jackson, Mississippi Genl. Johnson has fallen back to some station between Jackson & Vicksburg and says he is prepared to meet them in any force they may bring before him. he says he is confident of success. the health of the troops is very good now indeed, the weather is very fine. If I have not answered your last letter untill [*sic*] now I hope you will excuse me for this time lost since sometime before the fight has been in confusion, write soon. I will be very glad to hear from you.[5]

Far from the gory scenes at Chancellorsville and Fredericksburg, the Jarrett women waited for peace amid dwindling comforts. A letter to Lizzie from Cousin Mary Alice McComb in Bellview, Florida, is full of family news, and she finally mentions the impact of the war in saying: "Have you had any homespun dresses yet–I have three or four People that never thought of having such a thing as a homespun dress before the war now think they are very well off if they have homespun. Thread is 30 dollars a bunch. I heard calico was 9 $ per yard Worsted is 15 $ a yard."[6]

As the war continued, a great many items became costly and scarce. In the Tugaloo area, coffee and tea were replaced by a brew concocted from "parched grain or okra ground up" or various herbal beverages. Ink, paper, and button became hard to find, and homemade molasses became the standard sweetener. Pins and needles were carefully saved.[7] Despite such inconveniencing shortages, however, the Tugaloo area residents appear not to have suffered great hardships before the final days of the war. When Floride

Clemson, granddaughter of John C. Calhoun and a cultured young woman in her early twenties, arrived in Pendleton in January of 1865, she reported:

> The ladies look a little shabyly [shabby] & old fashioned but there seems little real want…Luxuries are almost unatainable [sic], sugar, & meat dear…but there is plenty of corn, flour, salt, sorghum, & even poultry, about here…The ingenuity of the people is wonder full in making things, & furnishing "substitutes," which is a word in every ones mouth.

Floride went on to offer a comment on the Confederate situation: "The greatest want, alas! is of men. Men to fight. There are scarce any out of the army now, & too few there. The people, as far as I have seen, are dispirited now."[8] If the Jarrett women wished to assist in the war effort by caring for wounded "heroes," they could climb in the wagon and drive across the river to Pendleton, where a one-room house near the railroad station had been converted into a hospital. There, "many a suffering soldier received good nursing."[9]

Another of the few remaining Jarrett letters from the Civil War era was that from Robert Jarrett to his wife, Elizabeth, written from Asheville, North Carolina, on September 5, 1862. Robert informed her: "I arrived here day before yesterday after a very rough road and painful journey the road from Clarkesville to franklin [sic] is very rough it had like to have worn me out." On the next leg of the journey, Robert had suffered greatly in his hips and back, he reported, but he hoped to be restored to health at a springs. He was cheered by the war news: "We have just heard of the battle of manassus [sic] plains our men have whiped [sic] Pope and McClellan the report is that 7000 of our men are killed and fifteen thousand wounded and the Yankee loss is immense."[10]

Regarding the farm, Robert instructed: "Tell york to put up fatning [sic] hogs all that will do and feed them what they will eat of the small corn and what they cut out of the fodder roads." After returning to the theme of his suffering, he closed with the news that he could not obtain a cap for his son, "little Devereaux." Perhaps the disability referred to in this letter was the cause of Robert Jarrett's death in 1864.[11]

In the last days of the Southern rebellion, the terrors of war finally visited the people living in relative seclusion in the Tugaloo neighborhood. For many months, Tugaloo residents observed with growing alarm the gradual decline of the slaveowners' cause. When General William T. Sherman led a burning, looting army across Georgia in 1864, determined to divide the South in half and show the Southerners the hopelessness of their fight and the bitter fruits of warfare, people in the Tugaloo area developed an increasing fear and hatred of their enemies. What would happen if the Yankees were to bring destruction there?

By February of 1865, Floride Clemson found the people "despondent… and…at heart conquered." Even necessities had become "ridiculously dear, & almost impossible to get." On February 19, she reported Pendleton to be full of "consternation" over the danger of Federal raids, and when Columbia, South Carolina, was "laid in ashes by the Northern Vandals," she fearfully anticipated the same for the Tugaloo neighborhood. On April 21, Floride confided to her diary: "Oh these are dreadful times to live in. I suppose we may expect raids now anyday, & God only knows how we are to bear it, for the country is starving now…I suppose we will die of starvation." On May 1, she wrote, "We scarcely ever see a news paper, & are bewildered groping in impenetrable darkness, & mystery."[12]

These fears were realized with dramatic suddenness. Confederate President Jefferson Davis fled Richmond in April, desperate to reach the trans-Mississippi region, where recalcitrant Southerners hoped that the war could be perpetuated. With Davis was a small escort and an indeterminate amount of gold from the Confederate treasury. He headed for the Southwest by a route which would take him across the Tugaloo somewhere between Traveler's Rest and Petersburg. On April 27, United States Secretary of War E.M. Stanton telegraphed General George Thomas, ordering him to see to the capture of Davis and the estimated $6 to $13 million in gold. Stanton cabled: "Spare no exertion to stop Davis and his plunder. Push the enemy as hard as you can in every direction."[13]

Thomas immediately passed the order on to General George Stoneman, commander of the headquarters of the Department of Cumberland at Knoxville, and on the same day, Stoneman ordered Generals David Tillson, Simeon B. Brown (both at Asheville), and William J. Palmer (at Cowpens, South Carolina) and their three brigades to pursue Davis. Stoneman exhorted, "If you can hear of Davis, follow him to the ends of the earth, if possible, and never give him up."[14] Greatly agitated by the rumors of vast hordes of gold, the eager Union troops headed for the Tugaloo, "living off the country." Crossing the Tugaloo at Hatton's Ford, somewhat north of Davis' Abbeville crossing, Palmer's brigade scrambled to reach Athens ahead of Davis, who was forced to halt at Washington, Georgia, disband most of his men, and turn back to the east. He was soon captured.[15]

During and immediately following their efforts to head off Davis and the gold, the overly excited Union troops made life extremely traumatic for residents of the Tugaloo. For the Jarretts and their neighbors of the wealthy planter class, the Yankees' arrival signaled the end of an era and a way of life which they had struggled desperately to preserve. Although only a few scraps of paper have survived to provide frustrating hints of the Jarretts' lives during those days of change, it is possible to obtain a deeper impression of how they must have felt from a number of sources which have been published. Several accounts from nearby in South Carolina vividly portray the adventurous, dangerous events of the Yankees' arrival at the Tugaloo. Since these records were kept by people of the same socio-economic class as the Jarretts, they can speak for that family, to a certain extent. Hence, they are especially valuable for the student of Traveler's Rest.

On May 1, 1865, Clarissa Adger Bowen, a young woman who lived at Ashtabula Plantation, near Pendleton, decided to begin a diary in order "to have a record of our every day life during these months of uncertainty, gloom, and suffering." The diary brings alive the impact of war upon this previously isolated community a few miles from Traveler's Rest. For weeks, the atmosphere had been permeated with "wild rumors." Already some-what terrorized by the free-booting soldiers of Joe Wheeler's Confederate cavalry,[16] by spring, the Tugaloo people were dreading the approach of loot-ing and burning Union troops. On May 1, they arrived, and forty soldiers rode up to Ashtabula, opened the stable, and took two horses. The Bowen family hurriedly poured out their liquor and hid guns and silver:

> In about twenty minutes three more of the wretches rode up, rush-ing at O. [Bowen] who was under an oak tree and tore his watch from him. One of them dismounting took him aside and imperious-ly demanded firearms and specie [coin money]. With drawn pistols they rushed into my room and the work of pillage began—jewelry firearms and specie seemed their principal desire but other things such as flannel shirts, shoes, wine, coffee, tea, loaf sugar, etc. were not despised. They even took the strawberries, bread, etc. out of the storeroom but we are yet in too much confusion to know what is tak-en and what is left. Only thank God, no blood was shed and O. was not taken prisoner. It was all as sudden as a clap of thunder.[17]

Few of those who had possessions the Yankees might value got much sleep during those early may nights. To her diary, Clarissa Bowen exclaimed, "What trials we are now enduring!" The Bowens and most of their wealthy neighbors slept with their clothes on, dreading a return of the Northern ma-rauders. The people had no way of knowing that the often drunken, thiev-ing, abusive, violent soldiers would commit no further barbarisms, such as burning or even worse. Floride Clemson delicately expressed the fear that must have preyed on the minds of many, saying, "We…were dreadfully afraid of personal insults."[18]

At Rivoli, home of Clarissa's father, Robert Adger, fifty Union soldiers appeared on May 1 and demanded "18 millions of treasure which they 'knew was hidden in the cellar' or to capture 'the President and Cabinet who had been at the house for two days!'" When the soldiers told Adger they knew exactly where the gold was, he told them, "Then go take it." Instead of digging, however, the officers led their men in plundering the house.[19]

The raiders also visited Boscobel, nearby home of Robert Adger's brother, the Reverend John D. Adger. There, they demanded horses and watches. Adger taunted them, asking, "Does your government send you all through this country just to rob private citizens?" To this, the Yankee spokesman replied, "Do you suppose I would go riding all about here and not take anything home to my family?" Upon going inside, he then told the tense Adger women, "Don't be afraid, ladies, we've seen ladies before. We only want to get pistols and gold watches." The soldiers ransacked the house, pocketing everything valuable and portable. As the spokesman climbed on his horse to depart, however, his rifle discharged, blasting a hole through his neck and head. The minister was nearly shot on the spot by the Yankee's surprised compatriots, but Adger reversed the situation: "I clapped my hands over their heads and said, 'The hand of God is on you, men. Give me back my watch.'" He also recovered his daughter's watch, and the chastened thieves then departed.[20]

Clarissa Bowen wrote that the Northerners had discovered some cases of liquor in Anderson, South Carolina, drinking until they had become "perfect demons." Louise Vandiver's *History of Anderson* tells of the drunken Union soldiers shooting down one young man as he crossed the street, and others were tortured to reveal the locations of their secret savings: "The drunken, rowdy soldiers entered everywhere, taking whatever of value they could carry away, wantonly destroying much that they could not."[21]

Young Caroline Ravenel described the Yankees' visit to her family in Anderson in a letter. They threatened to hang her grandmother, should she refuse to give them her purported gold: "She told them they could hang her, but as she had no gold, she could not give it up." The soldiers then looted the house:

> They went down, carried old Uncle Henry to Mama's room, put a noose round his neck, & hung him to the bedstead three times, that is, the tips of his toes alone touched the ground…Aunt Mary loosened the rope once, which so enraged them that they threatened to hang her too, and abused her so that she saw her presence was anything but a protection to Uncle H., & at last was obliged to come out. We did not know what was going on then. They came upstairs again, & oh! they abused Aunt Mary & Grandma, & Aunt Elizabeth dreadfully, saying they would give $50,000 if Aunt Mary was a man they might hang her too, & threatened her so much that I was very uneasy. They told us that they didn't believe "those fine ladies," meaning Aunt Maria, Aunt Carrie, Maria & I would tell a story & they would not

take $2000000 if we were to give it to them, but they <u>would</u> have that old man's gold, & they would hang him for lying & break his neck. They called down the most awful, awful curses on themselves if they did not kill the old man. Oh! Belle, you can never imagine the horror of those moments, words cannot describe it; even now, I cannot realize what I suffered then. Oh! it was dreadful…

Then, Belle, after abusing us, they went down in the room below. You may think you can imagine our feelings: first, we heard Uncle Henry's voice, then a pistol shot & a fall; we thought he was dead. But directly we heard his voice again, then a great struggle, a heavy fall, & dead silence! After a while the men rode off, & some went down. They had knocked Uncle H.'s face with a shovel, with their fists, & beaten his head against the wall, when, finding that they were killing him, he told where the gold was. Oh! it wasn't worth the anxiety we underwent.[22]

Naturally, *The History of the Fifteenth Pennsylvania Regiment* does not dwell on such incidents. Of the alcoholic refreshments at the Anderson Courthouse, the regimental history merely comments, "We got it all. Nearly all our men had a canteen full, and barrels of it were emptied in the gutters by standing orders from Gen. Stoneham [*sic*] who was fearful of its demoralizing effects on his troops." Apparently, the "whole force" had become intoxicated in North Carolina, and "Stoneman wanted no more of it."[23]

Certainly some of the Union officers tried to control their men, and the Reverend Adger reported seeing four of his light-fingered visitors being held as convicted thieves and prisoners.[24] There can be no doubt, however, that the Northern soldiers were guilty of considerable excesses. General William Palmer's May 6th report from Athens to Stoneman tells of sending Brown's brigade to guard all the crossroads, bridges, and ferries on the Tugaloo, "to feed there as long as possible without starving the people."[25] Forage was scarce, and Palmer recommended that Brown's men return to Tennessee as soon as could be arranged, for

> their officers for the most part have lost all control over their men. A large number of the men and some of the officers devote themselves exclusively to pillaging and destroying property. General Brown appears to have given them carte blanche in South Carolina, and they are so destitute of discipline that it cannot be restored in the field and while the command is living on the country.[26]

So went the Civil War adventures of people on the Tugaloo. Jarrett's bridge and Traveler's Rest were undoubtedly visited by a detachment of

Brown's rambunctious troops, as a letter written by Lizzie Lucas Jarrett to her niece, Zadie Jarrett, during those frightening days says,

> I am so anxious about the arrival of our "five hundred friends" that [I] shall have to defer our visit to Mrs. Jarres to another day. Na is going to Mr. Ramseys & Doyles come & go with her your Uncle K [Kennedy] has not come yet, & I had rather wait until he gets home as there is so much passing and confusion in the country. I wish I was a thousand men. I expect we will have to go to Milledgeville for arms & ammunition for the men say they "have none and someone ought to go."[27]

The Jarretts experienced further excitement in May, when Robert Toombs, a leading Georgia politician and member of the Confederate Cabinet as secretary of state, hid from Federal troops for a week at Joseph Prather's house. From Prather's, Toombs moved to hide at the Rembert's near Tallulah Falls, where he passed as Major Luther Martin and killed time by hunting deer. He soon fled the country by way of New Orleans and Cuba to Europe.[28]

Whatever actually happened at Traveler's Rest during the early May excitement, however, legends inevitably sprang up. Mary Jarrett White later offered this account of the Civil War days at Traveler's Rest:

> "Uncle Harry" the faithful negro slave took the twenty-two fine horses [these do not appear in the census schedules] to the woods where he said he would hide them from the Yankees. He kept them hidden three lonely months. He said "Miss Lizzie dey ain't no Yankee gwine to git dese horses long as I can hold a gun. I knows how to shoot same as dem old Yankees does."
>
> Harry was well taken care of during his long bigil [sic], food being taken to him by loyal slaves. Then came a sad day for Harry and all the Jarrett family. A "free nigger" which the Yankees picked up led them to where "Uncle Harry" and the beloved horses were hidden. They came by the house in a gallop waving and grinning at young mistress as they passed. "Uncle Harry" followed with tears streaming down his face he said, "Miss Lizzie, I sho am sorry, but I couldn't kill all dem Yankees. Dey was such a "garm" of the old devils which I believe riz up out of hell, whar dey will all go back to and I don't keer how soon." They took the meat that was buried, all the corn and wheat and killed the hogs and chickens and turkeys etc. They also took an old clock to pieces looking for money and valuables. Fortunately they did not burn the house which still stands. Nothing left for the family or porr [sic] negroes who were "Free."

This terrible blow was almost more than "Young Mistress" and "Young Master" could bear. Reconstruction and Carpet Bag days added to their other troubles.

A company of Yankees campted [*sic*] on the place near the Tugalo River toll bridge [Jarrett's] expecting to capture Jefferson Davis, but he evaded them and crossed the river several miles below.[29]

For plantation families such as the Jarretts, Adgers, Clemsons, and Bowens, difficult adjustments were just beginning, however. "The feeling of humiliation and constant apprehension I will not attempt to describe," wrote Mrs. Arthur M. Huger of Greenville.[30] With the defeat of the Confederacy, the Southern people's future became a maze of uncertainties. What would the conquerors do? Would the Rebels' land and other property he confiscated? And above all these questions loomed that of emancipation.

For Southern African-Americans, the future was just as uncertain as for their former masters, although perhaps not so ominous in some respects. When Clarissa Bowen wrote on May 1st that "the negroes are all much demoralized," she probably meant that they were excited, confused, and difficult to control. The former slaves were inclined to fraternize with the Union soldiers, and many African Americans left the area altogether. When rumors circulated that emancipation had somehow failed to be enacted by Congress, Clarissa wondered, "How will the negroes feel if things settle down and they are left as they were!"[31] This was not to occur, however, and blacks and whites were soon struggling to adjust to the irreversible end to slavery. Even for many former slaves who were accustomed to hard times, 1865 was a year of "bitter suffering and sorrow."[32] Clarissa Rosen reported, "our danger is now more from the poor people around us, than from the Yankees, as they are going about stealing what they please."[33]

In June of that year, the former rebels were forced to swear their allegiance to the federal government or lose their lands. Clarissa wrote,

We are conquered and the government is all powerful. How will they use that power? Perhaps they will deal gently, try to conciliate, but who knows! It is singular how in trying to avoid evils which are comparatively sell we plunge into unknown gulfs of misery and how little we reflect that it may be wiser to "bear those ills" we have, than to fly to "those we know not of." It seems to me that the mistake our people are making now is to indulge in guilty, sinful brooding over second causes. "If such and such things had not been done, we would have succeeded," they say, forgetting that they are thus dethroning God from Providential Sovereignty of HIS OWN WORLD. Forgetting that the Lord reigneth, they venture to dictate what the procedure of infinite love and wisdom should be. Let us beware lest we bring on ourselves a still more severe chastisement.[34]

Also in June, matters with the former slaves still had not been settled, and Clarissa's diary notes that the "negroes are so much demoralized that they will not work; fears are entertained that there will be but little corn made." Former masters had great difficulty in conceiving of their servants as free human beings, and Caroline Ravenel wrote upon imagining former slaves at her family home in Charleston: "Sometimes the idea is so ludicrous that I can't help laughing, & then again it is so dreadful, when I think of our old cook sitting up in the drawing room entertaining company!"[35]

Conditioned to horror at the idea of racial equality, the Southern whites were determined to keep African Americans in a state of inferiority and servitude. At Rivoli and Ashtabula, the Adgers and Bowens spent three days devising a contract for their house and field "people." The one-time household servants immediately signed, but the field hands were upset by the terms of the contract and delayed action. By morning, however, the lack of alternatives had prompted them to sign the proposal, by which the freed people agreed,

> to perform good faithful service as heretofore, submitting themselves in all respects to the control and direction of their former masters, never leaving the place without permission, abstaining from the use of liquor on the place and never becoming intoxicated while away. The former master on his part agreeing to give all, both workers and non-workers, good comfortable clothing, quarters, fuel, and medical attention as heretofore. The freedmen are to retain the products and patches of corn, gardens, chicken yards, etc. as heretofore.[36]

Such terms, dominated as they were by "as heretofores," make it easy to comprehend the field hands' reluctance to sign the agreement, and they must have wondered about the much-anticipated glories of freedom. Yet, undeniably, slavery had ill-equipped them to understand the concept of liberty, and believing that freedom meant "freedom from all restraint, surcease from all work,"[37] a great many expected to adopt the leisurely lifestyles of some of their former masters. On July 26th, Caroline Ravenel wrote a letter describing how, when presented with a work contract "the oldest negro on the place...was exceedingly indignant, & said Missis belonged to him, & he belonged to Missis, & he was not going to leave her...& he was not going to do any work either, except make a collar a week."[38]

Such attitudes as these ominously indicated that both races were to experience great difficulty in coping with the African Americans' freedom.

The Reverend John Adger resolved the dilemma for himself by sending his slaves away. In his memoirs, he wrote,

> I had announced to my slaves that they were all free. The coming of emancipation had been talked of all through the summer, and they had made inquiries about it of myself, and I had told them that, whenever it was determined, I should inform them of it. It was, perhaps, in August that the action of the State of South Carolina settled the question, and I told them I could no longer employ them, and that they must find homes for themselves. They were about thirty in number. One of them, a man named Morris, had a wife and a number of children, several of them grown boys. He alone of the whole number objected very much to the terms of their emancipation, having this large family to support. In general, they received the announcement with indifference. To Morris it seemed that the government had treated him very badly, in setting him free without "giving him a start," as he expressed it…The whole company very soon scattered, and I lost sight of them all.[39]

Others, however, felt a greater sense of responsibility toward their former slaves than did Adger. Considering his indifference, one need not wonder why his niece, Clarissa Bowen, was moved to comment: "Poor creatures. Truly the future looks dark for us, but it is blacker for them."[40]

Disappointingly few details have survived to tell of the travails and arrangements between the Jarrett family and their former slaves. Among the family papers are two contracts, faded with age, made between Charles Kennedy Jarrett and African American workers. One is nearly illegible in its entirety, but the other, made in August of 1865, bound Kennedy to pay Jasper Jarrett "five dollars per month to be paid in corn at (1) one dollar per bushel," or amounts [illegible figures] of pork and syrup. Jasper, on his part,

> binds himself to do good work at all times unless accidentally sick commencing work at sunrise and continue until sunset except two hours at twelve o'clock during the long days and one hour in the short day–said Jasper binds himself to keep good order at all times and to account for and return all tools which he may use when called for.[41]

Primary sources reveal many former slaveowners to have been neurotically sensitive about signs of African Americans' expectations of equality and potential arrogance, and Caroline Ravenel was offended at the idea of "colored belles" enjoying their freedom at picnics.[42] Another episode demonstrated the potential for overt hostility between the races, told by

Clarissa Bowen in her diary: "Col. Parker's negro threatened Mrs. P with an axe and when she pled for quietness for the sake of her son who was ill was told that they cared nothing for her son, that white people must now give way to coloured, etc....We begin to realize we are a conquered people and expect humiliations and insults." Clarissa's words were indeed accurate: "This is truly a world of change."[43]

In July of that year, Floride Clemson wrote that the Tugaloo was experiencing "a terrible drought, & many say the corn crop is already ruined… the prospect for winter is terrible. The negroes being free–almost everyone is turning them away by the hundreds to starve, plunder, & do worse. The times ahead a[re] fearful."[44]

Clarissa reported in October that the country was in a "very unsettled state." So-called "regulators" used violence to reinforce the racial "status quo ante-bellum." During this same period, Floride Clemson wrote that "this country is getting very unsafe. People are constantly called from their houses at night & shot." In mid-December, Floride was still pessimistic: "Every one expects trouble about Xmas: with the negroes, who expect land. Matters are pretty quiet now except casual disturbances and murders." Floride did not again mention her fears about starvation, so it is probable that shortages were not as extensive as she had predicted in July. By the summer of 1866, she was extremely anxious to leave Pendleton, and when her father, Thomas Calhoun, considered settling down at Calhoun's Fort Hill, she wrote, "One might as well be buried alive."[45]

Yet violence, uncertainty, despair, and dullness was not an unbroken pattern at the Tugaloo in the months after the end of the Civil War. In October of 1865, former General Wade Hampton was visiting the South Carolina side of the river, and a mock "tournament" was performed at Pendleton during his visit, attended by Clarissa Bowen, Floride Clemson, and perhaps some of the Jarretts. Hampton "looked and rode well as Don ____ in his blue velvet yellow satin and point lace," wrote Floride Clemson. "Calhoun [Clemson Calhoun] and young Ben Crawford were his knights, and the latter, Ivanhoe, won the crown and chose his queen of love, Miss Sue Lewis"—"a mere school girl," reported the piqued Floride.[46]

The Jarretts may or may not have been prepared to participate in such "chivalric" festivities at this time, however, as Kennedy Jarrett's barns, cotton gin, and mill had apparently been burnt during the springtime visit of the Yankees. Then, according to legend, "a storm blew down the carriage house where the coach was left and also the bridge was blown down."[47] Whatever the actual extent of the Jarretts' losses, Traveler's Rest and the Tugaloo Crossroads were never again to be as prosperous as in antebellum days.

# NOTES

[1] The upper age limit for military draft set by the Confederacy was originally thirty-five, but was soon raised to forty-five, then fifty in February, 1862. Governor Joseph Brown, who wanted Georgia to have an army of her own, got the legislature to pass a draft law conscripting all those from sixteen to sixty (December, 1863). Thomas P. Jarrett (born 1812) may have served in the "Rome Guard." Robert and Charles Kennedy's bad health precluded their active service. See Coulter, Georgia, *A Short History*, pp. 330-31. Confederate Microcards, Georgia Department of Archives and History; Lillian Henderson (ed.), *Roster of the Confederate Soldiers of Georgia* (Hapeville, Ga.: Longino & Forter, Inc., 1960), Vol. IV, p. 623.

[2] Traveler's Rest papers, Historic Preservation Section.

[3] Ibid.

[4] Ibid.

[5] Ibid.

[6] Ibid.

[7] Louise Ayer Vandiver, *Traditions and History of Anderson County* (Atlanta: Ruralist Press, Publishers, 1929), p. 237.

[8] Floride Clemson, *A Rebel Came Home*, Charles M. McGee, *Jr.*, and Ernest M. Lander, Jr. (eds) (Columbia, S.C.: University of South Carolina Press, 1961), p. 74.

[9] Vandiver, *Anderson County* , p. 238.

[10] Robert Jarrett papers at his home on Tugaloo, now in possession of the Henry and Elizabeth Hayes family.

[11] Ibid.

[12] Clemson, *A Rebel*, pp. 75, 77, 81, 83.

[13] *Official Records of the War of the Rebellion* (Washington, D.C.: Government Printing Office, 1897), Series I, Vol. XLIX, *Part I*, p. 546.

[14] Ibid.

[15] Ibid., pp. 547-50.

[16] Mary Stephenson (ed.), *The Diary of Clarissa Adger Bowen, Ashtabula Plantation, 1865: The Pendleton-Clemson Area, South Carolina, 1776-1889* (Pendleton: Research and Publication Committee, Foundation for Historic Research in the Pendleton Area, 1973), p. 73; Vandiver, *Anderson County*, p. 243.

[17] Stephenson, *Diary of Clarissa Adger Bowen*, p. 73.

[18] Stephenson, *Diary of Clarissa*, p. 73; Clemson, *A Rebel*, p. 81.

[19] Stephenson, *Diary of Clarissa;* John P. Alger, *My Life and Times* (Richmond: The Presbyterian Committee of Pblication, 1899), p. 339.

[20] Adger, *My Life,* pp. 342-43.

[21] Vandiver, *Anderson County,* p. 239.

[22] Daniel Elliott Huger Smith, ed., *Mason-Smith Family Letters* (Columbia, S.C.: University of South Carolina Press, 1950), pp. 211-12.

[23] Charles R. Kirk (ed.), *History of the Fifteenth Pennsylvania Volunteer Cavalry* (Philadelphia: 1906, no publisher), p. 512.

[24] Adger, *My Life,* p. 345.

[25] *Official Records,* Vol. XLIX, p. 551.

[26] Ibid.

[27] Traveler's Rest papers, Historic Preservation Section.

[28] Pleasant A. Stovall, *The Life of Robert Toombs* (New York: Cassell Publishing Company, 1892), pp. 304-07.

[29] Traveler's Rest papers, Historic Preservation Section.

[30] Smith, *Mason-Smith Family Letters,* p. 206.

[31] Stephenson, *Diary of Clarissa Adger Bowen*, p. 73.

[32] Ibid., p. 74.

[33] Ibid.

[34] Ibid., p. 75.

[35] Ibid.

[36] Stephenson, *Diary of Clarissa Adger Bowen*, p. 77.

[37] Coulter, *Georgia: A Short History*, p. 350.

[38] Smith, *Mason-Smith Family Letters*, p. 181.

[39] Adger, *My Life*, pp. 345-46.

[40] Stephenson, *Diary of Clarissa Adger Bowen*, p. 76.

[41] Traveler's Rest papers, Historic Preservation Section.

[42] Smith, *Mason-Smith Family Letters*, p. 181.

[43] Stephenson, *Diary of Clarissa Adger* Bowen, pp. 76, 79.

[44] Clemson, *A Rebel*, p. 93.

[45] Stephenson, *Diary of Clarissa Alger Bowen*, p. 79; Clemson, *A Rebel*, pp. 95, 96, 105. The Ku Klux Klan, violent defenders of "white supremacy," first appeared in Georgia in 1868. They were especially virulent in north Georgia; Coulter, *Georgia: A Short History*, p. 371.

[46] Stephenson, *Diary of Clarissa Adger Bowen*, p. 80; Clemson, *A Rebel*, p. 94.

[47] Traveler's Rest papers, Historic Preservation Section.

# Chapter 10

## Traveler's Rest During Reconstruction

This chapter in the history of Traveler's Rest and the Tugaloo Crossroads is the story of Charles Kennedy Jarrett's family, a story told in tax and land records, a handful of letters, and legends. Although the tax and land records show a slowly shrinking property, the letters offer almost no clues as to the causes of this decline. The fact that the South as economically devastated by the Civil War was surely a contributing factor in the Jarretts' financial woes, which were worsened by crop losses in 1865, 1866, and 1867. Since Traveler's Rest was no longer at a crossroads, perhaps the lack of passersby had as much to do with the Jarretts' fortunes as it did with the demise of the stagecoach inn. In any case, the break-up of the South's large plantations was, as E.M. Coulter puts it, "inevitable" after the end of slavery.[1]

It seems logical to connect the decay of Traveler's Rest as an inn with a general decline in travel in northeast Georgia. Apparently, the glorious "Grand Tour" of antebellum days was no longer so attractive to those who could afford it (or not within the means of those who wished to go). The Tallulah Falls Hotel, approximately twenty miles away, frequently mentioned in early travel accounts, was defunct by 1874, when George Walton Williams's *Nacoochie and Its Surroundings* referred travelers to "Mrs. A's," six miles from the falls. Mrs. A did not keep a hotel, but "accommodates travelers to the best of her ability." Williams relayed the innkeeper's complaint that travelers were too often fault-finding and that they should realize that in the upcountry towns, no guests would come for days, and then they would come in a flood and expect too much of their hosts.[2]

The Civil War cost Charles Kennedy Jarrett his slaves, but it left him with a good family and a sizable farm. He still owned several thousand acres on the Tugaloo, but if the barns, bridge, and carriage house were down, it would have cost quite a bit to replace them. The bridge, at least, was replaced.[3]

The South was a conquered territory, and a new relationship would have to be established with the federal government. President Lincoln had planned that formerly rebellious Southerners could regain full citizenship by applying for a pardon and taking an oath to support the Constitution and the Union. After Lincoln's assassination, President Andrew Johnson continued this program of pardoning, although excluding from amnesty fourteen classes of persons who were required to write special requests for pardon. Kennedy Jarrett wasted little time in dispatching this letter:

> Georgia, Habersham County
> To his Excellency Andrew Johnson President of the United States of America The application of Charles K. Jarrett of said County most respectfully sheweth, that he is forty five years old five 01 inches high blue eyes. Auburn hair fair complextion weight 175 lbs. Post office address "Walton's Ford Habersham Co. Georgia" That he comes under the first class of exceptions contained in your proclamation of the 29th May 1865 by reason of having been the Post Master at Walton's Ford Habersham Co. Ga. an office that he had long held for the convenience of the neighborhood before and after the beginning of the revolution. In the year 1864 he was also purchasing agent buying beef cattle for the use of the Army. With regard to the property qualification. At the time the State of Georgia passed what is commonly called the Ordinance of Secession, He was worth more than twenty thousand dollars including slaves. He is not now worth twenty thousand Dollars though other persons might estimate his property worth more. No proceedings have been instituted against him that [he] is aware of. I am a farmer by occupation. And now accept the existing state of affairs intending in good faith to abide the law and the Constitution. As the best evidence of his future conduct. He respectfully refers you to the annexed Oath which he has sollemly [sic] taken and And [sic] intends faithfully to keep, and observe. Therefore he most respectfully asks, and makes application for pardon and that he may be restored to the rights and privileges of a citizen.
>
> Respectfully subscribed<br>
> *Charles K. Jarrett*<br>
> Aug. 18th, 1865[4]

The acreage indicated for Jarrett in the 1870 Census Agricultural Schedule (100 acres) cannot be correct, as it differs greatly from the 1870s tax digests (3,700 acres). The war had cost Kennedy considerably in livestock. In 1870, he had four horses, five cows, two oxen, eleven cattle, thirty sheep, and eighty hogs, and the family grew only 800 bushels of corn, three bushels of peas and beans, 140 of oats, ten of rye, forty of wheat, twenty of Irish potatoes, and 100 of sweet potatoes. The farm also produced 100 gallons of molasses, 100 pounds of honey, eight pounds of wax, thirty pounds of wool, and 400 pounds of butter.[5]

The Census Population Schedule offers an idea of the plantation's household. By 1870 Kennedy and Lizzie had four children, and also residing with them were Lizzie's mother, two women named Duke, and an African American cook, Mickey Jarrett.[6]

The 1870 Population Schedule also provides some scanty details concerning a handful of the Jarrett and Prather freed people. A few of the African Americans had laboring skills which kept them out of the fields, including Coleman Prather, a stone-and-brick mason; Mickey Jarrett, the Jarretts' cook; Henry Jarrett, a miller; and Brown Jarrett, a blacksmith. Most, however, are listed as farm hands. The Agricultural Schedules slightly augment this meager information; while no freed people are listed in the 1870 schedule, four men are named in the 1880 schedule. "R. Jarrett" rented a small farm of twenty acres, and James Prather, and William and Jasper Jarrett were sharecroppers. The latter three operated fifteen- to twenty-acre farms, on which they grew corn, oats, and a bit of wheat and sweet potatoes. William added cotton and sorghum to his production, as well as six sheep.[7]

This information, sketchy as it is, conforms to the data which appears in Alan Conway's *The Reconstruction of Georgia*. As that work points out, Southern blacks and whites were bonded by proximity, affection, and economic necessity, simultaneously at odds because of racial antipathy and conflicting interests. At the war's end, Georgia did not immediately enact a harsh "black code" like Mississippi's, but the state's grudging provisions for the freed people's legal status were designed to keep "the Negro in political oblivion, social inferiority, and superficial legal equality." In the emotional confusion of the situation, some white Georgians bitterly predicted race war or wishfully forecasted the extinction of African Americans. A writer in Clarkesville decreed: "The race will die out—in 50 years a black face will be as rare as an Indian's is now."[8]

The African Americans' situation tended to substantiate old American ideas concerning the importance of personal property and social mobility for a free people. In short, what ex-slaves, whose training was almost entirely farming, needed most was land. Unfortunately, those who held the land had strong reasons for not wanting former slaves to obtain any of it. On the one hand, the prevalent racial ideology included the belief that African Americans could not farm independently; on the other, the freed people's acquisition of land would have necessitated some program of confiscation, simultaneously rendering the much-needed labor force less available and tractable.[9]

Sharecropping, the system arrived at for Traveler's Rest and for most of the South, is explained by Conway as "a compromise which enabled Southern whites to keep control of the land and with it Negro labor, but also a system which enabled labor to be obtained without wages," for which the landowners lacked capital. Sharecropping was a product of necessity—as seen by the landowners—the necessity of preserving white supremacy and holding on to the land. For the African Americans, it was a poor substitute for the acquisition of their own acreage. As a Georgia planter observed in 1867, "They [African Americans] will almost starve and go naked before they will work for a white man if they can get a patch of ground to live on and get from under his control." An ex-slave added, "As soon as we can buy two or three acres of land and build a cabin on it, we will work for ourselves and work hard." Even those African Americans who managed to struggle into an economic position to buy land, however, had trouble obtaining it from the reluctant whites.[10]

When combined with the devastation of the backward Southern economy, the African Americans' economic helplessness and the whites' determination to preserve it were sufficient to perpetuate Southern poverty for generations. Both races were trapped—the whites surrounding themselves with "indolent, thriftless, irresponsible tenants" whose attitudes could only be improved by opportunities for social mobility, a solution the whites dismissed out of hand because it threatened white supremacy. This trap had unfortunate consequences for the people of Traveler's Rest, as the economic woes of the South were visited upon the inhabitants of the Tugaloo Crossroads.

Apparently the Burnett Gold Mine no longer produced enough to keep the Jarretts "flush." Here again, the documentary material is piecemeal and disappointing, but the evidence does show that the Jarrett-Patton partnership to mine the property continued. During the Civil War, in September of 1863, Jarrett and James Patton made another agreement for maintaining the partnership. The contract does not explain why a new arrangement was needed, but since all the originally-named Pattons had disappeared from the new document, it can be surmised that the former partners had died. Patton and Jarrett agreed in this contract to work a mine on 900 acres located on Bean Creek in Habersham County, "being the tract or tracts recently owned by Jesse Siler, the late Patton, the late D. Jarrett." Full authority was given to Kennedy to work the mine for a quarter share for twelve years while Patton was to receive $\frac{1}{28}$ of all gold or other metal mined.[11]

A scrap of paper shows that in February of 1867, E. L. Patton and C. K. Jarrett agreed to terms on selling the Burnett Mine; if they sold it for $30,000, the two would receive a commission of $5,000 each; for every additional $10,000, they would be commissioned $5,000 more.[12] These plans, however, were never consummated.

For a few years, Jarrett and Patton nursed high hopes that the mine would make them a small fortune. By October of 1867, the men were excited about a possible $100,000 purchaser from New York, and in a fit of enthusiasm, Patton suggested to Jarrett that it might be wise to hold out for $250,000, inasmuch as all New York was interested in Georgia gold, or so Patton thought. Jarrett had apparently expressed some urgent need to raise money, however, and was considering a Kentucky company's offer of $30,000, for Patton requested that Jarrett hold out, if at all possible. He even offered to buy out Kennedy's share for $30,000 if Kennedy had to have cash so desperately, in order to prevent the latter from selling to anyone else.[13] Instead of this course, in December of 1867, Jarrett sold Edmund Patton of Abbeville District, South Carolina, one-fifth of the Burnett Gold Mine—"being two lots of land," Lots 23 and 24 in the third district, Habersham County, for $3,840.[14] This transaction, however, did not involve the total of the Jarretts' interest in the Burnett Mine, and on February 18, 1871, E. L. Patton wrote to Kennedy that he was not "adverse" to leasing the Burnett Mine for a short time. Patton was much more eager to sell the property, though, saying that if they had to rent, it would be preferable to do business with the "man from New York City" rather than with the "German," who might be an "adventurer." Patton urged Kennedy not to become discouraged, noting that "the mine is *immensely* valuable, and can be sold for, at least, one hundred thousand dollars." The property would be even more precious after the Atlanta and Charlotte Railroad and the road from Athens to Clarkesville were completed.[15]

An 1872 letter to [illegible] in New York City from Kennedy Jarrett also involved the Jarrett gold. He wrote, "I have visited the Nacoochee Gold Mine for specimens to send you. But there being no work going on and the tunnels being all filled up I could not obtain a suitable specimen. I expect to commence again there about the first of next year when I shall be able to send you specimens [illegible] the mine."[16]

The family letters suggest that Jarrett went to New York in the 1870s, but if so, he failed to sell the mine while there. Shortly after his death, Lizzie deeded her family's remaining share to A.K. Childs and Reuben Nickerson of Clarke County, for $1,500. The deed says that Elizabeth "assigns twentieth one undivided six (6/20) interest in lots 23 & 24 in 3rd district of originally Habersham known as Jarrett's Gold Mine (500 acres)."[17] So far as is known, this transaction ended the Jarrett family's career in gold-mining.

Not one to give up his wealth easily, Kennedy Jarrett tried a number of plans to reverse his family's dwindling fortunes. Realizing the importance of reestablishing the Tugaloo Crossroads, he took an active interest in the arrival of the railroad. The Atlanta and Richmond Airline Railroad Company was formed in 1870, in order to complete a line between those cities, through the Tugaloo area. Perhaps because the South was so economically troubled, however, the tracks only reached the spot which then became

Toccoa by the summer of 1873. Tracks were to run right across the Jarrett farm, and in August of 1871, Jarrett sold 500 acres of land just east of Toccoa to the A&R Airline Railroad for $750. On the same day, he deeded the railroad 100 feet on each side of the projected tracks in return for $5.00 and the benefits he would derive from the construction of the railroad. In addition to securing free, lifetime passes for his family, Kennedy was apparently interested in having the tracks close enough to Traveler's Rest so he could hear the trains go by.[18]

In October of that year, Kennedy wrote to an acquaintance, the Reverend C. D. Smith, about the proposed route. Jarrett pointed out that "crossing the Tallulah Cr. near the juncture of the two rivers, passing within two miles of this place, striking the ridge between the Tugalo and Broad River, some 8 or 9 miles from here" would be a considerably shorter route than the proposed one by way of Tallulah Falls.[19] Actually, the Atlanta & Richmond Airline Railroad crossed the Tugaloo just below Ward's Creek, then it crossed that creek and ran along it toward Toccoa.

During this same period, Kennedy also looked into getting the Tugaloo River improved for navigation. Progressive Southerners had realized that one key to the recovery of the South's economy lay in programs of internal improvements. During these years of "Reconstruction," the United States Congress had acquired the habit of handing out subsidies to encourage the development of the country; unfortunately, most of these appropriations went to the West and not the South, even after the Presidential election and the Compromise of 1876, which guaranteed internal improvements for the South. The defeated section was not wellfavored in Republican circles; therefore, when Kennedy approached his congressman, H.P. Bell, about improving the Tugaloo in 1874, he was doomed to disappointment. Bell replied that appropriations could not be had in the current session, but advised that Jarrett continue his efforts. Kennedy did so, as a follow-up letter from Bell in the winter of 1874-75 attests, but apparently the results Kennedy expected did not occur.[20]

Perhaps the depression of the mid-1870s made Jarrett desperate. Clearly, he was casting about for ways to make money during this time. A curious letter from an A.R. Ewing in November of 1876 shows that Jarrett was looking far and wide for economic opportunities. Ewing, "comfortably seated in front of one of my Patent Chimneys," wondered if Jarrett would be ready to start selling them soon. Kennedy was offered "full control of the state" as his sales territory. Ewing apparently was a family friend, for he concluded: "When is Sally G. coming—all join in Love to all." No other evidence has been found regarding this enterprise, however, so it probably did not flourish.[21]

In March of 1876, Kennedy ended his ten-year retirement from the postmastership. The Walton's Ford post office had been discontinued at

Jarrett's retirement during 1866, but it was reinstated later that year with J.T. Mulkey as postmaster. Mary Duke, a Jarrett dependent, became post-mistress the following year, but the office was again discontinued in 1869. Mulkey was reestablished in a couple of months and held the post until Jar-rett returned to the position in 1876. The name of the station was changed to Tugaloo in 1874, and Charles Patton Jarrett succeeded his father as post-master in 1879.[22]

The family letters provide a few glimpses of the Jarretts' personal lives. The girls were sent to school in Athens, and the boys were sent away to school, also, perhaps attending Americanna School near Adairsville, Ga. In 1874, Kennedy got a letter from the master offering to receive Jarrett's sons at any time: "I have a very clean set of boys and young men with me now," he stated, "and think your sons will find their associations here *very* pleas-ant, while I will do all I can to promote their intellectual and moral culture." Kennedy may have decided against Adairsville, however, for it appears that Charles Patton was already attending college at Athens. A letter dated April 27, 1872, to Kennedy from Miller Lumpkin offered to get young Charles a scholarship to Athens, and to qualify, he needed only to be able to read and "cipher." The Jarretts apparently applied in haste, for the acceptance of fourteen-year-old Charles Patton is dated May 1, 1872.[23]

Other family letters written during the depression years give impres-sions of life during Reconstruction. The family appears to have been strug-gling to adjust to an economic decline—but certainly not having "to do without," as were many neighbors. A letter from Grace Lucas to her daugh-ter "Lissie" [Lizzie] at Traveler's Rest, dated December 7, 1866, is interest-ing. Mrs. Lucas showed a nineteenth-century person's preoccupation with health: "Lissie's" brother was suffering from "gastrick fever," confined to his room, and not expected "to be himself" until after Christmas. As for Grace herself, "I am taking a bad cold but hope to avert it by taking gum goac-cum." She planned to visit the Tugaloo as soon as would be convenient to Lizzie, and she asked her daughter to make Sally Grace, Lizzie's ten-year-old daughter, a "cloack or jack" out of Grace's old cloak. Lizzie must have still done her own sewing, for her mother continued, "I have sent some scraps of cloth & have some more for you which will help to make it out but I think you can get a sack cloth out of it and trim it with velvit [sic] ."[24]

Apparently some hogs had recently been slaughtered at the Jarrett farm, for Grace commented, "I wish we had some of your hog killing doings here. Fred has no hogs to kill he had three to kill but killed them some time ago." The Jarretts also slaughtered some sheep, about which Grace queried, "Did you try any mutton hams, they are as good as venison."

Lizzie's mother was also helping with preparations for Christmas at Traveler's Rest:

I will try to get some little things for the Children, there was no money left after getting the things you wrote for, I borrowed three dollars and a quarter from Brother Jefferson, two dollars for a pair of shoes for Charley and one and a quarter to pay Mr. Weatherly for tuition. I have two dollars that I borrowed from Frederick which I Intend to get some things with for the Children for Christmas. I want to go into town [Athens] tomorrow and get them & leave them at the store so they can be sent by the first opportunity, I wish I had money to get you a good many things, did the things I sent in the bundle get there safe [They were to be sent from the Lucas store in Athens by wagon up to the Tugaloo.]…I sent some clothes and a good many other things, some little doll things and ribbons I believe for Sally G. Sally ought to have some flowers in front of her hat or some small plumes.

Grace added in the letter that she would buy as many "things" as "my money will get which will not be much."

Another letter from Grace, written five years later, continues the saga of Jarrett family life. It, too, stresses matters of health:

My Dear Lissie

I intended to have written you a long Letter this time but have Commenced this for a note only as I do not feel well enough to write much. I hope I shall get a letter from you this evening as it is regular Mail Day, I was up at Sarah's on Saturday evening I did not go in the house as it was late, she was looking for Mr. Prather home that evening but I have not heard wether [sic] he came or not She said she would send me word how you all were, I want to hear how you all have got with your Colds, and how much Sally Grace weighs and how tall and large Mary Lissie is as you have never sent me her Measure yet, did Sally G Come home and how did her and her visitors enjoy themselves did they go to the fall tell Sally to write to me and give me a description of the trip and the names of the Company that came home with them did Charly [sic] and Freddie go with them— have you any school at there yet if you do not get a Teacher before Commencement I expect you can get a good one among the Graduates, what church does Sally attend I hope she has not lost any of the good impressions made on he[r] mind two years ago, how does the Preacher Mr. Worley get on with his congregation I hope they are all doing well, there is a great Italian or something now in Augusta quite a number of Athenians returned yesterday Monday, the schools generally had and are still having Picknicks [sic] instead of May parties they have one they call a festival but have no queen it is great saving of expense, I told your Aunt Mary and Helen what you said about going to the Franklin Springs they say it is two [sic] lonesome and solitary they say all you invalids ought to go to the liveliest place you could find to cheer up your spirits, Helen is not well. She looks very bad indeed she is almost as poor as I am, and Dick is sick with a bad cold, he Just returned from Canida [sic] a few day past and took a Violent Cold. The knight [sic] before he got home he said he did not have a pain nor on the while he was gone, he Laid down and went to sleep and sombody [sic] hoisted a window over him and he has a most dreadful Cold your Brothers family are all pretty well my health is not verry [sic] good nor has it been for some time, I wish I knew whether you were going to the Springs or not and if you are when you will go as I want to go by Mr. Clevelands to see sister if I can Frederick says he will send me there any time that I wish to go. I do not feel well enough to travel much now without it was in a comfortable way, Cannot you come down your self and stay a while it would help you as much as the Springs at present and go to the Springs in the heat of Sumer Come if you possibly can Mr Singletons health is verry bad indeed She [sic] cannot walk across the room without help and she has a dreadful Cough Mat thinks of going to see he next week She is in Griffen [sic] at Mr Winkfelds.

Sue Kellom is no better do not think she will ever be able to get away from Macon there is a great Deal I want to write if I could think of it let me know if you come down or if you can meet me at your Aunties when will Mr. Jarrett come down when any of you come put a pillow in the Carriage, how is your Fruit and Vegetable did the Frost injure them tell your Folks to raise a great many Tomatoes [sic] how did your potted Fruits keep, if it is Convenient have two pair of gine cotton stockings knit for me, tell my Dear Boys they must make a crop of Some king [sic] how does their Ducks Come on and how many Chickens have they and who is the chicken feeder Freddy is the chicken raiser he takes care of the eggs sets them and takes them off when they hatch they have upwards of a hundred chickens whitish or gray Colour something like Mrs. Kellys only larger they must give Mary Lissie one hen and Chickens and let her have the proceeds of it for her own all your kinsfolks and Friends here send much Love to you and I do the same I wish I was at home with you all my Love to all and every body that knows or cares for me, I am at Brothers at this time they are preparing to Lay the corner stone of the Souldiers [sic] Monument on Friday next I expect there will be a great many people here to see it it [sic] will be put where the Old liberty pole stood I have not written half what I want to but must stop for want of strength to proceed Bless you all your affectionate Mother. G Lucas[25]

Lizzie Lucas Jarrett always seemed to be in bad health, and to combat her chronic illnesses, she would try to recuperate at a health springs. Three letters among the Jarrett family papers were written from Lizzie to her husband and mother from Franklin Springs, a sizable health resort nine miles southeast of Carnesville. On Saturday (no year given), Lizzie wrote to Grace:

> Ma, You don't know how bad & lonely I felt after Mr. Jarrett left me [at the springs] that day—the Baby [Mary Elizabeth] cried to go home to see & Grand Ma & all the folks & her daughter & poor Buddy Freddie & Charlie & Cousin Mollie was a bad girl didn't put any pockets in babys apron. Mrs. Duke cried too, but she has got reconciled. & I laughed and cried too. I thought it best to stay, but I don't think it will do me much good.

She had been "right sick" the night Kennedy left, she said, "& on friday was quite sick with one of those weak nervous spells and bad feeling in my stomach & breast." Lizzie apparently knew what to do in the face of such distress, however: "Mr. Bond gave me some Asafoeteday [sic] & taking other things I got over it and slept well last night." Her weak stomach prevented a healthy appetite. Half-hearted about her stay at Franklin Springs, she said in one sentence she might as well go home, and the next, she suggested that Sally Grace get her father to "bring her and her books down here." Lizzie's unpunctuated style of writing touched upon many aspects of her life:

> Tell Mickey [the cook] to Make a nice loaf of Bread & send down by Mr. Jarrett if the flour is not nice enough get enough of nice to make a loaf & send a part of it. I guess all got back from the shore I was sorry Mrs. Duke could not go I do want to see you all so bad I have been uneasy about you fearing you would get sick but be careful with yourself & maybe you will get on a spell. I wish you could be down here I think it would help you. The baby is fat as she can be she talks about you all all the time...There is a Jar of Marshmellons in Brine [probably pickled watermelon rind] in the pantry I think if they are not all spoilt fill one of those small gallon jars with some of the nicest & send down by Mr. Jarrett when he comes down...I wish I had some of the bitters Dr. Doyle gave me but I cannot get it now & I'll get some from Athens this week.[26]

On Sunday evening, Lizzie wrote to "Dear Father," apparently her nickname for her husband: "You don't know how lonely I felt after you left me that morning. The baby cried to go home with Father. Mrs. Duke cried & I had to do all sorts of aways to keep from crying right it is so lonesome."

Mrs. Williams, the landlady at Franklin Springs, was nice, Lizzie said, but in bad health,

> almost as bad as I am. & we have no way to take any exercise only to walk & we have n t much strength for that & it has been so cool I can not take much water not over a dipper full in the day if that much & then even it makes me feel an oppressed or crowded feeling in my stomach. I have no taste or relish for water at all though I drink as much as can & try to get better.

Lizzie went on to suggest that she would like to come home to "you & the children," and indeed her plight appears pitiful:

> You don't know what a desolate feeling it is to be away off from home & family sick like I am if I felt that I was improving any, it would be different but as it is, I don't see much use in staying here on expenses, but it seems that I am just an expense now any how, & any where, but if we had a school here & I could have the children with me, & see you I could do better, but dear Father to be from there all the time now, when I feel so bad, & feel that I cannot get well, & will soon have to leave them forever & when there [sic] company & yours would be such a great comfort to me, is a sad desolate feeling.

Nevertheless, Lizzie reconciled herself to staying at the springs. "I will try to be satisfied…I wish I had some of the Bitters Dr. Doyle gave me. I have only Dogwood now." She cheered up then and made a few requests: "I wish I had some of our grits ground fine & some more of that beef—if there is any bring me a piece of it, I'v [sic] no fish nor squirrels yet, & bring me a bottle of whiskey."[27] About this time, Kennedy wrote to daughter Sally Grace: "Mother & Baby is at the Franklin Springs—will not be here until you come home… Budy [Charles Patton Jarrett] is suffering. Has two boils on Him."[28]

Another letter from Grace Lucas to Lizzie on January 22, 1871, provides a further glimpse of the Jarretts during Reconstruction. She commented that she expected a visit from the Prathers [Kennedy's sister, Sarah Ann, and her husband Joseph] and hoped

> You would either bring or send Sally Grace with them to go to school to Madame Scomaska. She has the reputation of a first Teacher, do

send her off someplace that she can have good advantages for she is loseing [*sic*] precious time that can never be regained she is getting too old to lose any more.

The letter also mentions that "Mr. Jarrett" was about to go to New York, and next Grace referred to "the Dear little Mary Lissie," who later claimed not to have chosen that name for herself until she was eight years old, having been born in 1866 or 1868. Grace passed on some salutations, including one from an old friend, Mrs. Childs, perhaps the wife of the Childs who bought the gold mine.

Do try to send them furs down as soon as possible and I will get yours made anyhow and Sally Gs if I can and get some more skins if you can…Tell Mary Lissie never mind she shall have a fine horse and saddle when she gets large enough to ride…And sister Sallie shall have one also and when Brothers are done going to school they shall have a fine horse and saddle apiece and ride with their sister to church and anywhere they please.[29]

In 1875, Lizzie received from her concerned brother, F.W. Lucas, a letter in which he said he had heard that Kennedy's bridge (in Clarkesville?) and "part of his land is advertised for sale and imagining that you are all in trouble." Lucas would have been glad to lend them something, he said, but was himself broke. This came during the national depression of the mid-1870s, which hit the South especially hard. Lucas wondered if Kennedy was selling to meet old debts, which he thought had been paid, and he advised that it was a rather bad time to sell at public auction. Jarrett, Lucas said, should pay off the debt with some kind of property at "fair valuation rather than have it sacrificed." Apparently Lucas found relief from the troubled times through religion: "We had a glorious meeting at our church a short time since when the holy spirit was manifest in our midst."

Returning to the family troubles, Lucas commented, "He [God] may find it best to take our property in order to humble us…and to save our souls and to save our children." No post-Civil War evidence remains concerning the stagecoach tavern or the country store, but it is possible that the harsh times of the 1870s may have driven them out of business.[30]

In 1874, the Jarretts had their last child, George Devereaux. While the older boys attended the state college at Athens, Lizzie apparently brought the children to live there during the school term. The following letter was written to Kennedy, who remained at Traveler's Rest:

Friday Night

Dear Father

I wrote this morning but did not say all I wanted to say—I wanted to tell you we could not all go in the wagon at one time, there will be 8 of us & Sarah wants her trunk & we will be obliged to carry some of our clothes cant help it we must have them & then about the house it will be bad to have to pay rent for the two months we are gone, it will not do, I was just thinking if you could rent the house from the time in July we go home till winter it would be better for me & all but the boys to go home & stay I can do more at home than up here but if I come back I shall take boarders get Mr. Winefry to attend to it & collect the board for me, I am so uneasy about you have not heard a word from you since you left us & have heard such bad accounts of freshets the Bridge, railroad, Wheat, & every thing else that it keeps me almost in a fever, write to me all about it or get Cousin William to write tell him not to send any more papers for we do not get any at all. What have you done about the Dooly case get it all fixed right father before you leave get it done yourself & dont trust any one you know every one is for himself & you will have to start up here before the first Teusday [sic] & if there is a single gap left open they will jump right in try & get it fixed up. Chickens up here are 20cts & very scarse [sic], no butter no eggs, dont know how they would sell, every one is busy as can be getting ready for Commencement. I am sitting up in my soon old dress & look like a little whipperwill [sic] I am so thin but I will soon fatten up, am getting a good appetite & getting so can walk about & will do the best I can for us all. I can eat meat & corn bread there have been some nice Beef & Mutton but I didnt get any. You had better bring what eggs, butter, & chickens you can from home, for you cant get them nor fresh meat without money—& bring all the vegetables you can—cabbage, beets, potatoes (irish) & any thing else you can get, apples too for we can cook them & every thing of that kind has to be brought up here you will have to begin several days ahead to get up what you need. That Miss Julia Wills that was so sick when you were here died this morning she was taken sick before George was. George is as fat as he ever was I believe, he is doing finely Baby is improving too both have splendid appetites. Let me know about the cloths for Charlie P immediately, if you have got no money I dont know what they will do for Bud has to speak & I think Freddie too. They all have to be out on the stage, let me know what to do. Ill send him out to see if he can get a cheaper suit, but he thought that was a good & a nice suit too. & would last well. I hope you have been successful in finding some one who wants to get a mine or will let you have something for it Col Hand & his party have not returned yet. I didnt know they were gone till today, have some more Honey taken before it gets too late. ours is nearly gone. bring us butter & eggs if you dont chickens, but I think if you can you had better bring all from home. If you cant leave home or Clarksville [sic] till after the first Teusday [sic] in July you had better let Jack or some one who knows the fords start Friday with the wagon for we have nothing much here to eat now I will write I dont [want] to worry you dear Father but it is so far off—& I cant see you & when you were hear [sic] it hurt me to talk or any one to talk to me & these things ought to be attended to before sunday week as that is the commencement Sunday, first Sunday in July & it is nearly here so please write just as soon as you get this, & tell me your plans How is Brother Patton. give our love to him children all send love to you & all, write immediately or get Cousin W_____.

I wish I was with you tonight or all the time for I know you bothered almost to death, & the way we are fixed up we can be not much comfort to you.

Good night darling, your
Affectionate wife
*Lizzie*[31]

Among Kennedy Jarrett's papers can be found a highly interesting character evaluation, "a "Phrenological Chart of Character" by William A. Lore. Kennedy's skull contours apparently produced this evaluation of a long list of qualities. He was only "moderately" endowed with "veneration," "tune," and "marvelousness," and he was "average" in his secretiveness, destructiveness, "ideality," weight, time, and "eventuality;" but fully "pro-genitive," "inhabitive," concentrative, "alimentative," acquisitive, self-esteemed, conscientious, benevolent, constructive, mirthful, "localized," "languaged," and "causualtied." When it came to "amativeness," adhesiveness," combativeness, cautiousness, "aprobativeness," hopefulness, firmness, "sublimeness," imitation, individualization, calculation, form, color, and order, Kennedy was downright "large." Furthermore, he was "very largely" endowed with comparison and size. The phrenologist noted that Jarrett should marry a person of "nevous [sic] temperment," and that Kennedy's own nervous temperment "gives acute and fine preception [sic] with great mental activity, but when pure, lacks the capacity for long endurance."[32]

Perhaps this "nervous temperment" accounts for Kennedy's death at the age of fifty-eight, but whatever he died of, it was apparently lingering and painful. A letter that seems to be about his death mentions a visit to the unknown writer in Orlando, Florida:

When he wrote me he was going to be operated upon I gave him up, for I felt sure he could not stand it; he had one very severe spell while he was here, sometimes I did not think he could stand the suffering many hours, but Mr. Austin bathed him every night, and we all waited on him day and night—rendering every possible comfort.[33]

Kennedy's main concern seems to have been that "he might sometime [sic] become a burden to his children." The Jarrett papers yield a yellowed newspaper clipping which includes an obituary for Kennedy. In a typical, flattering style, it is an outstanding example of late nineteenth-century journalistic prose:

## IN MEMORIAM

Death, has again visited the house of affection, and borne their best loved one away. How strange it seems, how hard to realize, that the form of one who has been associated with our childhoods earliest recolections [sic] now sleeps in the silent tomb. Mr. C.K. Jarrett, whose name is a synonym for tender hearted kindness has gone from us forever. Death came as a strange guest into the family circle; although the weary sufferer had been fading from their sight for many days, yet when the messenger came and bore the kind husband and loving father away, fond hearts were shattered as if suddenly awaken[ed] to the "coming of the bridgroom [sic]." He will be sadly missed we know full well, first, by the sorrowing wife who for twenty years has walked beside him sharing his pleasures and weeping his tears; Then by his children who will arise and call him blessed, and again by the sick and suffering of the whole community to whom he was ever an earnest sympathizing friend, his great heart reaching out to all who were cast down. May the blessed reflection—that the dear one is not lost but gone before—shed a bright ray of hope and consolation through the gloom that now overshadows the desolate household. Oh, thou who hath said earth bath no sorrows that Heaven cannot heal, grant comfort to the bereaved, and mercifully show that whom thou Invest thou scourgest. Telegraphy of soul to Heaven should be so perfect that the subtlest touch of the hand Divine should bid us respond. Speak Lord thy servant heareth. Submission of our will to His, tunes our hearts within us like a sacred harp that knows no touch, but hands Divine; that breathes the melodies of Paradise alone and throbs its most triumphant strains as earth recedes and Heaven lies open to the view. Faith leads us to believe that this was the blessed experience of this noble man.

Mamie P.***[34] [The asterisks appear in the clipping.]

No will has been discovered for Charles Kennedy Jarrett, but the following is his appraisement, dated August of 1877:

| | | | |
|---|---|---|---|
| one yoke of oxen | 35.00 | 2 men saddle | 5.00 |
| 2 broken wagons | 25.00 | plow gears | 5.00 |
| 1 old stage | 15.00 | lot of plows and plow stocks | 15.00 |
| 1 spring wagon | 20.00 | lot weeding hoes | 1.25 |
| 1 old buggy | 5.00 | 3 ditching shovels | 1.00 |
| 1 corn sheller | 3.00 | 2 cross cut saws | 5.00 |
| 1 lot of hogs | 125.00 | 2 [?] | 1.00 |
| 9 sheep (in the woods) | 9.00 | 2 drawing knives, 2 augers, | |
| Bull, Cow, & calf | 15.00 | hand saw & & foot adge | |
| Red Bull, cow & calf | 15.00 | brace, sundry small tools | 3.00 |
| red sided cow | 13.00 | 6 axes | 3.00 |
| piped Heifer | 10.00 | 21 bushels oats | 10.00 |
| young bull | 6.00 | 6 bu. rye | 4.50 |
| 3 yearlings | 12.00 | 1 lot of boxes and barrels | 4.00 |
| mare & colt | 100.00 | | |
| bay mule | 50.00 | Number of Acres in Habersham and | |
| light bay mule | 75.00 | Franklin Cos. | |
| grey stallion | 70.00 | 4,800 | 19,000.00 |
| 1 feed cutter | 5.00 | 400 acres on Clarkesville Road where | |
| gin at Prather's | 5.00 | Wm. Clark now lives | 800.00 |
| 1 threser [sic] at Prather's | 10.00 | one note on J. E. Rutherford for | 200.00 |
| 1 fan | 5.00 | one note on Jas. P. Phillips for | 147.25 |
| 1 fan | 8.00 | another Rutherford note for | 5.00 |
| 1 set wagon geer [sic] | 6.00 | | |
| 1 scythe and cradle | 1.00 | 6 Be[illegible]ums | 7.50 |
| 1 cotton gin | 100.00 | 10 bushels wheat | 10.00[35] |
| One bark mill & | | | |
| other tanyard fixtures | 20.00 | | |

## NOTES

[1] Coulter, *A Short History*, p. 349; Alan Conway, *The Reconstruction of Georgia* (Minneapolis: University of Minnesota Press, 1966), p. 117.

[2] George W. Williams, *Nacoochie and Its Surroundings* (Charleston, S.C.: Walker, Evans & Cogswell, Printers, 1874), p. 24.

[3] Traveler's Rest papers, Historic Preservation Section.

[4] Ibid.

[5] Habersham County *Tax Digest*, 1872, District 440; U.S. Census 1870 Agricultural Schedule, Habersham County, p. 32.

[6] U.S. Census 1870 Population Schedule, Habersham County, p. 696.

[7] Ibid., pp. 90-96; 1870 Agricultural Schedule, District 130, pp. 3132; 1880 Agricultural Schedule, pp. 1, 3, 10, 12, 13. The Agricultural Schedule also shows Colbert, Ben, Joseph, Jesse, and Sol Jarrett as sharecroppers.

[8] Conway, *Reconstruction of Georgia*, pp. 55-56, 62, 64, 68.

[9] Ibid., pp. 72-74.

[10] Ibid., pp. 105-09.

[11] Traveler's Rest papers on microfilm, Historic Preservation Section.

[12] Ibid.

[13] Ibid.

[14] Ibid.; *White County Deed Book A*, p. 578.

[15] Traveler's Rest papers, Historic Preservation Section.

[16] Ibid.

[17] Habersham County *Deed Book BB*, p. 285.

[18] Ibid., an interview with Rose Jarrett Taylor.

[19] Traveler's Rest papers, Historic Preservation Section.

[20] Ibid.

[21] Ibid.

[22] National Archives and Records Service, U.S. Post Office Records, Vol. 26, pp. 92-93: Vol. 42, March 13, 1874, March 23, 1876, February 15, 1877, January 28, 1879.

[23] Traveler's Rest papers, Historic Preservation Section.

[24] Ibid.

[25] Ibid.

[26] Ibid.

[27] Ibid.

[28] Ibid.

[29] Ibid.

[30] Ibid.

[31] Ibid.

[32] Ibid.

[33] Ibid.

[34] Ibid.

[35] Ibid.

# Chapter 11

## Third-Generation Jarretts and "The Old Home Place"

Lizzie Lucas Jarrett became a widow in 1877, a woman in her early fifties with five children ranging in age from three to twenty-one. The oldest, Sally Grace; Charles Patton, in his late teens; and Fred Lewis, who died a few months after his father, were born before the Civil War. Mary Elizabeth was a spritely child of about eleven years, and George Devereaux, apparently a pleasant surprise for his middle-aged parents, was the much-loved baby.

The remnants of the Jarretts' economic mini-empire were thrust upon the former "Southern belle," and with admirable practicality, Lizzie set about turning most of the faded enterprises into cash, in hopes of maintaining the farm while she reared her family. In addition to selling her share of the gold mine for $1,500, she soon parted also with the other Jarrett mine, receiving $1,000 from A. K. Childs, and within the next few years, she sold about 2,250 acres of land for $7,700. (See Map 14.) In spite of raising all this cash, however, the Jarrett family's economic decline continued. Perhaps the Jarretts had developed a higher standard of living than their income from the farm and the depressed Southern economy would allow.[1]

According to the 1880 Census Agricultural Schedules, Lizzie Jarrett's farm had 145 tilled acres and 3,000 acres in forest. By the early 1880s, however, the farm encompassed only several hundred acres, and during the late 1880s and into the 1890s, the place totaled 450 acres. In 1880, the farm had two horses, four mules, two oxen, four milk cows, five cattle, twenty-eight hogs, and 125 chickens. It produced 150 pounds of butter that year, along with fifteen bales of cotton, 2,000 bushels of corn, eighty bushels of oats, and 105 bushels of wheat. Fifty peach trees grew on the land, as well as 400 apple trees.[2]

Although tradition has it that Lizzie mismanaged her farm, it remained a good-sized enterprise with large harvests. In the late nineteenth century, the Jarrett corn-shuckings made a vivid impression on young Mary Elizabeth. In later life, she recalled,

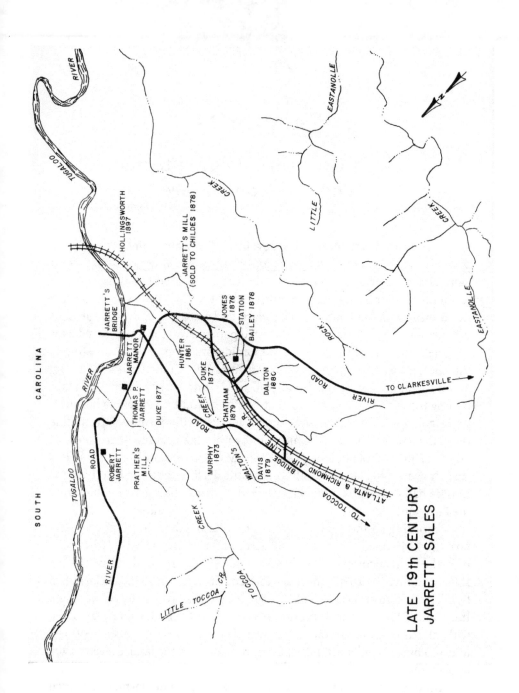

**Map 14:** Late Nineteenth-Century Jarrett Sales

Large bonfires were built adjoining the cribs where several thousand bushels were to be shucked, by both colored & whites. Songs and music and whiskey was in evidence. At the "Big House" Traveler's Rest an enormous supper was being prepared by negro women. When the corn was shucked about two or three o'clock in the morning they would catch the owner and ring and dance around him.[3]

Like her brothers and sister, Sally Grace, the oldest child, apparently enjoyed the best—if not more—that her family could afford. "Daughter," as she was usually known by the Jarretts, went to school at Madame Sosnowski's "Home" for young women in Athens. Among the family papers are party invitations addressed to Sally, indicating that she may have been an active "belle" in her own right. In the late nineteenth century, she lived mostly at Traveler's Rest, taking care of her feeble mother.[4]

Existing papers indicate little about the second child, Charles Patton. Born in 1858, he was often known as "Buddy" or "Bud." He became postmaster at Tugaloo in 1879 and held the position until 1883, after which he lived for a time in Athens and Atlanta, although he always paid his poll tax in Habersham County. In Athens, Charlie successfully "engaged in the general delivery business." Perhaps a graduate of the college at Athens, he never married.[5]

Much more information has been found concerning Mary Elizabeth, often called "Baby" by family members. Her "memoirs" relate a happy childhood, and Grandmother Lucas claimed that "Baby…never cries without she is hurt." According to a tract on her childhood by Ella Cooper Garner:

A chubby, cheerful infant, Mary Elizabeth, lovingly shortened to Mary Lizzie, grew into happy childhood.

The father died when she was five years old [inaccurate; see note 6], leaving a vast stretch of ten thousand acres of land for the frail widow to care for. An older brother took over the family and attending responsibilities.

He saw to it that "Baby" as Mary Lizzie was known to her family, had pets of all kinds. Squirrells [sic], lambs, pigeons, goats, pea fowls, and even a raven, were in her household of pets.

Growing up in the surrounding countryside were young friends. They gathered often and in the age old high ceilinged rooms of Traveler's Rest, they played at acting. Tableaus were the mode of the day. On one occasion Mary Lizzie was playing the part of the Sleeping Beauty. The stage was set, and the "Beauty" was placed on a cot for the benefit of the audience, which happened to be the neighbors. As the curtain rose, so did Beauty, thereby spoiling the show.

Hoping to do better the next scene, a tea was in progress, by the young actors. Not enough training had been given, however, for Mary Lizzie again exploded the show with—"Is this all we'er [sic] going to eat?"[6]

Mary Lizzie wrote this quaint letter to her "Mama" in 1878:

I want to see you so bad. I thought I would ask you to get me a doll that is worth 25¢ ask Susy to show you where the store is get the wax doll come home soon give my love to Julie Christy tell her I want to see her. Dont show any body this letter make Susy come home with you Ask her if she went to the fair tell her that I went. what did aunt Matt bring susy and Joe bring me something nice. Send love to all

Your Loveing [sic] daughter[7]

Mary Lizzie was sent to school in Athens at Lucy Cobb Institute and Madame Sosnowski's, where "she stood highest in her classes, carrying off most of the honors among the girls." The family papers include some of her school notes and tests, one test in history containing the following remarkable questions: "What great general is buried in a coffin made from the mast of a ship?" and "Who was it that swallowed the heart of a king of France?" Unfortunately, the answers to these macabre queries are not given.[8]

While Mary Lizzie attended school in Athens, her mother kept her informed of news from home. The following undated letter from Lizzie Lucas Jarrett to her daughter, probably written in the early 1880s, provides some interesting glimpses of life at Traveler's Rest during that period:

Dear Darling Baby

I know you will be disapointed [sic] when I tell you I cant come down this week bless you [sic] Dear sweet little heart Mama misses you so much, we all miss you from little George says mama what shall I do for little sister I do want her to come back so bad let her come back & play & read with me. I went to the association saw so many of Dear papas old friends Mrs Smith & family all went with me in the wagon. She & the children & Miss Willow & Mr. Williford spent yesterday with us Willie P [Thomas Patton Jarrett's son] came in the evening & they all went to the river & Miss Willow—Willie P—& all took a boat ride

Sallie Mass came Teusday [sic] night with Cousin Ida to uncle Pattons. I spent today with them & they are all coming down here tomorrow. Zaidie & children came down this evening they are coming down too. Ill have a housefull [sic] Daughter had not come yet look for her in a day or two let me know what you need. You can take lessons in Elocution if you wish & music too. I wrote to Miss Millie about the Music let me know what you would besides what you study & all that you need & Ill get it all fixed up I ought to have sent you some money but thought Id go down this week. I will come as soon as I can. & if you need any thing go to your uncle Fred & get money tell him I told you—& Id return it when I came down for books or any thing else you can tell Miss Millie—what I say about elocution—or I can write to her about it. I have no one here but Classe & Georgia Ann—Jim & George Washington have been very sick. I thought about you in the storm Saturday night & Sunday & wondered how you managed without Mama. Daughter said she was awfully frightened. Willie Patton's corn was injured more than ours I am sorry for him but he is jolly. Tom Scott & Johnny Hunter dined with us yesterday He was out electioneering, have you got your nice dress from Cousin Fannie & how does it fit how do you like it—get a sun bonnet from where they get theirs. Mary Newton can tell you where—Write & let me know how you are pleased & how fixed up & all about it give much love to all & keep a world full of yourself all send love to you

your own mama

Have you clothes enough & how does your aprons & under-clothes do. Ill bring the rest when I come. Much love to all the friends who were up here dont let any one see this.[9]

According to her memoirs, Mary Lizzie was a considerable coquette, though given to great modesty in her youth:

Music was made by the fiddlers and Mary Lizzie continued to be the reigning Belle of the valley. When the young men vied for her atten-tions, she coquetted with them all.

One day she had a date to go to church with one fellow she liked better than the others at the minute. About half way up the road to the little country church attended by the Methodists, they saw com-ing down the road toward them a black splotch. As they drew nearer, they saw to their horror that it was one of Meely's fatherless ones, without a rag of clothes on!

Both Mary Lizzie and her Beau's faces turned redder than the Fall leaves on an oak tree, and they looked like they'd burst.

Mary Lizzie was so embarrassed she never spoke another word all day, and after that she would never go with that boy again.[10]

Such were the travails of Victorian virtue. Another passage from the family papers elaborates upon Mary Lizzie's romantic "career":

Mary Lizzie grew into beautiful young ladyhood. She was known the country over for wit and beauty. No one in the whole country had such glorious, wavy auburn hair. Her blue eyes danced and sparkled in their mischeviousness [sic]. She was sweet and kind to all, but she could use a sharp tongue when necessary.

Beaux without number surrounded her—she was known as The Belle of Traveler's Rest. Many sued for her hand in marriage.

Her brother was constantly teasing her. On one occasion, when Mary Lizzie was most anxious to put her best foot forward in entertaining an especially prominent young Beaux [sic], her brother rowed them over to an island in the middle of the river at its widest point. Then on some pretext he left them.

He stayed away till almost dark, causing the young Mary Lizzie much embarrassment. In those days unchaperoned couples were looked on darkly.

When he finally showed up the couple was distressed beyond words—on being reprimanded by the mother for playing such a trick the brother replied—"Little Sister paid me to do it," whereupon Mary Lizzie chased him with a broom.[11]

Such episodes may have been remembered by a much-older Mary Lizzie with rose-tinted glasses. An actual corroboration of her attractiveness can be found in an incomplete, unsigned letter written to her from Rome, Georgia, in 1891. First, the writer expressed a wish to make another visit to "Old Tugalo—a choice spot," and then reference was made to a minor tragedy at Traveler's Rest, where "Mr. Adams had his poor little finger cut off" at the mill. The writer was sure of the cause. "I guess you and Miss Eugenia was enough to excite a poor old Bachelor till he'd loose [sic] control of head and heart and hand and feet. I know if it had been me I would have been ruined."

The writer, perhaps a minister, unabashedly declared his interest in Mary Lizzie: "O no, I am not going to fall in love with a long nosed girl here. My Big long nosed girl on Tugalo is about as much nose as I can bear." The outcome of this romance is unknown.[12]

George Devereaux Jarrett was, by all accounts, the family's "fairhaired boy." Born in 1874, little "Georgie" had the benefits of three mothers and, after 1877, no father. He, too, went off to school, probably in Athens. Like his sister Mary Lizzie, George apparently enjoyed a relatively carefree youth at the Tugaloo. One picture of his family's life in the late-nineteenth century can be found in a letter written by George to his mother and sisters at

Traveler's Rest. Written at a camp where Charles P. Jarrett and Sam Adams were working on a contract for a railroad sometime in the late 1880s or early 1890s, the beginning of the letter is lost, unfortunately, and no location is given. The remainder provides an entertaining account of George's life in camp:

> … all howdy she's doin jes tollerbul,' [sic] she's been in the woods ever since she left home. Says she has seen watermelons enough pass here to damn [sic] up Tugalo river.
>
> Just train-load after train-load of watermelons pass here every day going north. I reckon Bud [Charles Patton Jarrett] is enjoying himself at home, he left here Wednesday and has not put in his appearance since.
>
> Aunt Manda says to tell Uncle Henry's Lizzie to pick her enough blackberries to make about four gallons of wine and get the sugar and make it and she will pay her when she comes home.
>
> Mr. Adams says maybe he will be over in that country in a few days.
>
> Aunt Manda says tell Jaspers Mandy howdy; to write her.
>
> *George Jarrett*

> We are situated in the majestic forests of the Empire state of the South where Tecumseh and the screech owls held undisputed sway so recently followed by tigers and polecats; and when we hear the grand old watermelon trains come roaring up and see Arch and all the mosquitos that ever died had suddenly come to life and were taking vengeance on us for their murder.
>
> Oh! This is a sentimental place here surrounded by dump carts, wheel barrows, axle-grease, all the constitutions for the last century; all the rusty nails, maddocks, [sic] wrenches, chains, bolts, taps, brads, rings, plows, hooks, whetstones used in the manufacture of Noah's ark.
>
> And we are eased to sleep by Arch's musical laugh with a dozen others and the pleasant reverberations of the passing watermelon trains on the Great East Tennessee, Virginia, and Georgia Rail-Road, etc., etc., etc.
>
> We have two beds, one in a wagon body, the other on some planks. We also have in the tent about 30 bushels of oats, 3 bushels of rusty tools in a Smith's bile beans box. 4 cracker boxes, a saddle, in numerous small boxes to hold about a peck 13 packs for dump carts, two or three dozen shoes, 5 lanterns, two trunks, 2 valises, an umbrella and a looking glass all in a tent 9 x 7 feet together with socks, peach-cans and dirt. Oh! there's no place on earth like it.[13]

A letter from June of 1890 indicates the type of guest-entertaining roles the "manor house" was performing in the late nineteenth century. Helen, in Atlanta, wrote to "Cousin Lizzie," asking if her family could stay at Traveler's Rest that summer. "Are you going to take boarders this summer if so, will you board us for 2 weeks? What would be your group price for five of us?" Clearly, Traveler's Rest had come far from the days of the wayside inn, but nonetheless, this and other letters indicate that the large old house remained an attractive retreat for the Jarrett family and friends. Helen added the conjecture that "George of course he is wild over his freedom and delighted to be home again."[14]

George did well in school. He set his sights then on West Point, becoming a participant in the Southerners' return to military patriotism in the late 1890s. Passing his entrance exams, he gained admission to West Point in 1894 and went off to learn the "trade." "He was handsome in his West Point uniform," it was said.[15]

While George studied and drilled, his middle-aged brother Charlie fought "consumption"—tuberculosis. The struggle was arduous, and by November of 1897, Charles decided on a strategic change of climate, retreating to Silver City, New Mexico. Two letters have been found which were written to his mother during the winter of 1897-98, the first indicating that he was at least healthy enough to ride and court. He was surprised, if not shocked, by the riding style of his woman friend, however:

> When her horse was brought out—it had on a mans saddle, she walked up and put one foot in the stirrup and threw the other foot over just like a man, and rode astride. They have suits made for that purpose and a great many of the best people ride that way. It is the custom and no one thinks any things about it. That like everything else out here causes no comment and the neighbors dont care what they do so long as it does not concern them.[16]

Charles's letter of February reports that he had a fine time at a dance: "If I stay out here next winter I think we had better get an Adobe and all kinder [kind of] camp out in this country next winter."[17] Instead, during the following summer, Charlie came home to die. A letter from September of 1898 mentions that "Bud's" mother and sisters nursed him day and night for weeks, "knowing all the time that it would be impossible for him to recover." As the letter points out, the Jarretts' only consolation was their religious faith. A family friend who wished to comfort the family during their time of sorrow sent the following poem:

> Go tell it to Jesus
> He knoweth thy Grief
> Go tell it to Jesus

He'll send the relief
Go gather the sunshine
He sheds on the way
He'll lighten the burden
Go weary one, pray.[18]

A sevety-five-year-old scrap of newspaper in the Jarrett papers stated that "clever Charlie Jarrett is no more:"

> This announcement will carry sorrow to the hearts of his many friends in Athens, who knew and loved him for his many genial and charming traits of character. Mr. Jarrett passed away yesterday morning at ten o'clock at his home in Tugalo, Ga., after an illness of several months. His death was not unexpected and he was surrounded by his near relatives when the last moment came. A few months since he contracted consumption and sought to secure relief by going west. His trip did him no good and a few weeks since he came home to die.[19]

George wrote home from West Point, describing his grief and urging his mother to bear up and carry on. He commented, "John will have to manage things for a while. Mr. White can help and advise him about things he is in doubt about."[20]

Devereaux Jarrett's oldest son, Thomas Patton, died the same year as Charlie Jarrett. He had farmed the Turnbull place for over fifty years.[21]

George's attendance at West Point may well have "contributed significantly to the family financial decline." Be that as it may, he was graduated in 1899, 52nd in a class of about eighty. Assigned to Cuba, he arrived there too late to win any glory in the Spanish-American War, and his military career, recounted in Walter L. Williams's article, "A Southerner in the Philippines," was "in a military sense, not significant." In Cuba, Georgie's greatest triumph was in wooing and winning Victorine Paillett, a daughter of "a French diplomatic official turned plantation owner." Letters indicate that "Victo," as she was known, was politely received by the Jarretts when she visited Tugaloo with George on a month's leave in 1901. Mama described Victo as "quite an artist...she is [a] sweet little girl & is learning english right well & fast...They seem devoted to each other."[22]

While not pursuing romance, George found time to serve on courts-martial, as supervisor of prisoners, and as ordnance officer. His letters tell more of his duties than of his courtship, and in the Jarrett photograph album are a number of pictures of George's Cuban assignment locations.[23]

Letters to George from home, mostly written by "Mama," "Baby," and "Daughter," tell something of the life at Traveler's Rest at the turn of the century. The earliest dated one is from "Baby," also called "Little Sister," on March 27, 1899. In it, Mary Lizzie told of how continued rain made it so that "the farmers can do nothing." The day before, she had attended "preaching here yesterday." A call by a Mr. White, her favorite suitor, was mentioned. "[I]t was warm enough for us to sit on the piazza," Mary Lizzie said. Mama's health was a topic of concern, as usual: "I went to Toccoa on the freight train after some medicine for Mama." An adventure had occurred worth relating, also:

> Friday night an old tramp stayed here and he ate so much supper that Daughter [Sally Grace] was sure he would be sick, so in the night I heard her jump up and run to the sitting room door and try to un-lock it, and that waked Mama and she jumped up (to make the fire) and Daughter said in a very excited manner that the old man was bad off sick & that he was calling some of us. She ran to Johns room [John B. Watson was living in the house and running the farm at this time.] and made him get up to go up stairs quick to see the old man. John grumbled as he went and came on down stairs and Daughter (with her eyes as big as saucers) asked him what was the matter with the old man, He said he was sleeping so sound he hated to ask him.
>
> Every body in the house was awake and fearing around except the old man who was quietly sleeping. Mama got to fussing then about Daughter waking her and I went into hysterics. You can't say tramp to daughter now.

Mary Lizzie concluded her letter with what George was accustomed to by now from his maternally-minded sister, "Every body sends love to our precious darling sweet boy."[24]

Just before the turn of the century, Mary Lizzie chose from among her suitors. As the "memoirs" have it:

> After finishing school in Athens Mary Lizzie met the distinguished Virgil Arthur White. Her heart fluttered, but not her head. She was steady in her admiration for him, and love blossomed.
>
> They were married in the parlor of Traveler's Rest with all the young folks the country round attending. There were sad hearts among the young men, but they wished her happiness. They wore their best grey suits to the wedding with derby hats. The girls wore leg-o-mutton sleeves and wide ruffles on their skirts. Arthur White was ever a patient and loving husband.[25]

Born in 1860, White was postmaster of the Tugaloo post office, hav-ing held the post since 1884, and thus must have known Mary Lizzie well before she returned from Athens. Postmaster for over twenty years, White is shown on the 1900 militia district map as V.A. White, living at "store & res." slightly southeast of Traveler's Rest, just across the railroad tracks from Deercourt Station.[26]

Another perspective, and a more contemporary one, on the wedding of Mary Lizzie and Virgil White is revealed by a letter to her from her future brother-in-law, Samuel C. Adams. Writing from Pensacola, Florida, on October 18, 1899, Adams joked,

> You ask me what I think of the match—it is all right if you and Mr. White are satisfied—I see you have commenced to boss him already by pulling him off to toil his life away in the city.—You say he has quit his cranky ways—now don't laugh at what I say—has it ever crossed your mind that you have grown cranky yourself and don't see Mr. White's ways as you did several years back—alls well that ends well crank or no crank.[27]

Lizzie Jarrett's family made frequent use of the free railroad pass acquired when her husband sold land to the railroad in 1871. Perhaps Mary Lizzie and Virgil utilized it on their honeymoon or at a later date, as the couple did find opportunity to travel. An undated letter from Lizzie to Mary Lizzie was written during one such trip. Its contents reveal the continuing hard times at the Tugaloo, as well as Lizzie's willingness to share whatever she had:

> My Precious Darling Baby
> Mama is trying to write & It is a "trying" in fact for I can neither think nor write. I have been better for the last few days—only weakness—& that has gone to my head I guess as I cannot think of anything to say as usual, this is a cold morning rather windy almost frosty day. It rained a little early in morning—but sun shines bright now, we have a gay time some days, folks arriving in to see us to see how "pretty["] I am & how good & then they "want["] a "little chaw of Backee" & ["]children wants a little piece of bread"—they dont trouble much tho
> Lizzie Jarrett [Thomas Patton Jarrett's daughter] is at home she & Gus [Turnbull] called to see me I did not know her at first—I believe she & Gus are going to marry Mack Jarrett is terribly in love with Anna Turnbull. I hear of no weddings. Had a big Strawberry Pie eating the last few days—but today had berry eating—no Pie—had several galons [sic] of nice Berries all picked & capped nicely brought to us we are canning them, they are not large—as they used to be, but great many of them—we had for dinner not much & just as all was

cleaned up some one came in for something to eat there was an old lady & her daughter Mrs. Cheek [?] called with some nice berries & we gave them dinner & after they got through a darkie came in who has been living with Willie Patton [Jarrett] for ten years—on his way down to Willies—& he had dinner & now we have one more to feed our cook she has been washing today—& did not come in to dinner never does & has had none [dinner] yet we are going to have company now Mr. Edge—old man Lit Edge [one-time Jarrett overseer] is coming, & just as he was ready to go in came John Haddock [?]—Mr. Carter spent about half an hour or little more—& I think that is a true list of our visitors—very interesting is it not? You must write and let us know when to look for you—want to know when—where & how to meet you my dear darling child, we want to see you but must see—& know all you can & enjoy it all for it is all dull here Zosie [?] Ward has a beau a young widower—dont know his name—a nice fellow they say.

It would give you trouble to go buying & trading & daughter can get things we need in Atlanta—just cloth (white) & we have not money now & something to make me a dress but dont want you to bother with it now I know it would be a pleasure to you darling—but mama knows it would worry you so dont mind or think of it at all will be so glad to see you & my boy Arthur [White] bless his dear soul we are all very well—good bye—God bless you both & take care of you & bring you safely home—your loving Mama[28]

Still in the Cuba in January of 1900, George received a letter from his cousin Lizzie Jarrett, a school teacher in Mt. Airy, Georgia. Having been at Tugaloo for Christmas, she wrote,

Well, I spent xmas at home but was sick most all the time and didn't get to be with the folks very much. They certainly had a big time I think they had a dance every night. I went to several but was feeling so tough didn't enjoy very much.

Lizzie went on to claim that although she had not yet whipped a student, "I always give it to them when they need it."[29]

George's letter to Sally Grace, addressed to "My Dear Sweet Little Daughter," on March of 1900, expressed concern over Mary Lizzie's health: "You must write to me and tell me how Little Sister is, what she is suffering with etc. Do not allow any faith or so called magnetic nonsense to be tried on her." Mary Lizzie was experiencing an attack of "peritonitis," apparently an inflammation of her stomach lining, and a letter from Sally Grace told

George that "Little Sister" was almost dying of the malady.[30] Mary Lizzie must have recovered rapidly, however, for in July of that year she wrote to George, "I have been busy making blackberry wine. I have made sixty gallons, and Daughter has made about forty. We are not going to get on a big spree." Perhaps it was not peritonitis, after all.[31]

George's correspondence from his mother is not dated by year; but from these letters it can be learned that Lizzie was not too old or feeble to participate in canning. One letter to Cuba told "Little Georgie" of her canning cherries, "rasberries [sic]," strawberries, and "huckberties [sic]." On August 29th, probably in 1900, Mama mentioned a steady flow of relatives visiting the Tugaloo area. Another letter told that "times are hard in the country now Wish we could brighten it up—we have had *great rains* & wind—crops not very promising—fruit doing well—but *vegetables no account.*"

On June 6th, a letter described a heavy rain that had hit Traveler's Rest but none of the other farms in the area. The downpour had almost produced a freshet, and it "looks as if a freshet was coming today," Lizzie said. She was not too worried to eat "plenty of fried chicken," however. On June 20th, Lizzie described an overflowing Tugaloo River, the creeks and branches being almost impassable, and a full-scale freshet was feared. Some of the farmers had planted their cotton, and the "Bottom lands [were] most all under water." She wrote: "We feel interested in our fish nets & traps fear they will be washed away & we all love fish, wish we could send you a nice basket of our country dishes—right hot & all fixed up our fashion." A letter on January 25th reported: "Some folks running around trying to sell cotton and many to get corn—we have corn & have about sold what we can—but so little money—wish we had money plenty."[32]

Early in 1901, George and Victo left Cuba, spent a month at Tugaloo, and then went on to San Francisco and the Philippines. There, too, George missed most of the action, arriving at the end of the American suppression of the Filipinos' struggle for independence in April of that year. He stayed in the Philippines until the end of 1903, serving as ordnance officer, temporary post commander, and with the court-martial detail.[33]

One letter from Lizzie to George reveals that she still followed politics—and with a discerning eye. Members of the United States Senate were debating the passage of the treaty settling the late war and endowing the United States with an overseas empire—the Philippines. Some Southern senators had argued that it would be a serious mistake to acquire another population of subject "colored" people, and this reasoning brought the racial question into the Senate debate. Thus, Lizzie wrote to George: "We can't tell from the papers much if anything about the military affairs—but we look for *terrible things* as they are mixing up *color & politics.* Though we want peace—we want it in a nice big piece."

Like most white Southerners, the Jarretts apparently wanted African Americans to be politically quiescent, but Lizzie's sarcasm about American territorial aggrandizement is striking.[34] As Walter Williams' *A Southerner in the Philippines* points out, George Devereaux Jarrett's letters home often reveal a casual racism somewhat shocking to the modern reader. George referred to the Filipinos as "a number of monkeys or other animals without reasoning power." In another passage, he sought to amuse his mother with a "joke" about his pets: "With our two dogs and monkey and ducks and chickens and filipino and chinamen we have quite a menagerie, Haven't we?" Considering his opinions, one need not wonder why George found the "white man's burden" too heavy to bear.[35]

To ignore the offensive racism revealed in such comments, however, would be to overlook an important aspect of the history of Traveler's Rest—and of Southern history itself. Reared as slaveowners and slaves, the Jarretts of both races paid the complex and bitter price of their unfortunate historical relationship. At their best, three generations of black and white Jarretts lived through mutual support, but all too often, however, the record reveals examples of condescending *noblesse oblige,* as in Sally Grace's turn-of-the-century remark, "The little 'niggers' have all paid their Xmas call and gone"—a revealing statement of the races' love-hate relationship, their interdependency. Another comment from the same era, by Lizzie Lucas Jarrett to George, evokes a strong nostalgia: "We had a cornshucking, but not like the old ones Jasper & Juber not there."[36]

All the information presently on hand concerning the late-nineteenth-century lives of the African American Jarretts of the Tugaloo community comes from the United States census records and Habersham County tax digests. The latter are available from 1872 through 1900, along with some property statistics. These sterile numbers, however, provide sparse clues to the existence and lives of these people.

The 1872 Habersham County Tax Digest reflects the continuing paternalism demonstrated earlier in Kennedy Jarrett's contracts with the freedmen (no women are shown in the 1872 digest). For every group of freedmen shown, a white "employer" is also named. The records were prepared to enter various kinds of personal property, yet seven African American male Jarretts owned no property worth listing, but all paid the poll tax. Employed by C. K. Jarrett were Colbert Jarrett, a farmer who was thirty-three years old in 1870, still listed in 1880; and Harry Jarrett, listed as a thirty-six-year-old miller in the 1870 census, gone by 1881. Jasper Jarrett, a thirty-two-year-old farmer in the 1880 census, was employed in 1872 by Will Young; Bill Jarrett, a sixty-two-year-old farmer in 1880, worked for L. F. Young. All these men were married and had families. Thomas Patton Jarrett employed Solomon Jarrett, a sixty-three-year-old farmer, in 1880; Elizabeth A. Jarrett, Robert's widow, employed Major Jarrett and Harry Jarrett [perhaps the miller]. Each of the white Jarrett families employed African Americans who were not Jarretts, but their records have not been traced.[37]

For the duration of the nineteenth century, African American Jarretts came and went in the census records and the tax digests, and their efforts to accumulate property fluctuated dramatically, as did the American economy as a whole. There were never more than eleven Jarrett African Americans listed in the tax digest (1877), and never fewer than four (1873 and 1886).

In 1874, six African American Jarretts owned a total of $490 in unspecified property. Brown Jarrett, listed as a thirty-one-year-old blacksmith in the 1880 census, appears in 1874 for the first time, owning $60. Henry Jarrett, worth $280, was by far the richest. The average property value for these men was $81.61 in 1874, but it dropped to $26.36 in 1875 and did not surpass the 1874 level until 1883. Henry Jarrett, perhaps the much-loved "Uncle Harry" of the Jarrett legends, no longer appeared in the records by 1881.

Long-term residents not already named include Ben, a twenty-seven-year-old farmer in 1880; Snurl, who appeared in 1876 and lasted into the 1890s; Juber, a farm hand, seventeen years old in 1870; Jesse, a sixty-year-old farmer in 1880; Butler, thirty years of age in 1880; Randal; Rachel, perhaps the forty-five-year-old wife of Jesse in 1880, who appears in the 1889 tax digest as the first woman property holder ($175, mostly in livestock); and Joe, a fifty-year-old farm hand in 1880. All the men were usually listed as having paid the poll tax.[38]

Property for the African American Jarretts was listed as "household and kitchen furniture," livestock, tools, and miscellaneous. Over the years, Henry and Brown were the most prosperous. After 1883, the average property-holding value dropped steadily to $49.75 in 1886, but the next year it jumped to $94.25. Then the average mounted to $110.62 in 1889, only to decline every year thereafter, reaching a dismal $12.62 in 1892 and $33.00 in 1893. These were years of serious depression for the whole nation, with Southern and Western farmers suffering especially hard times.

In 1895, the average African American property holding began to recover, and reached a new peak in 1899 at $159.89, with Brown Jarrett's $1,138 distorting the average. Randal, who appeared in the records for a brief time in 1876, returned in 1881 as the first Jarrett freedman to own land. Holding twenty acres worth $100 in that year, he was not listed in the following year, but he appeared in the 1883 records without his acreage, which had apparently been purchased by Brown. In 1884, Randal had three acres; in 1885, neither he nor Brown held any, but in 1886, Randal once again owned twenty acres. A year later, his thirty acres were worth $200, but by 1890, the total was once again twenty. So it went, and Randal had disappeared from the records after 1895. Manda owned two acres in 1894; Brown was the owner of 100 acres in 1899.[39] These figures show that although the

Jarrett freed people were able to accumulate a bit of property throughout the late nineteenth century, they had difficulty in retaining it. Those with the most marketable skills, such as Brown and Henry Jarrett, were the most successful. (For a listing of this information, see the appendices.)

Lizzie and her daughters wrote to George in 1901 of the usual parade of weather, illness, crops, and visitors. A letter written January 6 from Mama said, "Christmas has gone—the young folks had number of parties & dinners [illegible] but none hear [sic] Mama [herself] could not have them & so many of [them] wanted to have them here as they always enjoyed them here." Lizzie's health was better than usual:

> though little Sister is quite sick in bed for about 5 or 6 days—she has been going to parties and took a cold—affected her teeth, some Dentist—had filld & did not half do his work—they inflamed & absess [sic] formed at the root & in the roof of her mouth & then it seemed she would go crazy—oh such intense pain & suffering & then an attack of inflamation [sic] of stomack [sic] & Bowels.

To compound her problems, Mary Lizzie was also suffering from "a (bad one too) nervous attack."[40] The family rapidly became dissatisfied with George's military career. Letters from Georgia began to express wishes for his return. Mama wrote, "Wonder when this foolish war will be over, soon, I hope & then we will have a happy time at home all of us together." Apparently George had been thinking of an early retirement, as he commented then to Mama, "Daughter wrote that [she] wanted me to get a position in civil life in the states. If I could get a good one I would gladly accept it." He must have been considerably moved when his mother wrote: "The old home looks real desolate—place all run down & worn out & not much money—but I think when we all get well it will soon be right." She also told of the boys hunting "turkey, possens [sic], etc." Sally Grace wrote that John Watson was "still running the farm."

Unable to abide the South Sea climate, Victorine "Victo" Jarrett returned to the United States and Traveler's Rest in early 1903. George contracted malaria at some point in his Philippine sojourn, but since the serious illness is not mentioned in any of his letters, it seems likely that it occurred just before he left the islands. He was then stationed at Fort Logan, Colorado, where he was joined by Lizzie, Sally Grace, and Victo. Mary Lizzie wrote to Colorado of her plans to visit Fort Logan. Soon after, Victo returned to Cuba for a stay with her family. Tragically, the lingering effects of George's malaria destroyed what should have been a joyous reunion. On February 15th, George "killed himself while insane and suffering from the effects of acute malarial poisoning."[41] According to a military report,

Lieut. Jarrett had been on sick report since February 9, 1904; at the access of his fever, and while suffering, he terminated his life.

His disease was contracted in the line of duty during his long service in the Philippine Island.[42]

Victo did not learn of her husband's death until February 24th. In broken English, she wrote to Sally Grace the next day:

> Yesterday came for me the terrible news! My hart [sic] and life are broken; I cannot understand nothing except that I will never see again my poor George. He died when I was far from him, without I see him a last time! Without I know he was so sick...
>
> Only you, you can imagine how I was sad to stay so long away from my home! Every day I told to my sister, I must not stay any longer here. I must go with my husband; but I had no energy enough to go because my family dint [sic] want me to go there during the winter and youself [sic] my poor sister you wrote to me so many times, that it will be better for me to wait a little longer.
>
> I cant imagine that...I left George healthy and looking well and I will never see him again, there is no consolation for me and for you too.
>
> I wrote this morning to Mrs. Williams and asked her about you and mother. How are you? how is poor mother, what she says? Does she understand the terrible malheur?
>
> I want to see you so much and cried with you our poor George, tell me what are you going to do? do you expect to come back home soon? I will go soon that I will receive your letter.
>
> I have to think of poor Baby too, how she received this new I will wrote to her to day and will do what she will do.
>
> If you can, please write to me my dear sister soon as possible and remember you that your sister loved you all always.
>
> I want to see you soon, please write me or ask to somebody to write me about you very soon my place is not here but it is near you.
>
> I wrote to you last Sunday. how you will be sad to read my letter full of hope in the future!...
>
> With a heart full of love from my family and from your sister Victo Write to me soon.[43]

The stricken Jarretts kept the news from frail "Little Mama," and apparently Virgil White and Mary Lizzie went to Colorado to bring home Lizzie and Sally Grace, who were both ill. A relative named Marguerita wrote to Mary Lizzie in Colorado of meeting the train with George's "remains" in

Atlanta. "Such a different homecoming from what we had all planned," she lamented. Lizzie Lucas Jarrett died soon after the suicide of her youngest son, and they were buried side by side.[44]

## NOTES

[1] See Habersham County *Deed Books:* BB, pp. 156-58, 255, 285-86, 485; CC, p. 585; FF, p. 392; EE, p. 361; and White County *Deed Book D,* pp. 174-75 (500 acres in original Habersham County).

[2] U.S. Census 1880 Agricultural Schedule, Habersham County, District 130, p. 10.

[3] Traveler's Rest papers, Historic Preservation Section.

[4] Ibid.

[5] Ibid.

[6] Ibid., Mary Lizzie Jarrett White was the source of this short paper by Ella C. Gamer. "Baby" was not five years old when her father died in 1877, for she was born in 1866 or 1868 (see U.S. Census 1870 Population Schedule and cemetery records in the Traveler's Rest papers, Historic Preservation Section).

[7] Traveler's Rest papers, Historic Preservation Section.

[8] Ibid.

[9] Ibid.

[10] Ibid.

[11] Ibid.

[12] Ibid.

[13] Ibid.

[14] Ibid.

[15] Ibid.

[16] Ibid.

[17] Ibid.

[18] Ibid.

[19] Ibid.

[20] Ibid., The "John" referred to by George was John B. Watson, who appeared in the Habersham County Digest these years as the Jarretts' agent.

[21] Ibid.

[22] Ibid.

[23] Ibid.

[24] Ibid.

[25] Ibid.

[26] Jarrett cemetery records, Historic Preservation Section; National Archives Records, U.S. Post Office Records, Appointment of Postmasters, Vol. 42, May 22, 1884, Vol. 68-A, July 20, 1905.

[27] Traveler's Rest papers, Historic Preservation Section.

[28] Ibid.

[29] Ibid.

[30] Ibid.

[31] Ibid.

[32] Ibid.

[33] Williams, "A Southerner in the Philippines."

[34] Traveler's Rest papers, Historic Preservation Section.

[35] Ibid.; Williams, "A Southerner in the Philippines."

[36] Traveler's Rest papers, Historic Preservation Section.

[37] U.S. Census 1870 and 1880 Population Schedules; 1872-1899 Habersham County Tax Digests.

[38] Ibid.

[39] Ibid.

[40] Traveler's Rest papers, Historic Preservation Section.

[41] Ibid.

[42] Ibid.

[43] Ibid.

[44] Ibid.

# Chapter 12

## Mary Elizabeth Jarrett White
## and Jarrett Manor

After 1900, Traveler's Rest was several decades removed from the wayside inn at the Tugaloo Crossroads. Mary Lizzie recognized this fact in 1915 when she changed the now of the old house to Jarrett Manor. (See Map 15.) She and Sally Grace were the survivors of Kennedy Jarrett's family, Mary Lizzie being the dominant figure of the twentieth-century history of the site.

On the death of her mother, Sally Grace Jarrett finally relented to the persistent courtship of Sam Adams, who had waited for her "yes" for twenty-five years. Annoyed by the large crowds at the big house, Adams built a small cabin nearby, called the "son-in-law" house, though neither of his parents-in-law were living at the time. Sally became known as the "lady with the lantern," for leading wagons on the nearby road from the cabin down to the river crossing.[1]

In spite of the many tragedies in her life, more sadness awaited Mary Lizzie. She and her husband lost more than one baby; then, in 1911, Arthur White himself died. Yet Mary Lizzie had plenty of Jarrett spirit, and her subsequent career shows that she was undaunted by the many tragedies. Her memoirs sum up "Baby's" response to her difficult situation:

> She had the care of the many acres thrust upon her. The country store [White's store; see Map 15], where the countryside gathered and discussed the doin's of the day, was now her responsibility. The community's Post Office, a part of the store, made her Post Mistress of Deer Court.
>
> Her friends feared for her safety when she would climb the steel framework to hang out her bag of mail for the baggage master on the trains to "grab."
>
> She looked like a pioneer of the olden days. Racing from this to that.

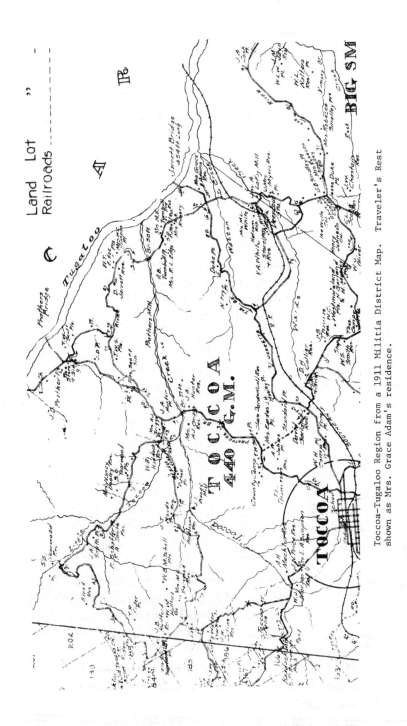

Toccoa-Tugaloo Region from a 1911 Militia District Map. Traveler's Rest shown as Mrs. Grace Adam's residence.

**Map 15:** Toccoa-Tugaloo Region from 1911 Militia District Map

Her efforts were rewarded. She soon won recognition among the interlect [*sic*]. People came from far and wide to see what a woman had done.[2]

Mary Lizzie was immediately recognized as a rich widow, and this fired the hearts of some unusual suitors. In a carelessly written memoir, she later recalled two special ones:

A few years ago a man wrote me from a town in S.C. …beginning his letter "Dear Sugar Babe, you haint never seed me, but I seed you oncet in Toccoa and I axed [asked] some body who you was as you passed.

You was the *purtiest* thing I ever looked at Sugar Babe and I want to marry you. I will be over Thar in two weeks and we will git married Sugar Babe.

I know nuthin that ever wuz made is as purty as you ar Sugar Babe." Your devoted lover

Another one wrote me from Atlanta saying that he 'wanted to git married and supposed that I did too. I [the suitor] am 38 years old and "read and rosey." Weigh 200 lbs. Have a 14 year old son. I policed a while and worked some on R.R. When employed I make $3.00 per day. When you come to Atlanta let me know where you stop at and I will see you. You have been highly recommended to me.[3]

Spurning such offers, Mary Lizzie, with Sally Grace's help, attempted to maintain an agricultural operation at Jarrett Manor. Some of their practices have been recollected by Velma Brackett Yearwood, who worked for the Jarrett sisters as a youngster:

Daughter…was head of the milkhouse where I worked when I was twelve years old [ca. 1920]. My job was to draw water to keep the milk cool. After the milkman did milking, the milk was strained in crock pitchers and a white cloth tied over them. Next they were put in wooden troughs and tubs. I drew water from the well all day long. When the water would begin to get warm, the stopper was pulled from the end of the trough. The warm water would drain out and fresh cool water *was* drawn and poured in the trough. The process was continued throughout the day. Guests were always served fresh cool milk.

Perhaps this labor-intensive refrigeration had been handed down from stagecoach days at Traveler's Rest. Mrs. Yearwood's memories reinforce the impression that Mary Lizzie did her best to keep the old place jumping:

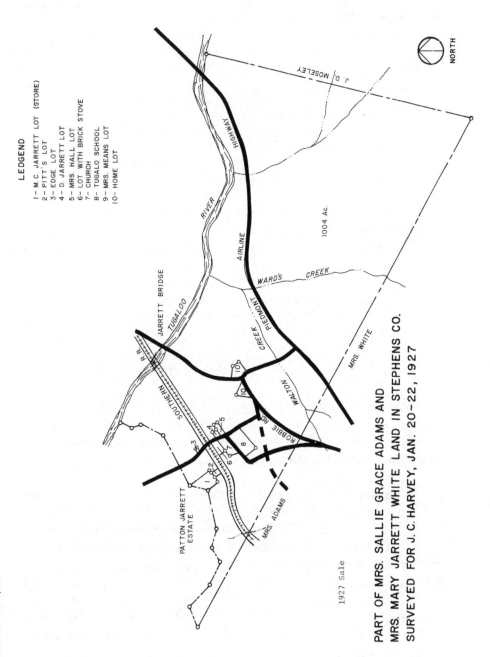

**Map 16:** Part of Mrs. Sallie Grace Adams and Mrs. Mary Jarrett White Land in Stephens County Surveyed for J.C. Harey, January 20-22, 1927

My mother always did the washing and ironing for Traveler's Rest. There were so many guests that much linen was used. Sometimes she would have to wash on Sunday, and I helped her.

One day Miss Babe [Mary Lizzie] said, "Velma, get on to the chickens. The Campfire girls will be here tonight for supper." Laws a me. I killed and dressed chickens all day. When I finished, I had ready 25 chickens. My, my those were the good old days. I have picked many gallons of blackberries along Tugaloo River.

This way of life was vastly different from that of the dangerous days of Jesse Walton, Ben Cleveland, and hostile Creek warriors. Some aspects of farm life, however, had not changed so drastically. Asked if she had "ever hoed corn & cotton," Mrs. Yearwood recalled, "Mercy, mercy, mercy, yes. A many a day I have spent in them old bottoms, all the way from Prather Bridge to the furtherest [sic] bridge south. I have had my feet on every foot of this land."[4] As long as the Jarretts owned land, people were available to work it for them.

Though she had no income other than from land sales, Mary Lizzie continued to live "in the manner to which she had become accustomed." She was not an economically practical person, and her part of Devereaux Jarrett's once vast plantation was "mismanaged." The Habersham County tax digests show only 200 acres for the C. K. Jarrett estate in the early 1900s, valued at $3,000. After the 1905 creation of Stephens County, Mary Lizzie appears as Mrs. V.A. White with 1,100 acres. The next year, Sally Grace appears as Mrs. S. C. Adams, a non-resident, holding 500 acres worth $3,500. Mary Jarrett White does not appear that year, but she was in the tax records in 1909, again in 1911, and from then until 1954. Sally Grace was a non-resident in 1910 and 1911, but a resident from then until her death in 1926.[5]

By that time, the two sisters' combined acreage was about 1,600, worth $14,500. In 1929, Mary Lizzie sold Jarrett's old bottomlands to Georgia Power Company for $45,000. (See Map 16.) After that, she held about 600 acres until 1940, when she sold all but ten. For these decades, the tax digests indicate that Mary Lizzie owned a car most of the time, several hundred dollars in town property, but never more than one or two cows. With all her political and social activities in Atlanta, it is highly probable that she paid insufficient attention to the maintenance of the farm.[6]

In spite of her dwindling estate, however, Mary Jarrett White promoted a successful image. A yellowed newspaper clipping from her personal effects reported the organization of a Federation of Business Women. "Efficiency" was to be the "watchword" of the organization, and Mary Lizzie was on the board of directors. The article commented,

An example of what women can do is shown in sidelights of some of those in attendance at the convention. Mrs. Mary Jarrett White of Tugalo, owns 1800 acres of land, which she oversees at a good profit each year. In addition she runs a general store, real estate office, keeps house, looks after her children, and, as she expressed it, "curses all week and preaches on Sunday."

Unfortunately, such exaggerations could not forestall the diminishment of her property.[7]

The memoirs and newspaper articles show that Mary Lizzie was busy with politics and romance. As the memoirs have it: "Her interest was aroused in politics. She wanted to see the 'little man' have a chance." Her most notable political coup, however, was for the "little woman." In 1920, a friend allowed her to register to vote before the ratification of the Nineteenth Amendment allowed women the ballot. On election day, Mary Lizzie was the only Georgia woman to vote, and due to this, she was named the state's "Woman of the Year." "Baby" enjoyed hobnobbing and working with politicians, who were often entertained at Jarrett Manor. She was on the Georgia Democratic Executive Committee, a campaign leader for successful gubernatorial candidates, and a Presidential elector for Franklin D. Roosevelt—all this despite the fact that she never voted after 1920.[8]

Such a woman of the world was bound to have admirers, and the memoirs recount the following:

She almost lost her heart in one of these heated campaigns. Many notables were attracted to the gay, attractive widow, who was Farmer, Politician, Post Mistress, Country Store Keeper, and Homemaker for her beloved son, Howard.

The man in the case was a candidate for the Office of the Georgia Senate, and she was campaigning for his rival! What must she dp [do]? Follow her convictions and fight for her party, or follow her heart, and succomb [sic] to the pleadings of the handsome man who wanted her for his wife.

Her sound judgment won out, and she went the way of a sacrificing fighter, and elected her man. Perhaps she wasn't in love anyway.

Acting on the State Executive Committee during the next Governor's reign, carried her to the capital city. There she was the Georgia Belle of the Ball room.

Her beauty was spoken of throughout the land.

She was too busy for more romance at the time.[9]

Mary Lizzie's romantic inclinations may have been satisfied later, with Howard's marriage to Mary Lou Edge. A truly chivalric affair at Jarrett Manor, the wedding was "typical of his mothers hospitality. Taking place in the parlor of the great house, the bridal procession, fourteen couples, marched down the great stair way, lined with ivy, and stood under a huge canopy of woods flowers."[10] They must have made a strangely incongruous picture, parading down the "great" stairway of the old frontier inn.

Letters from this period contain more concerning Mary Lizzie's private life than the state of affairs at Jarrett Manor. One striking letter written in 1924 reports that the woods nearby had been burning for three days.[11] A 1929 letter tells of the "liquid refreshments" served at one of her "bashes" (during Prohibition). Another letter is full of her eagerness to get a "water works" installed in the house and take on boarders.

When not busy with politics and entertaining, Mary Lizzie sought to help her African American neighbors, in whose problems she showed a continuing (if somewhat patronizing) interest. She was apparently ready to become thoroughly involved in the most traumatic affairs. One scarcely-credible but dramatic memoir survives to illustrate this practice:

Sitting on the quiet veranda of her ancestral home, our heroine was conscious of a car driving, very fast, in the direction of the Manor. Bouncing from the car to the ground came Sabrina Jarrett, a descendant of the slaves of the Jarrett family, who lived at Gum Log, a community in the same County, where also lived Isaac and Jacob, twin brothers of "Briny." "Miss Baby" she blurted out—"I have come to tell you terrible news" "Brother Isaac had to kill a man about his wife and the law come after him. I have brought him and hid him over yonder tuther side of them pine trees near the creek. Oh, Mistress, what's us gwine to do—I'se sceered to death." After a minute of thought our heoine [sic] said "Where is he—near the River?" Now the Tugaloo River being a State line M.J.W. [Mary Jarrett White] knew that once across the River, Isaac would be safe, or rather have time to make a complete get-a-way. Hastily gathering her wits, she told Briney to drive her, as fast as she could, to the home of Mary Jarrett, another one of her "cullod" friends and loyal worshipper of M.J.W. When they reached Mary's house MJW rushed in and said "Mary, give me one of your dresses and hats, and, quickly, Mary. Miss, what you'se gwine to do wid deco clothes." "Don't ask questions, Mary, and tell the law nothing, if they ask you." With bundle in hand MJW again set out with Briney to find the poor, bleeding Isaac crouched behind the bushes, far from sight and hand of the law. Hearing Isaac's story of how a "poor white trash" man had insulted his wife, she made

Isaac slip Mary's big plaid gingham dress on and donning Marv's best hat, they waited till dark then making him get in the back of the car, they drove full-speed to South Carolina and far enough to send him on his way unnoticed. She returned home, cautioning all darkeys to stay close by and say nothing.

Retiring early that night MJW hoped to have complete rest from the strenuousness of the day and from sheer exhaustion, soon fell asleep.

About 2:00 A.M. came another car—this time faster than the first one and again Briney, with tears streaming down her face, after begging for admittance, said, "Lord, Mistress, tis worse-er than ever now—the law done cum and took Jacob this time case [cause] they say they don't know one from the tuther and they had to have one. Jacob told them he warn't guilty but they taken him to jail, anyway."

At that hour of the night our heroine drove to nearby Gainesville to awaken and employ the best criminal lawyer in the country to defend Jacob, offering and agreeing to mortgage her home to help defend the poor darkey, and the lawyer consented only because of his admiration of her and her defense always of the under-dog.

The time for the trial arrived. So notorious was the case that all of the county folk jammed the stuffy courthouse which was taxed to capacity. Newspaper men from all over the country were there to report and the self righteous population of the county only laughed and said, "Why does MJW mix up in such things?" Not so, MJW. When the frightened Jacob was led into the court-room, who should take a seat in the witness stand near him but our heroine looking like a picture in a lavender hat trimmed with pink roses which brought out the natural beauty of her silver hair, her eyes reflecting the courage of her innermost soul.

A mistrial, which was the best the Attorney could obtain for Jacob, was the verdict and the dejected and starved Jacob was returned to his Jail cell.

A few nights later, a sullen and crazy mob, made up of poor whites who were revenge-hungry, formed and things looked dark for poor old Jacob, the innocent victim of the vagaries of his brother's wife...Fearing not only the law, but the mob of white men, Briney slipping quietly around in the night, put a messenger on a mule to ride 25-miles in black darkness again to tell her adored mistress of the terrible calamity. When the news came, our heroine was almost oversome [sic] with anxiety for the poor black who had shed no innocent blood. Never had she failed to help her colored friends and family before and she must not forsake them this time.

Slipping down to a cabin in the yard, she called John Smith, a white man who lived there—made him get up out *of* bed and said "John, don't you belong to the Ku Klux—now T want the truth?" and John admitted that he did. Telling him of Jacob's predicament, she sent him to the nearest "brother-in-the-clan" and thus in a short time the Klan was hooded and riding.

In a race between the vicious mob and the Ku Klux, the latter reached the Jail just as the Sheriff was about to deliver the keys to the mob. And what became of Isaac and Jacob—well, they are well, and doing well—in TEXAS.[12]

Surely, if this tale has an element of truth, the Klan had seldom been enlisted for such a cause before.

Mary Jarrett White was also involved in working on prison reform, volunteering for the Red Cross, and participating actively in the Daughters of the American Revolution. She founded the local chapter of the D.A.R., and her papers contain some short, patriotic speeches of little interest. Perhaps it was in the spirit of the Revolution that she held a costume ball at Jarrett Manor, related in the memoirs:

A party was held in her home, all members wearing lovely, colorful costumes. Mary Lizzie dressed as the beautiful Martha Washington. A state senator, as George Washington, fell head over heels in love with the Revolutionary Daughter, and asked for her hand in marriage. When she refused him, he was so heart broken he jumped off the river bridge near Traveler's Rest. He was saved by a friend. Still Mary Lizzie refused to marry him.[13]

So went life for the granddaughter of Devereaux Jarrett, until old age finally began to slow her down after World War II. As an old lady, Mary Jarrett White was much admired in the Tugaloo neighborhood, which still called her "Big Baby." Her promotion of the historical importance of Traveler's Rest, although it tended to be inaccurate and legendary, was a valuable legacy. In 1934, the Historic American Buildings Survey did line drawings of the house, and the National Register of Historic Places recognized Traveler's Rest as a National Historic Landmark in 1963. Mary Lizzie helped create an abiding interest in Traveler's Rest in the Tugaloo area, which came into fruition in the last years of her life. She died in 1957, about ninety years of age.[14]

In the winter, early in 1954, the Toccoa Chamber of Commerce secured an option to purchase Jarrett Manor for $10,000. Mabel Ramsey, Howard Tatham, and Ben Wiggins were leaders in this effort, according to the *Toccoa Record*. The original option called for the purchase of seven acres. The

Chamber of Commerce founded the Jarrett Manor Foundation, and an offer of financial assistance was obtained from the Georgia Historical Commission. It was agreed that the Foundation would raise half the necessary funds, and the Commission the other half. The State Properties Commission approved the purchase in 1955, and for $8,000, Traveler's Rest and somewhat less than three acres became the property of the State of Georgia. During the early 1960s, Hartwell Dam held back the Tugaloo waters to create Lake Hartwell. The fertile "river bottom" lands that had been the pride of the Waltons, Wylys, and Jarretts were covered by water, along with the sites of the Cherokees' Tugaloo Old Town. Traveler's Rest now stands only about a quarter of a mile from the lake.

Until 1974, Traveler's Rest was maintained and operated under the auspices of the Georgia Historical Commission. Mabel Ramsey, a Jarrett descendant, was curator of the museum. In 1965, the deteriorated outer shell of the house was removed, and the structure was protected by a clear plastic cover while its construction history was studied. In the summer of 1968, Mabel Ramsey retired, to be replaced by another lifelong resident of the Tugaloo area, Frances Wilbanks. After that, the replacement of the outside of the house was begun, and painstaking restoration work continued throughout the years that followed. In 1974, Traveler's Rest came under the management of the Georgia Department of Natural Resources, Parks and Historic Sites Division.

Its establishment as a museum once again returned Traveler's Rest to its optimum position—at a crossroads. Through its careful study and restoration, Georgia has made it possible for all people to have a unique example of the American heritage vividly preserved at a site of long-time occupation.

## NOTES

[1] Traveler's Rest papers, Historic Preservation Section.

[2] Ibid.

[3] Ibid.

[4] Cora Ledbetter, "Farm Chores are Reviewed," *Toccoa Record*, July 21, 1976.

[5] *Habersham County Tax Digests, 1900-1906; Stephens County Tax Digests*, 1907-1926.

[6] *Stephens County Deeds*, Book 18, p. 407; *Stephens County Tax Digests, 1927-1940.*

[7] Traveler's Rest papers, Historic Preservation Section.

[8] *Stephens County Tax Digests, 1920-1950*; Traveler's Rest papers, Historic Preservation Section.

[9] Traveler's Rest papers, Historic Preservation Section. Howard White was reared by Mary Lizzie, although he was not her own son, nor was he ever officially adopted.

[10] Traveler's Rest papers, Historic Preservation Section.

[11] Ibid.

[12] Ibid.

[13] Ibid.

[14] Ibid.

# Appendix A

## Traveler's Rest
## Stephens County, Georgia
## A Historical Architectural Analysis

Paul F. Buchanan
P.O. Box 2
Williamsburg, Virginia 23185

Prepared for the
Georgia Department of Natural Resources
May 20, 1978

On September 25, 1977, I traveled to Toccoa, Georgia, and spent three and one-half days investigating the structure called Traveler's Rest. Although the building had been heavily restored, it was still possible to determine the architectural periods and evolution of this structure. There are several basic periods in the development of this existing structure, but there were earlier structures on this site. Archaeological studies made by William J. Kelso show that at the southern end of the present structure, there was occupation by white settlers prior to 1815.

## PERIOD I

The first period of the present structure was built about 1815, plus or minus five years. (See Drawing 1.) This is determined by a combination of architectural design, building materials, moulding profiles, brick bond and structural techniques.

This first building was a two-story frame building, 18'2" x 50'10½", facing west with a five-bay shed-roof porch running the full width of the building on the west side. A similar shed was on the east, but only the center portion of this shed was a porch, as both ends of this shed were enclosed to create rooms. These sheds were designed this way because here there were to be open porches, the first-floor joists ran north and south and were supported by heavy summer beams. Where there were to be enclosed rooms, the floor joists ran in the opposite direction, supported by heavy wood sills. There were six wood posts on the west porch, with a balustrade between the posts, except in the center bay. At both ends, mortises for the balustrade rails can be seen in the corner posts of the building. The posts of the porch partially rotted and were covered with one-inch boards, a common method of repairing rotting posts. The posts were later removed and replaced in the restoration of the 1960s. They were replaced the wrong size, using the size of the original posts plus the cover boards. They give the building a heavy look, and I recommend that they be replaced with correct-size posts.

The roof of both sheds of Traveler's Rest were originally eleven inches lower at the building than they are now. They were given a steeper pitch when the building was enlarged ca. 1835-1840. The original fastening marks can be seen in the roof space.

The west wall of the building was covered with random-width, beaded tongue-and-grooved flush boards, with the tongue in the down position. This was poor building practice, because the groove could hold water, but was easier to erect, especially by one man. The bead on these boards is a bead that came into use after 1800. It has a flat quirk instead of the sharp quirk of the eighteenth century. This moulding detail occurs on all remaining original beaded mouldings of Traveler's Rest. The ceiling of the porch was also covered with flush beaded boards. There is very little of the original beaded

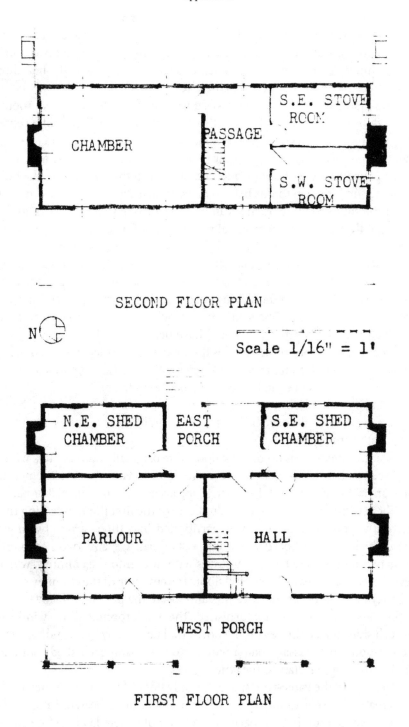

SECOND FLOOR PLAN

N

Scale 1/16" = 1'

WEST PORCH

FIRST FLOOR PLAN

**Drawing 1:** Traveler's Rest, Stephens County, Georgia. ca. 1815-1835

boarding remaining on the wall because when the building was added to, the fenestration was altered, removing all four windows and adding two doors and a window. (See Drawing 2.) When this change was made, the boarding was replaced with flush boards, not beaded.

The first floor of the original house was divided into two equal rooms with a door between them. Each of these two matching rooms had a center door and two windows on the west wall, a fireplace on the exterior end, with windows on each side of the fireplace and two doors on the east wall. One door opened to the east porch, and one opened to the shed room, the only difference in these two rooms being a quarter-turn stair in the northwest corner of the south room. Evidence can be seen for this stair in a patch in the ceiling of this room, on the original north wall of this room, and under the first run of the attic stair. The second-floor joists over the first run of the stair to the second floor were headed off, creating head-room. This head-room space was boarded with beaded boards. The stair was not as steep as the present stair as can be seen in the sloping cut of the wall sheathing on the original north wall of this room. The south room would originally have been called the "hail," and the north room would have been called the "parlor." This is reversed today. All four rooms on this floor had flush beaded boards covering the walls and ceiling, similar to the porches. Where altered or added to, the boards used were not beaded. There is no plaster in the building.

All nails in the house are machine-made cut nails instead of the handmade nails that would have been used if the building had been built in the eighteenth century.

The two shed rooms on the first floor were originally bed chanters with a fireplace and one window. There were two doors in each room, one entering the rear, or east, porch, and the other giving access to either the hail or parlor.

The second floor was almost a duplicate of the first floor, excepting that the south space over the hail was partitioned into three spaces by single-board-thick vertical boards, creating a stair passage and two bedrooms. These two rooms were heated by stoves with flues into the chimney, which never had a fireplace on the second floor. The covering of the chimney needs to be removed in order to prove this and locate the position of stove pipes so the rooms can be properly furnished. The north room had two windows on each side and a chimney on the north wall flanked by two windows. The second-floor stair passage had a window overlooking each shed roof and still has the original stair to the attic.

The attic in the gable-roof space was only floored over the southern half. This created another usable space which was not lit or heated. In order to get some ventilation in this space, two round holes were later (before 1835) cut in the weatherboards in each gable end. These holes have erroneously been called loop holes.

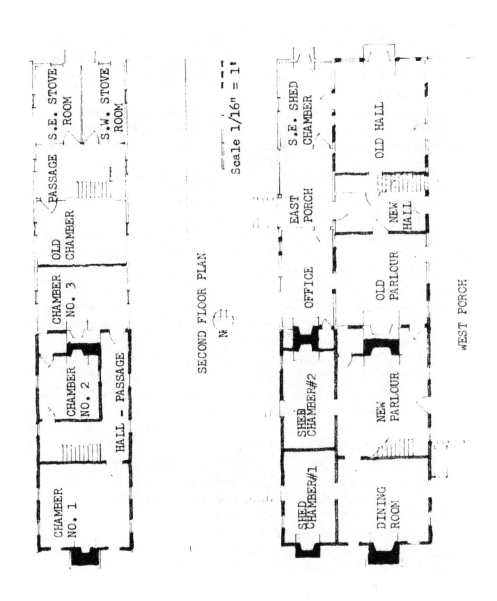

**Drawing 2:** Traveler's Rest, Stephens County, Georgia. ca. 1835-1850

The foundations of the building are stone around the perimeter, heavily repointed and replaced in the 1960s' restoration. The interior east and west walls are supported on masonry piers. The chimneys have stone foundations, but are brick otherwise. The two south chimneys are of American bond with varying numbers of stretcher courses, from five to eleven. They have stepped weatherings and are typical early nineteenth-century chimneys. The northeast chimney was completely rebuilt when the north addition was added, and much of the northwest chimney was rebuilt above the first floor at the same time, 1835-1840. This is evidenced by the different mortar types used in the two periods. The weatherboards on the original building has 6½" exposure to the weather and were moulded on the lower edge with a quarter-round moulding. This type of weatherboard was used between 1790 and 1825. Some original weatherboards still exist in the north gable, covered by a later addition, as all weatherboards now exposed on the building were new in the 1960s' restoration.

The framing of the original two-story building is unique, utilizing a different method of framing on the east and west walls. There are four corner posts and two (in the center of the east and west walls) posts that are a full two stories high. The two corner posts on the west side are L-shaped, hewn from a single timber. The center post on the west side is similar, but T-shaped, hewn from a 12" x 12". However, the matching three posts on the east side are made of two separate pieces each.

The solid L and T framing posts occur in the Southern states between 1780 and 1830, usually between 1800 and 1820. The location of the framing is a great help in locating later changes and has been used throughout this structure in order to analyze it.

## PERIOD II

Between 1835 and 1840, Travelers Rest was enlarged to the north and the original structure was altered. The building was thus over ninety feet long with a full-length shed porch on the west side. (See Drawing 2.)

The alterations to the original structure included the raising of the pitch of the east and west shed roofs by eleven inches, because the original roof slopes of the shed roofs were too low to keep the wood shingles from leaking. The stair to the second floor was removed and rebuilt so that the only access to the original second floor was through a new door opening on the west porch. This stair was completely enclosed by a new east-west partition across the old hall. The two windows on the west wall of the old hall were removed and closed in. The two south windows of the old hall were enlarged. The two doors on the east wall were closed, and another door was installed to the southeast chamber. All fireplaces in the original building were given new mantles of the Greek Revival design, which is the architectural period of this addition. The first part of the existing building was the "Federal' period or architectural style. A new passage or hail was created by a new partition across the old parlor, with a new doorway to the west porch. A new window was installed in the west wall of the old parlor, and all four original windows in this room were removed. The door to the north shed chamber was moved to the north. This north shed chanter must have been made the working office for the newly enlarged building, due to the installation of another window and a new mantle, the design for which concealed drawers in the panels. The office had visual control of the outside kitchen and a door to the rear porch. Two new doors were installed, one on each floor, to the new addition at the west end of the original north wall. The north balustrade of the original west porch was removed, making a very long shed porch with two bays without balustrades, giving two entrances.

The alterations of the original building on the second floor only occurred in the old chamber, which was divided into two rooms by a new board partition. The north room thus created was only accessible from the new north addition through a door that was inserted in the place of one of the two north-end windows that were removed. The southern room created was only accessible from the new stair from the west porch and was not heated. Thus, the second floor of the original now had three rooms that were either unheated or heated by stoves. These rooms, along with the attic space, were accessible only by an exterior door at the foot of the new stair on the west porch. This created a set of rooms or spaces to be used for the accommodation of less desirable travelers who could be denied the use of the first-floor public spaces.

The new addition doubled the size of the original building. A very important feature was the cellar kitchen and storeroom built at this time. The original structure had only an outside kitchen building. It was desirable for all large taverns to have a cellar kitchen for winter use. Service to the tavern above was by a steep stair through the floor of the new west porch. (See Drawing 2.) Evidence for this stair was almost obliterated by the 1960s' restoration. Only several marks for the nailing of the stair stringers now exist.

The first floor of the new addition had four rooms, each with a fireplace and a door to the outside. The framing construction of the new addition was very similar to that of the original building, with the exception that L and I posts were not used. The kitchen/dining room chimney is built of stone up to the chimney stack, which is brick. The chimney to shed chamber #1 is now missing, but it was probably stone with a brick stack. It was removed between 1850 and 1960. Not enough is known about this chimney to replace it. The chimney to shed chamber #2 was completely rebuilt in the period of 1835-1840. The chimney to the new parlor was partially rebuilt but added to in places.

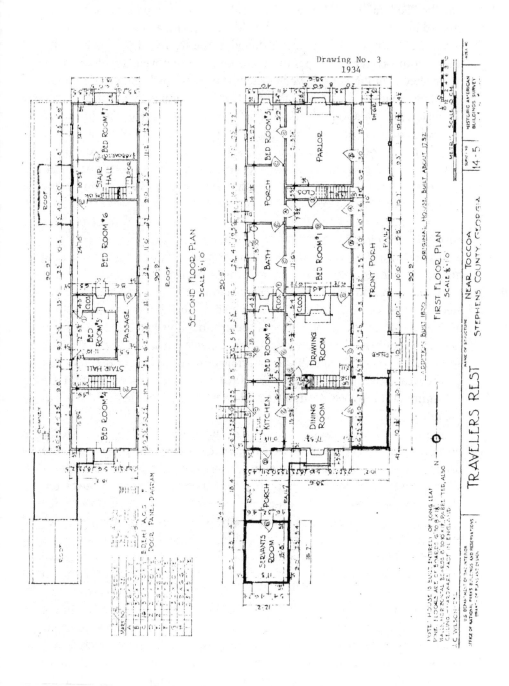

**Drawing 3:** Traveler's Rest, Stephens County, Georgia. 1934

The woodwork of this period has simple Greek Revival mouldings. The interior walls and ceilings are covered with random-width, flush yellow-pine boards similar to the original structure, excepting the boarding in the addition is not beaded. There is a simple open-string, straight-run stair to the second floor on the north wall of the new parlor. This stair has brackets of a continuous wave form. The mouldings and details are typical of the 1835-1840 period. The stair has rectangular balusters, two to a tread. The newels are tapered octagonal shape and the handrail is roughly octagonal and has awkward ramps and easements.

On the second floor of this addition are two heated bed chambers and a stair hall-passage. The passage was necessary to have access to chamber #3, which was created from the old chamber in the original building. Chanter #1 was the best room of the new tavern. It was light and airy, with a northern exposure and two windows on three walls. Chamber #2 used the space left after making a passage to chamber #3. It was dark, and only had one window on the east wall. This did not allow any cross-ventilation. Because of this, a window was built on the west interior wall. I was asked if I saw any evidence of chamber #2 ever having been used as a post office. I did not, and I think that logic would preclude a second-floor room being suitable as a post office.

It appears to me that the new north addition was primarily a family residence attached to a tavern, allowing the original building to be devoted to tavern use only.

## LATER PERIODS: 1850-1960

Architectural styles and details indicate that sometime after 1850, a separate building was built at the north end of the tavern. It was later connected to the tavern by an open porch. Later, when the tavern operations declined, the building became a large residence with a few bedrooms rented to boarders. Several other alterations were made which I will list:

1. The outside stair from the cellar kitchen was removed before 1920.

2. The two north bays of the west porch were enclosed or screened after the stair was closed, and later removed in the twentieth century.

3. A new interior stair to the cellar kitchen was installed when the exterior stair was removed.

4. A sun deck was cut in the shed roof over the east porch and the window on the east wall of the original passage was made a door. All this was later removed and a new window was inserted towards the north (probably in the twentieth century).

5. The partition between the two stove rooms was removed, and reinstalled in the 1960s.

6. The partition in the old chamber was removed.

7. The shed chamber #1 chimney was removed and a modern kitchen installed in the twentieth century.

8. The office was converted to an interior bathroom in the twentieth century.

### LAST PERIOD: 1960-1977

This building was heavily restored in the 1960s. The restoration was basically sound, except some weatherboards could have been saved, however. More photographs should have been taken, and records should have been kept on what was done. The partition in the old chamber should be reinstalled, with a concealed door, if passage is desired for interpretation. The porch columns should be replaced. (I have given Mr. A. Waylor of the Department of Natural Resources recommendations regarding maintenancc and climate control, which are beyond the scope of this report.)

### SUMMARY

Architecturally, this building, in its first two periods, was a combi nation of a residence and tavern. "Tavern" in this report means a structure that provides lodging, food, drink and entertainment for the traveling public. I doubt that there was a bar, and I saw no evidence of one. A table in any of the shed rooms would have sufficed. The amount of the building used for the family residence was very flexible and was controlled by the numbers and types of the traveling public who had to be accommodated.

This combined residence-tavern is very important to the State of Georgia, architecturally as well as historically. It is a good remaining example of early nineteenth-century pioneer vernacular architecture of the Georgia Piedmont and its growth up to the 1860s.

The structure is a good example of the simplicity of frontier building, which combined the minimum of purchased materials and tools with a building style suitable for the climate. The indigenous materials, stone, wood and clay for bricks were easily fabricated with the minimum number of tools. The purchased materials, nails, hardware and glass did not need skilled labor to build the resulting architecture. There was some foresight to adapt the two-story hall-parlor-plan type by adding sheds and porches, combined with carefully sizing and locating the doors and windows. This, with proper orientation, made the building suitable for the purpose and climate.

Paul E. Buchanan - Restoration Architect

# Appendix B

## Excavations at Traveler's Rest
## Toccoa, Georgia
## 1968

William M. Kelso
Archaeologist Georgia Historical Commission
Savannah, Georgia
February 18, 1969

The Traveler's Rest historic site (Jarrett Manor) is located six miles east of Toccoa, Georgia, near the Tugaloo River. The site includes 3.9 acres of ground and six buildings: the main house, the "loomhouse," two small cabins, a modern tool shed, and an old garage. A small creek on the north, the remnants of the Old King's Highway from South Carolina and River Dale Road on the west, Walton's Creek on the south, and an old cleared field on the east border the site.

## HISTORY

The Traveler's Rest site was part of the Cherokee Nation until May 31, 1783, when a treaty was drawn up ceding this area to the State of Georgia.[1] However, since no large representative group of the [American] Indians was present at the signing, the Cherokees, as a whole, were not satisfied with the agreement, which led to "a spirit of restless discontent [and]...many acts of ferocious hostility."[2] It was in this troubled area along the Tugaloo River that Major Jesse Walton, Revolutionary War veteran and founder of Jonesboro, Tennessee, was granted several tracts of land in the 1780s, and on the first tract, 400 acres on the river,[3] he probably built a residence. After the Treaty of Hopewell (November, 1785) was signed between the United States Government and the Cherokees fixing a boundary line in the Tugaloo Region,[4] Walton attempted to settle his newly acquired land only to find that the [American] Indian hostility had not subsided sufficiently to insure safety for his family. He apparently moved his wife and children sixteen miles from his original settlement soon after.[5] After that, Walton seasonally brought up a labor force to work his plantation on the River until he was ambushed and shot by Cherokee Indians on his land in 1789.[6] Three weeks later, he died from the wounds, leaving his household furniture and part of his land to his wife and dividing the remainder of his property among his children.[7] There is no mention in his will of his house, but presumably it went to his wife along with the furniture.

The land next went to Joseph Martin, Walton's son-in-law, who in turn sold out to James R. Wyly in 1818,[8] and in 1838, Devereaux Jarrett bought the property.[9] Soon after Jarrett acquired the place, he began using the main house as a stagecoach inn for the use of those traveling the King's Highway, and in 1844, a United States post office was set up in the house. The close proximity of the King's Highway and the river ford (Walton's Ford) made both the post office a necessity and the inn (Traveler's Rest) a success.

Traveler's Rest remained the property of the Jarrett family until June, 1955, when it was purchased from Mary Jarrett White by the State of Georgia. The Georgia Historical Commission presently [1969] administers the site for the State, and is carrying out a program of renovation of the main house and restoration and reconstruction of some of the outbuildings. As part of the site's development, archaeological excavations were carried out by the Commission in 1968, the findings of which are presented in the following report.

## PLAN OF EXCAVATION

The first season of excavations at Traveler's Rest was conducted May-July, 1968, concentrating on the area immediately around the buildings. The site was excavated by areas, using a grid system of 250-foot-square blocks, divided into fifty-foot squares. The major objectives of the excavation were to locate and date the various periods of construction of the main house, to locate and define the functions of the various out-buildings, and to learn something of the types of artifacts that were used by the inhabitants of Traveler's Rest through the years. The major emphasis during this initial season, however, was the main house.

## THE MAIN HOUSE

The main house at Traveler's Rest measures ninety feet by thirty-nine feet, has thirteen rooms in its two and one-half stories, a full-length open front porch, a basement kitchen and a dug wine cellar. Previous architectural study of the building suggested that it had experienced several periods of expansion and alteration, but only two major periods of construction, with the south half being built first (Period I) then the north half (Period II) extended later, doubling the original size. It was hoped that archaeology could aid the architectural research by uncovering anything pertinent to the various construction and alteration periods of the building. Therefore, areas under and around the main house were excavated.

The subsequent digging under the south end of the house and along the south foundation wall revealed features from prehistoric [American] Indian occupation and a backfilled toot cellar. The excavations uncovered an area of charcoal and burned clay under the front porch and several Indian-like post holes and shallow pits outside the present building. Any strati-graphic connection between the post-hole complex and the fire area underneath the main house has been destroyed by the construction of the south foundation wall and the erosion that had occurred outside the present building. Moreover, a graded driveway had been built just south of the post-hole complex, which further disturbed the evidence of the earlier [American] Indian occupation. Probably the post holes and fire area are all that is left of the extreme north side of an aboriginal structure, the remaining features totally destroyed by a combination of erosion and all of the various construction programs that have occurred at the site during the historic period.

On the other hand, the root cellar had remained undisturbed through the years, having been protected from construction disturbance and erosion by the house above it. The feature was seven and one-half feet square and two and one-half feet deep, surrounded by miscellaneous gouges apparently dug under the house by animals. A shallow slot had also been dug from under the front porch to the edge of the cellar, the purpose of which remains unknown. Both the slot and the pit had been backfilled level with the undersurface of the remainder of the house. Immediately below a shallow level of modern dust, a layer of rocks and chunks of red clay (clay chinking) had been thrown into both the cellar and the slot. Some of the rocks had been burned on one edge, indicating that both the burned rocks and the chinking had probably come from the destruction of an earlier chimney. Below the chimney-destruction level, a layer of dark humus flecked with bits of wood ash was found, probably representing a build-up of debris on the cellar floor during its occupancy. In addition to containing chimney debris and dark humus, the lower part of the chimney-debris level and the lower humus level contained early nineteenth-century artifacts, and, significantly, both layers ran under the present rockhearth foundation of the central chimney of the main house, i.e., the hearth foundation had been built on the fill of the cellar.

In the extreme southeast corner of the cellar, an area of the lower fill had become much more compact than the surrounding soil, indicating that this area had been trodden down as people entered and left. Directly outside the building in front of the present chimney stool in line with the compact area in the cellar, two fieldstone rocks had been laid on edge into the natural clay, perhaps all that remained of a stone walk leading to the cellar. On each side of the stones, about equidistant from each edge of the walk, a post hole containing fragments of early nineteenth-century ceramics was found. The posts may have supported a lean-to shelter above the stone-walk cellar entrance, thus creating a crude bulkhead. About three feet from the south foundation wall under the main house, still supporting the east and the west main house sills, two makeshift piers had been constructed out of wedge-shaped blocks. Apparently, these supports had held up the south end of the house when the south foundation wall was reworked. The reworking probably took place when the south chimney was added to the house at the point where the cellar entrance had been. At least, the piers (or jacks) had definitely been placed under the sills after the root cellar had been abandoned because the west pier rested upon the chimney destruction level that had been thrown into the slot and the cellar.

The artifacts found in the root cellar consisted of glass, ceramic, metal, and bone objects, and, studied as a group, provide the general date during which the pit was filled. An American military button, a Corps of Artillery button made in the period 1815-1821,[10] was the most datable item in the collection. Therefore, the backfilling of the pit had to have taken place sometime after ca. 1815. The European ceramics found were types being used from ca. 1790-1830,[11] i.e., creamware, shell-edged peariware, and blue and polychrome handpainted peariware ("Gaudy Dutch"). Three minute sherds of cobalt-blue, transfer-printed earthenware were also found, the presence of which suggests a deposition date after ca. 1810.[12] Also, a fragment of a free-blown wine bottle was recov-Bred from the fill, the style having been popular ca. 1790-1820[13] Several stamped brass buttons featuring raised lettering on the back and soldered loop fasteners were found in the fill, and these were types also used in the first quarter of the nineteenth century.[14] Therefore, the datable artifact material from the cellar suggests that it had been back-filled sometime in the period Ca. 1815-1825.

A quartz scraper, a broken stone celt, and several sherds of prehistoric Early Mississippian [American] Indian pottery (Woodstock, Ca. 1000 A.D.)[15] were also found mixed into the cellar and slot fill, all associated with the historic items. Apparently, the site had also been occupied briefly during the prehistoric period. Subsequently, the construction disturbance of Traveler's Rest mixed the early material in with more modern features and artifacts.[16]

In short, the sequence of events suggested by the excavations at the south end of the main house are: (1) prehistoric [American] Indian occupation (Woodstock), ca. 1000 A.D.; (2) construction; (3) backfilling of the root cellar after ca. 1815 and probably before 1825; and, (4) jacking up of the south sill to add the stone-based brick chimney after 1815 and probably before 1825. In addition, architectural evidence shows that the central chimney had to have been dismantled to at least the first-floor hearth level so that the fireplaces for the new north addition could be built into the north side of the chimney. This operation could have 291 created the chimney debris which wound up as part of the backfill in the abandoned root cellar. Therefore, it can be logically concluded that the central chimney was dismantled, the root cellar filled in and the south chimney added ca. 1815-1825, all as part of the more extensive program of expansion which climaxed with the main house being extended to double its previous length, i.e., addition of Period II.

The remaining undersurface of Period I of the main house was excavated, revealing a flat, hard and relatively undisturbed clay surface. No erosion or roof-drip lines were found to indicate that Period I had been built in more than one stage. Walnuts, straw, and a corncob which had been crushed down into the ground level when it had been open to the weather, and a two-foot-diameter hole containing an 1887 dime were the only features found in this otherwise-undisturbed area.

The excavations revealed that a builder's trench had been dug to lay the Period I foundation wall. However, the widest side of the trench was dug outside the building, all remnants of which eroded away along with about twelve inches of the surrounding yard. To remedy the obvious weakening effects of the erosion along the wall, the section along the southeastern back porch was underpinned sometime after ca. 1890. The effects of erosion were made more visible when a portion of the rear steps was excavated, revealing the protected mound of uneroded clay beneath. The fact that the clay under the step remained at about the same level as the undersurface of the main house indicates that these steps (or some protective structure) had been there at least as long as the house. However, the original stone steps themselves were replaced quite recently and relocated at the end of the present open front porch.

The excavations around and under the main house also revealed sets of the scaffold holes which had been dug when the south and central chimneys were built. No datable artifacts were found in the twelve holes that were excavated. However, the fact that it was necessary to erect a scaffold on the north side of the central chimney meant that this chimney had been built to the Period I section of the main house before the north section of the main house was extended. Therefore, the mere fact of location of scaffold holes in this case serves as further evidence that the south half of the existing main house was built first.

The excavations under the front porch of the north section of the main house (Period II) uncovered a worn path leading from the basement kitchen door directly to the well and southward along the foundation wall to a flat clay platform-like feature, probably the base for a stair. The present steps to the kitchen lead down from the parlor inside the building, but it Is obvious that these stairs were cut into the floor as an afterthought. Apparently, the first set of stairs led up through the front porch to the rooms above as indicated by the path and earlier stair base along the foundation outside.

There has been some speculation that the fireplace and the lower levels of the basement kitchen may have been part of a separate kitchen building serving the original early structure (Period I); then, when the Period II half of the main building was extended, the original kitchen served as its foundation. If this had been the case, one would expect to find the drip line from the original kitchen building along the east and west kitchen wall. No such disturbances were found.

## THE SMOKEHOUSE

The smokehouse foundations were located during the course of the excavations. This building was fifty feet southwest of the main house, had accumulated two distinct dirt floors over the years, and was eighteen feet six inches square. At some time, the west foundation had been underpinned to negate the effects of erosion. The earliest dirt-floor level contained some woodash, but not as much as one would expect to find on the floor of a smokehouse. However, the unevenness of the floor surface suggested that perhaps the ashes were periodically shoveled out completely to the clay floor, thus destroying most of the evidence of fire. The artifacts from this occupation level consisted mainly of red or purple transfer-printed earthenware, types usually considered to have come into public favor after ca. 1830. A layer of clean red clay was put down over the early floor, apparently when the building ceased being used as a smokehouse.

An excellent photograph of ca. 1890 shows the smokehouse superstructure complete with overhanging porch roof and hewn-log walls. A strikingly similar smokehouse still stands across the river in South Carolina at the "old" Ramsey home. When the ford was in use, this would have been the nearest dwelling to Traveler's Rest and, perhaps, both smokehouse structures were built by the same man. At any rate, the Ramsey smoke-house could serve as excellent precedent for reconstruction work on the Jarrett building.

## THE LOOMHOUSE

The other existing early building at Traveler's Rest, the half-planked and half-brick structure known locally as the loomhouse, was also investigated archaeologically, and like the smokehouse, it, too, had multiple dirt-floor levels. The upper levels could have been the floor when the lower story of the building had been used as a loom area, for several circular thread weights were found at this level. However, the earliest floor level, found some eighteen inches below the present floor, included features and artifacts that indicated that the building had been originally used as a dairy. A three-by-five-foot pit had been dug in the northeast corner, probably to serve as a cold-storage pit for dairy products. Three fragmented artifacts were recovered from the pit, two of which could very well have been lost in a dairy: a stoneware-crock handle and a round, metal-can lid. Further evidence for the building's use as a walk-in cold-storage room was the discovery of the remnants of the early wooden steps leading down to the earliest floor level. The artifacts in the mixed-fill level, although quite scarce, suggest that the building ceased being used as a cold-storage vault sometime after ca. 1850. A large sherd of a graniteware plate was found in the mixed-fill layer, probably having been thrown into the building with the fill that was used to raise the floor level. Graniteware rarely was used in America before 1850, but after that approximate date, it was both manufactured in the United States and imported from England by the ton during the third quarter of the nineteenth century. No datable artifacts were found in a context that would help date the original construction of the building. However, architectural features of the structure itself provide some clue as to when it was built. The fact that the first story of the building is built solidly of brick laid in American bond on a stone base suggests that it is contemporary with the only other similarly built feature on the site, the south chimneys of the house; i.e., stone base, brick walls laid in American bond. This fact is made more significant when it is recalled that the south chimney was built immediately after the early food storage area, the root cellar, was backfilled and abandoned. Therefore, the "loomhouse" was probably built to provide additional cubic feet of safer food-storage space. Assuming that the Period II section of the main house was also built at the same time along with its basement kitchen, it follows logically that the meat house and dairy would be built close by. In fact, a door is located to the right of the basement kitchen fireplace leading directly to the "loomhouse," fifteen feet to the north.

Light probing north of the loomhouse, and down the slope, indicated stonework beneath the surface. Therefore, several trenches were opened in this area. A stone terrace was subsequently uncovered. However, the artifacts and local information showed that this feature had been part of a garden built by one of the Jarrett relatives about 1900.

Excavations were also carried out beneath the wooden cabin standing near the northwest corner of the property as part of the construction program to renovate the structure. The work revealed that the house had been built on a deposit of early twentieth-century domestic refuse. Historical evidence indicates that the original occupant of this structure had also built the garden nearby; therefore, both date from this century.

The small cabin located immediately east of the main house was investigated briefly. A trench to the north of it showed that it had never been any larger than its present fifteen-by-twenty feet, and that its small fireplace had probably been built in the late nineteenth century. The idea that this could have been an early kitchen building was not in evidence archaeologically.

The well, located twelve feet northwest of the main house, was excavated from its modern twenty-three-foot level to forty-three feet. It had been filled to the that depth with modern domestic trash. A well borer was used to excavate below the water table (thirty-six feet), but this method of excavation was abandoned when large rocks were found at a depth of forty-three feet. There is a good possibility that the borer hit the original rock liner which had collapsed over the early fill in the well. However, equipment problems have delayed the excavations at the well until the next excavation season.

## CONCLUSION

One of the major purposes of historical archaeology is to add specific information concerning a historical site not already provided by the historical documents or architectural research. The archaeological work at Traveler's Rest successfully added the following information to the body of knowledge of the site:

1.  The site had been briefly occupied by Early Mississippian Period [American] Indians.

2. Period I of the main house had been built prior to 1815,

3. A root cellar had been dug under the south end of the main house with a crude bulkhead entrance where the south chimney now stands.

4. The root cellar had been backfilled and the main south chimney built after 1815 and probably in the period 1815-1825.

5. The south half of the main house (Period I) had been constructed before any other structure now standing at the site. The present back porch and rear steps were part of this early construction.

6. The smokehouse was specifically located along with enough documentary and architectural evidence to allow reconstruction.

7. The "loomhouse" was originally used for food storage, had ceased being used for cold storage after ca. 1850, and was probably built as part of the expansion program of ca. 1815-18258.

8. The wooden cabin and the rock garden located on the extreme north boundary of the property date from the present century.

Another purpose of conducting archaeological research is to provide insights into the lives of the occupants at a historic site. Unfortunately, very little information was found relating to the inn period of Traveler's Rest. However, the collection of artifacts found in the fill of the root cellar provides a glimpse of life at the site during at least the early nineteenth century. The simple tablewares and eating utensils testify to the unpretentious way of life experienced by those living on the northeast Georgia frontier. And, even the simplest items used by the early occupants, from buttons to bowls, were made in and imported from England. This fact serves as a reminder that like the Georgia frontier, the United States was far from industrial by the period 1815-1825, nor was the frontier or the nation, by any means, self-sufficient at this time. In short, the artifacts recovered from the early nineteenth-century context show that the early occupants of Traveler's Rest were leading the typical simple life of a pioneer, at least until the wave of the advancing frontier had rolled further west, bringing "civilization" and prosperity to Traveler's Rest.

The deposition dates supplied by the artifacts found in the fill of the root cellar make it highly probable that many of the objects had belonged to Joseph Martin, Jesse Walton's son-in-law, who had inherited the property upon the death of Walton's wife (1800). It is also quite probable that the actual backfilling of the root cellar and the extensive construction program carried out at the site thereafter was undertaken by James R. Wyly, who bought the property in 1818 and held it until 1838. In fact, the forementioned military button found in the cellar fill might well have belonged to Wyly, who had served in the War of 1812. Perhaps about 1829, he probably had to double the size of the residence at the site out of sheer necessity—he had thirteen children.[17]

Finally, like all historical research, historical archaeology attempts to discover facts which can aid in the broad interpretation of a given historical site so that the events that have taken place there and the culture that has disappeared can be viewed in its overall relationship to the general movement of history itself. In a limited extent, archaeological work at Traveler's Rest achieved this end by extending knowledge of the occupation of the site back through prehistoric [American] Indian and early frontier times. With our knowledge of the site now, in part provided by archaeology, Traveler's Rest can be presented as a living example of the frontier movement in American history. The sequence of occupation shows prehistoric Indian settlement followed by early simple pioneer settlement, climaxing into a full-blown, prosperous Southern plantation. The site, therefore, does not have to be looked upon as just another relic of North Georgia—but it can help define the role of North Georgia in the larger movement of the advancing American frontier.

Although the first season of archaeology at Traveler's Rest did meet with success in some areas, some of the various other outbuildings mentioned or hinted at in the historical documents were not located. Moreover, the archaeological excavations did not specifically uncover evidence which can be used to date the earliest construction at the site, although we now know that some of the main house stood at the site prior to 1815. Another season of archaeology concentrating on the area between the main house and the river might reveal some of the evidence remaining of the plantation outbuildings.

## THE ARTIFACTS

The artifacts recovered during the excavations at Traveler's Rest were mostly late nineteenth century and modern domestic items, except for those objects found in the root cellar under the main house or in the early floor level of the smokehouse. The root cellar contained an excellent representative sample of ceramic, metal, glass, and bone domestic items of the first quarter of the nineteenth century.

## THE ROOT CELLAR

The ceramics recovered from the cellar were mainly pearlware types either decorated with blue or green shell-edging, hand-painted designs in cobalt blue in the peasant manner, or polychrome hand-painted designs banded in brown. Some creamware in the royal pattern was also recovered with a few sherds of brown stoneware. The [American] Indian pottery types recovered from the cellar included a plain tan and a burnished type, and a linear and curvilinear prehistoric stamped type. Three molded clay tobacco pipes and one soapstone tobacco pipe were recovered from the cellar. Two of the clay pipes were molded into the shape of a human head and face, and the third was a plain type common throughout the nineteenth century. The soapstone pipe was fashioned, apparently, in an attempt to copy an earlier English export form. All were reed-stem pipes. Not one fragment of an English kaolin pipe or stem was found in all of the excavation work at Traveler's Rest.

A few glass objects were found in the cellar. Three fragmented cylindrical wine bottles were recovered along with the base section of a "patent" medicine bottle bearing relief lettering. Apparently, the medicine bottle had contained "Essence of Peppermint," an organic pain killer. Moreover, a fragment of the "sunburst" relief side panel from a liquor flask was also found. Near the root cellar, presumably discarded in association with it, a small pale-green bottle still containing traces of oil of wintergreen was recovered.

The root cellar also contained fourteen buttons; ten brass, three bone, and one pewter. Six of the brass buttons were simply flat disks with raised designs and lettering on the reverse side; two were concave on the reverse side with raised lettering and designs, and one, an American military button, had the design and lettering on the front side and was completely flat. All of the brass buttons had soldered loop fasteners, whereas one brass button had been made in two pieces and was bulbous in shape. The bone buttons were flat with single-hole fasteners, whereas the pewter button was made much like the brass buttons, i.e., concave on the reverse side, having a loop fastener. However, the pewter button was probably cast, but the brass buttons were stamped. One cast-pewter cuff-link made in a two-piece mold was found bearing a floral design on the front side.

Numerous iron objects were found in the cellar. Two padlocks were found, one heart-shaped and one circular. An iron pintle was also found, together with a varied collection of equestrian hardware, a bridle cheek-piece, half of a worn horseshoe, the footrest from a stirrup, part of a harness ring and two harness buckles. Some fragmented cutlery were also found, including sections of knives, a broken spoon, and a bone fork or knife handle. A few nails were found, all exhibiting manufacturing techniques common to the first half of the nineteenth century.

## THE SMOKEHOUSE

The ceramics found in the smokehouse floor level consisted mostly of semi-porcelain, transfer-printed in a willow pattern or a red floral border design. One sherd of polychromed, hand-painted peariware similar to sherds found in the storage pit was also found.

Note: Illustrations which appeared in the original report are omitted here. Punctuation has been added for clarity.

# NOTES

[1] Charles C. Royce, *The Cherokee Nation of Indians* (Washington, D.C.: Smithsonian Bureau of Ethnology, 1887), p. 130.

[2] Royce, p. 151.

[3] Franklin County Deeds, Original Plat Book N, on file and of official record of the Surveyor General Department, Office of the Secretary of State, Atlanta, Ga., p. 133.

[4] Royce, p. 152.

[5] Bryce Martin, personal correspondence with Lyman Draper, May 18, 1954, The Draper Manuscript Collection, No. 14 DD 16 (Tennessee State Archives), microfilm frame no. 16-3.

[6] Martin, frame 16-4.

[7] Franklin County Minutes of the Court of the Ordinary, Wills, Inventories, Etc., May 15, 1786 - September 6, 1813 (Georgia Department of Archives and History), WPA Project No. 5993, p. 3.

[8] Franklin County Deed Book B, 1818 (Georgia Department of Archives and History), p. 18.

[9] Habersham County Superior Court Book glb 1841-44 (Georgia Department of Archives and History), p. 237.

[10] William Louis Calver and Reginald Pelham Bolton, *History Written With Pick and Shovel* (New York: The New York Historical Society, 1950), p. 154; and J. Duncan Campbell, "Military Buttons Long Lost Heralds of Fort Mackinac's Past," *Mackinac History Leaflet Number Seven* (Mackinac Island, Mich.: Mackinac State Park Commission, 1965), p. 3.

[11] G. Bernard Hughes, *English and Scottish Earthenware, 1660-1860* (London: Abbey Fine Arts, n.d.), p. 126; and Ivor Noel Hume, *Here Lies Virginia* (New York: Knopf, 1963), p. 299.

[12] Geoffrey Bembrose, *Nineteenth Century Pottery and Porcelain* (New York: Pitman Publishing Corp., 1952), p. 23.

[13] George S. and Helen McKearin, *American Glass* (New York: Crown Publishers, 1941), pp. 424-25; and Ivor Noel Hume, "The Glass Wine Bottle in Colonial Virginia," *Journal of Glass Studies* (Corning, N.Y.: Corning Glass Center, 1961), Vol. III, pp. 101-05.

[14] Stanley South, "Analysis of the Buttons from the Ruins at Brunswick Town and Fort Fisher, N.C., 1726-1865," *The Florida Anthropologist*, Vol. XVII, No. 2 (June, 1964), pp. 113-33.

[15] Similar stamped patterns illustrated and discussed in Robert Wauchope, "Archaeological Survey of North Georgia," in *Memoirs of the Society.* American Archaeology, Number Twenty-One (Salt Lake City. 1966), pp. 60-63.

[16] A common occurrence on many historic sites near waterways.

[17] Cora Bales Sevier and Nancy S. Madden, Sevier Family History (Washington, D.C.: Kaufmann Press, 1961), p. 296.

[18] Similar examples have been recovered recently by archaeologists at New Echota, Georgia, the Cherokee Capitol, 1819-1836; Charles Fairbanks, "European Ceramics from the Cherokee Capitol of New Echota," Southeastern Archaeological Conference Newsletter, Vol. 9, No. 1 (June, 1962), pp. 10-16.

[19] Noel Hume, Here Lies. p. 299.

[20] Berebrose, p. 9.

[21] Hume, p. 296.

[22] Several examples of this ware have been recently excavated in Alex-andria, Virginia, by the Smithsonian Institution in a context of 1790-1820.

[23] Apparently, these pipes were made well into the nineteenth century, but they are strikingly similar to the eighteenth-century examples made at Bethabara, North Carolina, at least as late as 1789; Stanley South, "The Ceramic Forms of the Potter Gottfried Aust at Bethabara, North Carolina, 1755-1771," The Conference on Historic Site Archaeology Papers, 1965-66, p. 35. Some of these pipes had been traded to the Cherokees by the Nora-vians.

[24] Similar example illustrated in South, "The Ceramic Forms...," p. 50, fig. 10, no. 7.

[25] See note 13.

[26] An identical "Essence of Peppermint" bottle was recovered in the excavations at New Echota, Georgia, In 1955; Georgia Historical Commission Archaeological Study Collection, New Echota Visitor's Center, Calhoun, Georgia.

[27] According to the Suey Analytical Laboratories of Savannah, Georgia, slight traces of oil of wintergreen were still present in the bottle, and that oil of wintergreen was used as a rheumatism remedy in the nineteenth century.

[28] Similar sunburst motifs are illustrated in McKearin, American Glass, p. 263, plate 101.

[29] Similar stamped patterns illustrated and discussed in Robert Wauchope, "Archaeological Survey of North Georgia," in *Memoirs of the Society for American Archaeology*, Number Twenty-One, Salt Lake City, 1966, pp. 60-63.

[30] Similar types have been found at Brunswicktown, North Carolina, in an archaeological context of 1800-1830. See note 14.

[31] These types all illustrated and discussed in: Lee R. Nelson, "Nail Chronology as an Aid to Dating Old Buildings," *American Association for State and Local History Technical Leaflet Number Forty-Eight*, History News, Vol. 24, No. 11, November, 1968.

[32] Similar examples discussed and illustrated in Bembrose, *Nineteenth Century Pottery...*, pp. 9-10.

[33] Ibid., p. 23

[34] Ibid.

[35] See note 19.

## BIBLIOGRAPHY

### Books

Berubrose, Geoffrey. *Nineteenth Century Pottery and Porcelain*. New York: Pittman Publishing Company, 1952.

Calvet, William Louis , and Bolton, Reginald Pelham. *History Written With Pick and Shovel.* New York: The New York Historical Society, 1950.

Hughes, G. Bernard. *English and Scottish Earthenware, 1660-1860.* London: Libbey Fine Arts, n.d.

McKearin, George S., and MeKearin, Helen. *American Glass.* New York: Crown Publishers, 1941.

Malone, Henry T. *Cherokees of the Old South.* Athens, Ga.: The University of Georgia Press, 1956.

Noel Hume, Ivor. *Here Lies Virginia.* New York: Knopf, 1963.

Royce, Charles C. *The Cherokee Nation of Indians.* Washington, D.C.: Smithsonian Institution Bureau of Ethnology, 1887.

### Articles and Periodicals

Campbell, J. Duncan. "Military Buttons, Long Lost Heralds of Fort Mac-kinac's Past," *Mackinac History,* Leaflet Number Seven. Mackinac Island, Mich., 1965.

Fairbanks, Charles. "European Ceramics from the Cherokee Capitol of New Echota," *Southeastern Archaeological Conference Newsletter,* IX, No. 1 (June, 1962).

Nelson, Lee H. "Nail Chronology as an Aid to Dating Old Buildings," *Amer-ican Association for State and Local History,* Technical Leaflet Num-ber Forty-Eight, History News, XXIV, No. 11 (November, 1968).

South, Stanley. *The Ceramic Forms of the Potter Gottfried Aust at Beth-abara, North Carolina, 1755-1771,"* The Conference on Historic Site Archaeology 1965-66.

Wauchope, Robert. "Archaeological Survey of North Georgia," *Memoirs of the Society for American Archaeology,* Number Twenty-One. Salt Lake City, 1966.

### Unpublished Material

Martin, Bryce. "Personal Correspondence with Lyman Draper, May 18, 1954," in Draper Manuscript Collection on file at the Tennessee State Archives. Nashville.

Franklin County Deed Book B, 1818. On file at Georgia Department of Archives and History. Atlanta.

Franklin County Minutes of the Court of Ordinary, Wills, Inventories, Etc., May 15, 1786-September 6, 1813. Georgia Department of ArchiYes and History, WPA Project Number 5993. Atlanta.

Habersham County Superior Court Book g, 1841-44. On file at Georgia Department of Archives and History. Atlanta.

South, Stanley. "Analysis of the Buttons from the Ruins at Brunswick

Town and Fort Fisher, N.C., 1726-1865," Paper read at the Southeastern Archaeological Conference, Macon, Georgia, October, 1963.

# Bibliography

## I.
### Manuscript Sources

*Lyman C. Draper Papers, King's Mountain Papers, DD, and Tennessee Papers, XX.* The Draper Manuscripts are now in possession of the State historical Society of Wisconsin, Madison, Wisconsin.

*Traveler's Rest Papers.* State of Georgia, Department of Natural Resources, Historic Preservation Section.

*Thomas Lumsden Papers.* Clarkesville, Georgia.


## II.
### Southeastern Indians and the Colonial Frontier

Primary Sources

Bartram, William. *Travels Through North and South Carolina, Georgia, East and West Florida.* Savannah: Beehive Press, 1973.

Chicken, George. "Journal of the March of the Carolinians into the Cherokee Mountains, in the Yamassee Indian War 1715-16." *Yearbook of the City of Charleston-1894.* Charleston: Walker, Evans & Cogswell Co., Printers, 1984.

*The Colonial and State Records of North Carolina.*

*The Colonial Records of Georgia* (Atlanta, Ga., 1904-16), Allen I). Candler (ed.).

*The Colonial Records of South Carolina, Journals of the Commissioners of Indian Trade, 1710-1718* (Columbia, S.C.: South Carolina Archives Department, 1955), W.L. McDowell (ed.).

_____, *Documents Relating to Indian Affairs, 1750-54* (Columbia, S.C.: South Carolina Archives Department, 1958).

_____, *Documents Relating to Indian Affairs, 1754-1765* (Columbia, S.C. University of South Carolina Press, 1958), W.L. McDowell (ed.).

Mereness, Newton D. (ed.) *Travels in the American Colonies* (New York: MacMillan Company, 1916).

Williams, Samuel C. (ed.) *Adair's History of the American Indians* (New York: Promontory Press, 1930).

_____. *Early Travels in the Tennessee Country, 1540-1800* (Johnson City, Tenn.: Watauga Press, 1928).


## Secondary Sources

Alden, John Richard. *John Stuart and the Southern Colonial Frontier.* (Ann Arbor, Mich.: The University of Michigan Press, 1944).

Badders, Hurley E. *Broken Path: The Cherokee Campaign of 1776* (Pendleton, S.C.: Pendleton Historical and Recreational Commission, 1976).

Brown, John P. *Old Frontiers: The Story of the Cherokee Indians* (Kingsport,TN.: Southern Publishers, Inc., 1938).

Caldwell, J.R. *Appraisal of the Archeological Resources of Hartwell Reservoir, South Carolina and Georgia* (National Park Service, 1953).

Crane, Vernor W. *The Southern Frontier, 1670-1732* (Ann Arbor, Mich.: The University of Michigan Press, 1929; reprinted 1956).

Doster, James F. *The Creek Indians and Their Florida Lands* (New York: Garland Publishing, Inc., 1974), 2 vols.

Every, Dale Van. *Forth to the Wilderness, Vol. I of The American Frontier* (New York: Mentor Books, 1961).

Goff, John. "The Dividings," *Georgia Mineral Newsletter*, Vol. IX (1950).

Hudson, Charles. *The Southeastern Indians* (University of Tennessee Press, 1976, no location given).

Kelly, A.R., and Clemens de Baillou. "Excavation of the Presumptive Site of Old Estatoe," *Southern Indian Studies*, Vol. 12, October, 1960.

Meriweather, Robert L. *The Expansion of South Carolina, 1729-1765* . (Kingsport, Tenn: Southern Publishers, 1940).

Mooney, James. *Myths of the Cherokees* (New York: Johnson Reprint Corporation, 1970).

Myer, William E. "Indian Trails of the Southeast," *42nd Annual Report of the Bureau of American Ethnologists, 1924-5.*

Ramsey, Robert W. *Carolina Cradle: Settlement on the Frontier* (Chapel Hill, N.C.: University of North 1964).

Swanton, John R. "Indians of the Southeastern United States," *Bureau of American Ethnology, Bulletin No. 137,* 1946.

____. *The Indian Tribes of North America* (Washington, D.C.: Smithsonian Institution Press, 1968).

Willis, William S. *Colonial Conflict and the Cherokee Indians* (Ann Arbor, Mich.: University Microfilms, 1955).

Woodward, Grace Steel. *The Cherokees* (Norman, Okla.: University of Oklahoma Press, 1963).

## III.
## The Revolutionary Frontier and the Early Nineteenth Century

<u>Primary Sources</u>

Asbury, Francis. *The Journal of Rev. Francis Asbury* (New York: N. Rau and T. Mason, 1821), 3 vols.

Calendar of Virginia, State Papers and Other Manuscripts, 1652-1792, William P. Palmer (ed.)(Richmond, Va.: State of Virginia, 1875), Vols. 1-5.

Caughey, John Walton (ed.). McGillivray of the Creeks (Norman, Okla: University of Oklahoma Press, 1938).

Deeds of Franklin County, Georgia 1784-1826, compiled by Martha Walters Acker (Easley, S.C.: Southern Historical Press, 1976).

Dow, Lorenzo. History of Cosmopolite (Cincinnati, Ohio: Anderson, Gates & Wright, 1858).

Franklin County tax digests, other records on microfilm at the Georgia Department of Archives and History, 1798-1865.

Gilmer, George R. *Sketches of Some of the First Settlers of Upper Georgia, of the Cherokees and of the Author* (New York: D. Appleton & Co., 1855).

Hays, Mrs. J.E. (ed.). *Indian Depredations* (Atlanta: Georgia Department of Archives and History, 1938).

_____. *Indian Letters* (Atlanta: Georgia Department of Archives and History, 1938).

_____. *Indian Treaties, Cessions of Land in Georgia, 1705-1837* (Atlanta: Works Project Administration, 1941).

Lyman Draper Papers, Tennessee and King's Mountain Calendar and Papers, DD and XX (in possession of the Wisconsin Historical Society).

Milfort, Louis Le Clerc. *Memoirs, or, a Quick Glance at My Various Travels and My Sojourn in the Creek Nation* (Savannah: Beehive Press, 1959).

*Miller's Weekly Messenger* (Pendleton, S.C.: March 30, 1807 - September 8, 1810; some issues missing; located at Clemson University Library).

*Pendleton Weekly Messenger* [Formerly *Miller's*] (August 21, 1813 - December 1, 1830; some issues missing; located at Clemson University Library).

*Records of the Moravians in North Carolina,* Adelaide L. Fries (ed.), Vol. III (Raleigh: State Department of Archives and History; reprinted 1968).

"The Records of Washington County," *American Historical Magazine,* 1900, V. 5, pp. 326-81; V. 6, pp. 51-93, 191-92, 283-88.

Redd, John. "Reminiscences of Western Virginia, 1770-1790," *The Virginia Magazine of History and Biography,* 1899-1900, Vols. 6 and 7.

*The Revolutionary Records of Georgia,* 3 vols. (Atlanta, Ga.: Franklin-Turner Company, 1908-09), Allen D. Candler (ed.).

Wynd, Frances. *Franklin County Georgia Records* (Albany, Ga.: printed by author, no date given).

## Secondary Sources

Alderman, Pat. *The Overmountain Men: Early Tennessee History* (Johnson City, Tenn. Overmount Press, 1970).

Bailey, J. O. *Commanders at King's Mountain* (Gaffney, S.C.: Ed H. DeCamp, 1926).

Browning, Howard M. "The Washington County Court, 1778-1789: A Study in Frontier Administration," *Tennessee Historical Quarterly,* 2nd Series, Vol. I, 1942.

Cleveland, Edmond J., and Horace G. Cleveland. *The Genealogy of the Cleveland and Cleveland Families* (Hartford, Conn.: Case, Lockward & Brainard Co., 1899).

Coulter, Ellis Merton. *Old Petersburg and the Broad River Valley of Georgia* (Athens, Ga.: University of Georgia Press, 1965).

Dick, Everett. *The Dixie Frontier: A Social History* (New York: Alfred A. Knopf, 1948)

Draper, Lyman Copeland. *Calendar of the Tennessee and King's Mountain Papers* Madison, Wise.: The Wisconsin Historical Society, 1929).

_____. *King's Mountain and Its Heroes* (New York: Dauber & Pine Book Shops, Inc., 1929).

Driver, Carl S. *John Sevier* (Chapel Hill, N.C.: University of North Carolina Press, 1932).

Eggleston, George C. *Red Eagle and the Wars with the Creek Indians of Alabama* (New York: Dodd, Mead & Co., 1878). 264

Every, Dale Van. *A Company of Heroes, Vol. II of The American Frontier* (New York: Mentor Books, 1962).

_____. *Ark of Empire,* Vol. III of The American Frontier (New York: Mentor Books, 1963).

Fauche, Jonas. "The Frontiers of Georgia in the Late Eighteenth Century," *Georgia Historical Quarterly,* XLVII (1963).

Folmsbee, Stanley J.; Robert E. Curlew, and Enoch I.. Mitchell. *History of Tennessee* (New York: Lewis Historical Publishing Company, Inc., 1960), 4 vols.

Gilmore, James R. *John Sevier as Commonwealth Builder* (New York: D. Appleton & Co., 1887).

Goode, J.F. *History of Tugalo Baptist Association* (Toccoa, Ga.: J.S. Little & Ives Co., *Toccoa Record,* 1924).

Goodpasture, Albert V. "Indian Wars and Warriors of the Old Southeast 1730-1807," *Tennessee Historical Magazine,* IV (1918).

Halbert, H.S. and T.H. Ball. *The Creek War of 1813 and 1814* (Chicago: Donohue & Henneberry, 1895).

Hays, Louise Frederick. *Hero of Hornet's Nest A Biography of Elijah h Clarke* (New York: Stratford House, Inc.,1946).

Hill, Judith P.A. *A History of Henry County, Virginia* (Baltimore: Regional Publishing Co., 1976; originally published 1925).

*Kincaid,* Robert L. *The Wilderness Road* (New York; The Bobbs-Merrill Company, 1947).

Kiosky, Beth Ann. *The Pendleton Legacy* (Columbia, S.C.: Sandlapper Press, Inc., 1971).

Kollock, John, *These Gentle Hills* (Lakemont, Ga.: Apple House Books, 1976).

Landrum, J.B.O. *Colonial and Revolutionary History of Upper South Carolina* (Greenville, S.C.: Shannon & Co., 1897).

Logan, John H. *A History of the Upper Country of South Carolina*, Vol. I (Charleston, S.C.: S.G. Courtenay, 1859).

_____. *Logan Manuscript*, Joseph Habersham Chapter, Daughters of the American Revolution, Vol. II of *Logan's History of Upper South Carolina* (Atlanta: Chas. P. Byrd, State Publisher, 1910).

Mcclary, Ben Harris. "Nancy Ward: The Last Beloved Woman of the Cherokees," *Tennessee Historical Magazine*, Vol. 21 (1962).

Owsley, Frank L. "The Pattern of Migration and Settlement on the Southern Frontier," *Journal of Southern History*, XI (1945).

Pendleton District Historical and Recreational Commission. *Pendleton Historic District: A Survey* (Pendleton, S.C., 1973).

Pusey, William Allen. "General Joseph Martin, An Unsung Hero of the Virginia Revolution," *The Filson Club Historical Quarterly*, Vol. X (April, 1936).

Ramsey, J. G. M. *The Annals of Tennessee* (Knoxville, Tenn.: East Tennessee Historical Society, 1967; originally published 1853).

Rouse, Parke, Jr. *The Great Wagon Road, From Philadelphia to the South* (New York: McGraw-Hill Book Company, 1973).

Saunders, James E. *Early Settlers of Alabama* (New Orleans: L. Graham & Son, Ltd., 1899).

Sevier, Com Balea, and Nancy S. Madden. *Sevier Family History* (Washington, D.C.: Kaufmann Pantry Co., 1961).

Simpson, R.W. *History of Old Pendleton District* (Anderson, S.C.: Oulla Printing Co., 1913).

Turner, Francis M. *The Life of General John Sevier* (New York: The Neale Publishing Company, 1910).

Turner, Frederick Jackson. *The Frontier in American History* (New York: Henry Holt and Company, 1920).

Weeks, Stephen B. "Gen. Joseph Martin and the War of the Revolution in the West," *Annual Report of the American Historical Association*, Vol. 4 (1893).

Williams, Samuel C. "Col. Elijah Clarke in the Tennessee Country," *Georgia Historical Quarterly,* Vol. 25 (1941).

____. "The Founder of Tennessee's First Town: Major Jesse Walton," *East Tennessee Historical Society Publications*, Vol. 2 (1930).

____. *History of the Lost State of Franklin* (Johnson City, Tenn.: Watauga Press, 1924).

____. *Tennessee During the Revolutionary War* ( Nashville, Tenn.: The Tennessee Historical Commission, 1944).


## IV.
### Travel, Inns, and the Plantation Era

Primary Sources

*Athens Southern Banner,* 1830-1860.

Blake, William A., and Charles T. Jackson. *The Gold Places of the Vicinity of Dahlonega, Georgia* (Boston: no publisher, 1859).

Buckingham, James Silk. *The Slave States of America*, 2 vols. (London: Fisher, Son & Co., 1842).

Featherstonhaugh, George W. *A Canoe Voyage up the Minnay-Sotor* (St. Paul: Minnesota Historical Society, 1970 [1847]).

Gilman, Caroline. *The Poetry of Travelling in the United States* (New York: S. Coleman, 1838).

Habersham County Tax Digests, other records on microfilm at the Georgia Department of Archives and History and in the Clarkesville Courthouse, 1819-1905.

Hall, Captain Basil. *Travels in North America, 1827 and 1828*, 2 vols. (Philadelphia: Carey, Lea & Carey, 1829).

Hewett, Daniel. *The American Travellers; or, National Dictionary, containing an account of all the Great Post Roads of the United States* (Washington, D.C.: Davis & Force, 1825).

Lambert, John. *Travels Through Lower Canada and the United States,* 3 vols. (London: T. Gillet, Printer, 1810).

Mills, Robert. *Atlas of the State of South Carolina* (Columbis, S.C.: Lucy Hampton Bostick & Fant H. Thorney, 1938).

____. *Statistics of South Carolina* (Charleston, S.C.: Hurlbut & Lloyd, 1826).

Mitchell, Samuel A. *Traveller's Guide Through the United States* (Philadelphia: S.A. Mitchell, 1835).

Motte, Jacob Rhett. *Journey into Wilderness* (Gainesville, Fla. University of Florida Press, 1953), James F. Sunderman (ed.).

*Orion*, 1842-1844 [a Georgia literary magazine in Savannah edited by William C. Richards].

*Pendleton (S.C.) Weekly Messenger*, 1830s (located at Clemson University Library; many issues missing).

Richards, T. Addison. Appleton's Illustrated Handbook of American Travel (New York: D. Appleton & Co., 1857).

Sherwood, Adiel. *A Gazetteer of the State of Georgia* (Athens, Ga.: The University of Georgia Press, 1939; originally published 1827).

Stephenson, Mary (ed.) *The Recollection of a Happy Childhood*, by Mary Esther Huger (Research and Publication Committee, Foundation for Historic Restoration in the Pendleton Area, 1976).

United States Census records for Franklin, Habersham counties, 1800-1880.

White, George. *Statistics of the State of Georgia* (Savannah: W. Thorne Williams, 1849).

_____. *Historical Collections of Georgia* (New York: Pudney & Russell Publishers, 1854).

Zeigler, Wilbur Gleason and Ben S. Grosscup. *The Heart of the Alleghenies in Western North Carolina* (Raleigh: Alfred Williams & Co., 1883).

Secondary Sources

Boatright, Sherry L. *The John C. Calhoun Gold Mine* (Atlanta: Georgia Department of Natural Resources, Historic Preservation Section, 1974).

Brockett, L.P. *The Silk Industry in America: A History*; prepared for the Centennial Exposition, 1876 (New York: George F. Nesbitt & Co., 1876).

Carroll, Joseph Cephas. *Slave Insurrections in the United States 1800-1865* (New York: Negro Universities Press, 1938).

Coulter, Ellis Merton. *George Walton Williams, The Life of a Southern Merchant and Banker* (Athens, Ga.: The Hibriten Press, 1976).

Dunbar, Seymour. *A History of Travel in America* (Indianapolis: BobbsMerrill Co., 1914).

Earle, Alice Morse. *Stage Coach and Tavern Days* (New York: Dover Publications, Inc., 1900; reprinted 1969).

Flanders, Ralph B. *Plantation Slavery in Georgia* (Chapel Hill, N.C.: The University of North Carolina Press, 1933).

Green, Fletcher. *Georgia's Forgotten Industry: Gold and Mining* (reprinted from the Georgia Historical Quarterly, Vol. XIX, No. 2; Vol. XIX, No. 3, 1935).

Halasz, Nicholas. *The Rattling Chains: Slave Unrest and Revolt in the Antebellum South* (New York: David McKay Company, Inc., 1966).

Hammond, Edmund Jordan. *The Methodist Episcopal Church in Georgia* (printed by the author, 1935; no location given).

Kelso, William. "Excavations at Traveler's Rest," 1969 (Savannah: unpublished paper for the Georgia Historical Commission).

Lane, Mills (ed.). *The Rambler in Georgia* (Savannah: Beehive Press, 1973).

Lathrop, Elise. *Early American Inns and Taverns* (New York: R.M. McBride & Co., 1926).

Leggett, William F. *The Story of Silk* (New York: Life-Time Editions, 1948).

Phillips, Ulrich B. *American Negro Slavery* (Baton Rouge: Louisiana State University Press, 1969; originally published 1918).

Sears, Joan A. "Town Planning in White and Habersham Counties, Georgia," *Georgia Historical Quarterly*, Vol. 54 (1976).

Yoder, Paton. *Taverns and Traveler's: Inns of the Early Midwest* (Bloomington, Ind.: Indiana University Press, 1969).

## V.
### The Civil War, Reconstruction, and the Late Nineteenth Century

Primary Sources

Adger, John B. *My Life and Times, 1816-1899* (Richmond; The Presbyterian Committee of Publications, 1899).

Andrews, Eliza Frances. *The War-Time Journal of a Georgia Girl* (Macon, Ga.: The Archives Press, 1960).

Clemson, Florida. *A Rebel Came Home* (Columbia, S.C.: University of South Carolina Press, 1961, Charles M. McGee, Jr. and Ernest M. Lander, Jr. (eds.).

Kirk, Charles H. (ed.). *History of the Fifteenth Pennsylvania Volunteer Cavalry* (Philadelphia, 1906).

Smith, Daniel Elliott Huger (ed.). *Mason-Smith Family Letters* (Columbia, S.C.: University of South Carolina Press, 1950).

Stephenson, Mary (ed.). *The Diary of Clarissa Adger Bowen; Ashtabula Plantation, 1865, the Pendleton-Clemson Area, South Carolina, 1776-1889* (Pendleton, S.C.: Research and Publication Committee, Foundation for Historic Research in the Pendleton Area, 1973).

*The Summer of 1882 Among the Health Resorts of Northeast Georgia*, Richmond & Danville Railroads.

*War of the Rebellion: Official Records of the Union and Confederate Armies*, Series I, Vol. XLIX, Pts. I, II (Washington, D.C.: Government Printing Office, 1897).

Williams, George Walton. *Nacoochie and Its Surroundings* (Charleston: Walker, Evans & Cogswell, Printers, 1814).


Secondary Sources

Conway, Alan. *The Reconstruction of Georgia* (Minneapolis: University of Minnesota Press, 1966).

Henderson, Lillian (ed.). *Roster of the Confederate Soldiers of Georgia (1861-65),* IV (Hapeville, Ga.: Longino & Porter, Inc., 1960).

Stovall, Pleasant A. *The Life of Robert Toombs* (New York: Cassell Publishing Co., 1892).

Vandiver, Louise Ayer. *Traditions and History of Anderson County* (Atlanta: Ruralist Press, Publishers, 1929).

Williams, Walter. "A Southerner in the Philippines," *Washington State University Research Studies,* Vol. 39(2), June, 1971.

## VI.
### Miscellaneous Sources

Chappell, Absalom H. *Miscellanies of Georgia: Historical, Biographical, Descriptive* (Columbus, Ga.: Thos. Gilbert, Printer, 1874).

Church, Mary L. *The Hills of Habersham* (Clarkesville, Ga.: published by the author, 1962).

Coulter, Ellis Merton. *Georgia: A Short History* (Chapel Hill, N.C. The University of North Carolina Press, 1947).

"Cora Ledbetter's History Scrapbook," *Toccoa [Ga.] Record.*

Perkerson, Medora F. *White Columns in Georgia* (New York: Bonanza Books, 1952).

Sparks, Andrew. "Plastic Skin Reveals Secrets of Old Inn," *Atlanta Journal and Constitution Magazine,* November 13, 1966.

Stephens County Tax Digests, 1906-1960 (located at Georgia Department of Archives and History and the Toccoa, Ga., courthouse).

Trogdon, Kathryn Curtis. *The History of Stephens County, Georgia* (Toccoa, Ga.: Toccoa Woman's Club, Inc., 1973).

Utley, Francis Lee, and Marion R. Hemperley (eds.) *Place Names of Georgia.* (Athens, Ga.: University of Georgia Press, 1975).

# VII.
## Fiction

Kennedy, John Pendleton. *Horse-Shoe Robinson* (New York: American Book Company, 1937, 1852 edition), Earnest E. Leisy (ed.).

Richards, T. Addison. *Tallulah and Jocasse; or Romance of Southern Landscape and Other Tales* (Charleston, S.C. Walker, Richards & Company, 1852).

Simms, William Gilmore. *Guy Rivers, a Tale of Georgia* (New York: Redfield, 1355 revised edition).

# Maps

**Map 1:** Compiled from Charles Hudson, *The Southeastern Indians* (Uni versity of Tennessee Press, 1976), pp. 6-7; and William Harlen Gilbert, Jr., *The Eastern Cherokees* (Washington, D.C., Smithsonian Institute, 1943): 179.

**Map 2:** Mary Stephenson, (ed.), *The Diary of Clarissa Bowan, Ashtabula Plantation 1865, The Pendleton Clemson Area, 1776-1889* (Pendleton, S.C., Research and Publication Committee, 1973): 14.

**Map 3:** Adapted from George Hunter's 1744 copy of John Herbert's 1725 Map of South Carolina, from the Georgia Surveyor General's Office.

**Map 4:** John Brown, *Old Frontiers* (Kingsport, Tenn.: Southern Publishers, Inc., 1938), 1.

**Map 5:** Adapted from Hurley Badders, *Broken Path: The Cherokee Campaign of 1776* (Pendleton, S.C.: Pendleton Historical and Recreational Commission, 1976), viii.

**Map 6:** Drawn by Leonard Chester from William Kelso, "Excavations at Traveler's Rest," Figure 2, Historic Preservation Section files.

**Map 7:** From the Georgia Surveyor General's Office.

**Map 8:** Part of C.C. Royce's Map of the Cherokee Country, from the Georgia Sur veyor General's Office.

**Map 9:** From the Georgia Surveyor General's Office.

**Map 10:** From the Traveler's Rest Papers, Historic Preservation Section.

**Map 11:** Adapted by Leonard Chester from Hall's map shown in Kathryn C. Trog don, *History of Stephens County* (Toccoa, Ga.: Toccoa Women's Club, 1973), 8.

**Map 12:** Drawn by Leonard Chester from a map compiled by Robert Bouwman. The location of the tavern, store, blacksmithy, and tanyard are hypothetical.

**Map 13:** Part of Habersham County, District #3, adapted by Leonard Chester from the original from the Georgia Surveyor General's Office.

**Map 14:** Drawn by Leonard Chester from a map compiled by Robert Bouwman.

**Map 15:** Part of a 1911 Stephens County Militia District Map from the Georgia Surveyor General's Office.

**Map 16:** From Stephens County Courthouse, Plat Book 1, 49.

# Images

**Image 1:** Traveler's Rest: South View, 1977

**Image 2:** Traveler's Rest: Northeast View, 1977

**Image 3:** Traveler's Rest: Early Spring, 1977

**Image 4:** Devereaux Jarrett, proprietor of Traveler's Rest, in a photograph obtained from Jarrett descendants, date unknown.

**Image 5:** House of Robert Jarrett, 1977

**Image 6:** House of Thomas Patton Jarrett, 1977 (House has since been destroyed by fire.)

**Image 7:** Toccoa Falls, 1977

**Image 8:** House of Joseph Prather and Sally Jarrett, 1977

**Image 9:** Cradle

**Image 10:** Bed brought to Traveler's Rest by Lizzie Lucas Jarrett around 1852.

**Image 11:** "Indian Rock"

**Image 12:** Bent-wood Rocking Chair

**Image 13:** Corner Cupboard

**Image 14:** Detail of Main Stairway

**Image 15:** Traveler's Rest. Photo taken near the turn of the twentieth century.

**Image 16:** The Jarretts' Tugaloo River "bottom lands," facing northward toward the Appalachian Mountains. Photo taken about 1900.

**Image 17:** Sally Grace, date unknown.

**Image 18:** Mary Lizzie, 1890s

**Image 19:** Lizzie Lucas Jarrett and family, about 1898.

**Image 20:** Charles P. Jarrett and friends "camping in the Mountains of NE Georgia, 1894." Charles Jarrett is in the center in the vest.

**Image 21:** Charles P. Jarrett, camping in northeast Georgia, 1894. Charles, wearing a vest, is in the center.

**Image 22:** Charles Patton Jarrett with unknown women and girls, about 1898.

**Image 23:** Charles Patton Jarrett and an unknown woman, perhaps at Tallulah Falls, about 1898. The back of the photograph reads, "He and his girl all alone. Gloom and splendor crowned their comely faces."

**Image 24:** Left to right: Unidentified woman with dogs, Sally Grace Jarrett, and Lizzie Lucas Jarrett at Traveler's Rest in the early 1900s.

**Image 25:** Charles Patton Jarrett in New Mexico for his "consumption" in 1898.

**Image 26:** Victorine Faillett Jarrett, wife of Lt. George Devereaux Jarrett, location unknown. Photo taken in early 1900s.

**Image 27:** Neeley Jarrett, former slave. Date unknown. "Taken in front of her little cabin."

**Image 28:** Lt. George Devereaux Jarrett and Sally Grace Jarrett at smokehouse in early 1900s.

**Image 29:** Lizzie Lucas Jarrett and son, Lt. George Devereaux Jarrett, on front porch at Traveler's Rest in early 1900s.

**Image 30:** Lizzie Lucas Jarrett on front porch at Traveler's Rest in early 1900s.

**Image 31:** Lt. George Devereaux Jarrett on transport *Rawlings* in early 1900s.

**Image 32:** Lt. George Devereaux Jarrett at home in the Philippines in early 1900s.

**Image 33:** Lt. George and Victorine in the Philippines, about 1903.

**Image 34:** Lt. George and Victorine in Cuba, about 1901

**Image 35:** Steamboat on the Tugaloo River, date unknown.

**Image 36:** Unknown woman at small house near Traveler's Rest in early 1900s.

**Image 37:** Lizzie Lucas Jarrett in a small room at south end of Traveler's Rest in early 1900s.

**Image 38:** Lizzie Lucas and Sally Grace Jarrett in a small room in early 1900s.

**Image 39:** Family picture before the front porch at Traveler's Rest in early 1900s.

**Image 40:** Front view of unrestored Traveler's Rest. Photo taken in 1953.

**Image 41:** Rear view of unrestored Traveler's Rest in 1953.

**Image 42:** Basement Kitchen

**Image 43:** Upstairs "Common" Bedroom

**Drawing 1:** Traveler's Rest, Stephens County, Georgia. ca. 1815-1835

**Drawing 2:** Traveler's Rest, Stephens County, Georgia. ca. 1835-1850

**Drawing 3:** Traveler's Rest, Stephens County, Georgia. 1934

CPSIA information can be obtained
at www.ICGtesting.com
Printed in the USA
LVHW081700100620
657786LV00025B/1788